THE
PHOENIX
SOLUTION

THE PHOENIX SOLUTION

GETTING SERIOUS ABOUT WINNING AMERICA'S DRUG WAR

Vincent T. Bugliosi

DOVE
BOOKS

ISBN 0-7871-0682-8

Printed in the United States of America

Dove Books
301 North Cañon Drive
Beverly Hills, CA 90210

Distributed by Penguin USA

Jacket design and layout by Mauna Eichner
Text design by Stanley S. Drate/Folio Graphics Co., Inc.

Jacket illustration by Paul Corrigan

First Printing: March 1996

10 9 8 7 6 5 4 3 2 1

MAY I 6 I996

To those members of law enforcement
who have valiantly given their lives
in the war against drugs
so that the rest of us can live
in a safer and more civilized America.

Contents

Author's Note

The reader may wonder why this book contains a great number of legal references and citations. The answer is inferable from the text. *The Phoenix Solution: Getting Serious About Winning America's Drug War*, was written in the hope, albeit faint, that the solutions to the drug crisis it proposes will be carried out by our federal government. But in my discussions with members of America's drug-fighting agencies, and in view of established and long-standing federal policies, it has become clear to me that our country is unaware it has the legal authority to employ the recommended proposals. The legal references and citations, therefore, are intended not for the general reader or opinion-maker but as a legal road map for the authorities to follow if the decision is made to adopt and implement any of the measures set forth on the following pages.

These measures were first outlined in my 1991 book, *Drugs in America: The Case for Victory*. *The Phoenix Solution* brings the reader up to date on America's drug war and expands considerably on many of the matters and issues discussed in *The Case for Victory*.

Although the drug war has been going on for decades, with virtually no change in its fundamental complexion, paradoxically hardly a day goes by that something noteworthy does not occur in the United States, Colombia, Peru, Bolivia, or some other place of high drug intensity. This book takes the reader up to January 25, 1996, at which time my final draft was submitted for publication. Undoubtedly, in the interlude between that time and the book's publication, events will have taken place on which I would have liked to comment.

I wish to thank the many members of the various federal law enforcement agencies involved in the anti-drug effort for the tremendous cooperation they gave me in answering my endless questions and furnishing me with informative and timely publications on the drug problem issued by their respective offices.

Introduction

When my book *Drugs in America* was first published in 1991, I was asked by the host of "The Today Show" how likely were the prospects that the federal govern ment would implement the proposals to solve the drug crisis set forth in my book. When I responded "extremely unlikely," the host said, "Then why did you even bother to write the book?" My response was that the problem was severe enough to warrant the effort.

The drug problem remains the same today, as I predicted it would in 1991 if this nation did not take serious, as opposed to cosmetic, steps to solve it. Only some of the players and numbers have changed. The pervasive poison of illicit drugs continues to course through the nation's bloodstream, damaging or destroying everything in its wake and making it the most enduring and serious internal crisis this nation has faced since the Civil War. And yet, the most powerful nation on Earth continues to give the impression that it is helpless to do anything about it. But this is pure moonshine. The Persian Gulf War showed what this nation does when it's really serious about something. Within just months, we mobilized an incredible military force of 500,000 men and women (and persuaded 27 nations to join in the effort) to fight in some distant land. And all of this was to solve a perceived problem—an increase in domestic gasoline prices—that pales next to American's drug problem.

There is only one reason why America still has a severe drug problem, and that simply is the fact that this nation is not serious about solving it, and never has been. If the nation's electorate started throwing presidents out of office because of their failure to eliminate the problem, we'd quickly see dramatic steps taken to end the crisis. But since the drug problem is erroneously perceived to be incapable of solution and has become an accepted staple in our society, as immutable as taxes and the aging process, our nation's politically unthreatened leadership continues to get by with mere posturing as opposed to remedial action. Nothing is more cloying and smacks more of posturing and mere symbolism than our continued use of the "war" metaphor to characterize our fight against the drug menace. The fight, of course, bears no resemblance to a real war. For instance, at the 1992 drug summit in San Antonio, Texas, President Bush "asked" the presidents of Peru, Bolivia, and Colombia, the three nations responsible for virtually all of the cocaine entering this country, to make an effort to reduce illicit narcotic production in their respective countries by 50 percent within the next ten years. And the Latin leaders, mind you, refused to make such a commitment. Can anyone imagine this same president *asking* Saddam Hussein if he would remove 50 percent of his forces from Kuwait within the next ten years?

Make no mistake about it. The drug "war" is nothing but a neverending game between the parties to the war, with each side responding to the moves of the opposition. The only dynamic that distinguishes the drug war game from, let's say, NBA basketball competition is that although the drug traffickers may ostensibly fall a point behind here and there, they invariably end up on top. I say that because the object of the game for the traffickers is to get their narcotics into this country for sale. Law enforcement's goal is to prevent this. Yet every single year, without exception and despite record seizures by law enforcement, the traffickers get all the narcotics into this country that they need to satisfy their buyers, and then some. I say the traffickers "ostensibly" fall a point behind here and there because when, for example, law enforcement seizes a large cache of cocaine and drug money, the setback to the traffickers is illusory. Everyone knows by now that the traffickers look upon such events as merely part of the operating cost of doing business. Moreover, such large seizures are always misperceived by law enforcement as a victory. Instead of calling a press conference and rejoicing, as they never fail to do when they make a large seizure, why is it that law enforcement doesn't view these large seizures for what they truly are—evidence of defeat? If their year-in-and-year-out effort to stop the flow of illicit drugs into this country were succeeding, such large "record" caches of cocaine and other narcotics would not continue to be present in this country *for* them to seize. Since we know that whatever amount of drugs we seize has no impact on the amount still available, law enforcement's refrain, "We had our best year yet" (following a record year of seizures) should more appropriately be, "We had our worst year yet."

Since 1991, the same tired spinning of wheels that has been the hallmark of our "war" on drugs in the previous decades (and which can be analogized to the no-win Vietnam strategy we had), has continued to occur. The headlines of the past four years, like those before them, aptly reflect this sad reality. The following are just a few among thousands of never-ending headlines generated, year in and year out, without fail, by the war on drugs:

1991
(subsequent to the publication of *Drugs in America*)

"U.S.A.'s Illegal Drug Bill: $40 Billion"; "Success Bedevils Drug Traffickers"; "Morale Is Key to Local Police Fighting Drugs"; "Andean Anti-Drug Plan Called a Failure"; "Official Says U.S. Is Losing Drug War"; "Cocaine Traffickers Diversify with Heroin"; "U.S. Withholding Drug Aid to Peru"; "Thirty-five Suspects in Laundering of Drug Money Arrested"; "Drug Trafficking Spawns a 'Death Valley' "; "Cocaine Use on Rise, U.S. Survey Finds"; "Thai Heroin Cartel Frustrates U.S."

1992

"Doubts Raised on U.S. Andean War on Drugs"; "Bush, Latin American Leaders Announce Anti-Drug Initiative"; "Disagreements at Drug Summit Deal a Blow to War on Cocaine"; "U.S. Report Cites Gains in War on Cocaine, Plays Down Setbacks"; "Fighting the Drug War in the Skies over Peru"; "Panama's Free, but Drug Trade Thrives"; "Border Drug Seizures Setting a Record Pace"; "Remapping Latin America's Drug War"; "Experts Are Critical of Anti-Drug Program Touted by Bush Administration"; "Pot-Busting Season Underway"; "Four Years of Bush's Drug War: New Funds but an Old Strategy"; "U.S. Offering $2 Million Reward for Fugitive Drug Lord Escobar"; "Drug Agents Break Global Money-Laundering System"; "Across the U.S.A. Drug Enforcers Uproot a Bumper Marijuana Crop"; "Bush Seeks More Drug-War Funds"; "Battle Lags in Eliminating Peru's Poison"; "Prison Medical Crisis: Overcrowding Created by War on Drugs Poses Public Health Emergency"; "Federal Lawmen Gone Bad: Border Drug Smuggling Proves Tempting"; "Radar Trap on Border Nets Zero Drug Smugglers"; "Police in New York Shift Drug Battle Away from Streets"; "Chicago Steps Up Campaign Against Drugs and Violence in Public Housing"; "Coca Fields in Bolivia—the United States Tries in Vain to Fight Cocaine at Its

4	VINCENT T. BUGLIOSI

Source"; "2.5 Tons of Cocaine Seized: Bust Reported to be Biggest Along Texas-Mexico Border."

1993

"Drug Strategy Shifts Away from Interdiction"; "Drug Policy: It's Time to Try Something Very Different"; "New Bosses Taking Over Cocaine Traffic"; "Strategies for Treating the Nation's Drug Scourge"; "U.S. Cutting Funds for Latin American Drug War"; "Biden: Shift Drug Focus to Users"; "War on Drugs Shifting into Lower Gear"; "Report Faults Military's Drug War"; "Another Shift in Drug Policy"; "Studies Find Drug Program Not Effective"; "War on Drugs Shifting Its Focus to Hardcore Addicts"; "Drug Policy Adrift, Lawmakers Say"; "Democratic, GOP Senators Attack Clinton Drug Strategy"; "U.S. Losing Drug War on the Border"; "Swamped by Smuggling: Surge in Drug Seizures Forces Border Officials to Weigh Eased Guidelines on Prosecutions"; "FBI Arrests Thirteen in Money-Laundering Sting"; "Bay Area Mayors, Police Chiefs Say War on Drugs Failed"; "DEA Agents Seize Nearly Half-ton in Hashish"; "Heroin Now Rivals Cocaine in Deaths in Dade County [Florida]"; "Detective Drug Witness Fatally Shot in Court"; "Drug Seizure at Roadblock Is Ruled Illegal"; "Mexico, Drug Corruption from the Top"; "Survey Indicates Decline in Drug Use"; "Indoor Marijuana Farms on the Rise in Suburbs."

1994

"Illicit Drug Use by Youths Shows Marked Increase"; "Clinton Anti-Drug Effort Shifts Toward Treatment"; "Doctors Seek End of Drug Prohibition"; "Pentagon Is Scaling Back Its Drug-Fighting Activities"; "Nation's Drug Scene Again Degenerating"; "Nations Urge New Approach to Fight Drugs"; "Drug Dealing Arrests Increase 47% at Schools"; "International Sting Nets Cocaine-Cash"; "U.S. Says Probe Pierced Cali Operation"; "Crack Addiction Afflicts Us All"; "Crack: A Ruthless Ruler of the Streets"; "Bank's Suspicion Nails Corrupt DEA Agent"; "Lawyer Reveals Laundering Millions of Drug Dollars Offshore"; "U.S. Says 17 Ran Murder Gang that Ruled Heroin Sales in Bronx"; "Legalized Drugs an Idea to Consider"; "U.S. Halts Flights in Andes Drug War Despite Protests"; "Politicians and Drug Lords Said to Have Plotted Mexican Assassination"; "DEA Plans to Provide Teams to Help Control Gang Crime."

1995

"Tons of Cocaine Reaching Mexico in Old Jets"; "Seventeen Agencies Join to Target Desert 'Cocaine Corridor' "; "Prevention Is Casualty of Drug War"; "New Assault on Drugs, Old Debate on Tactics"; "Drug War on Losing Path"; "Border Inspections Eased and Drug Seizures Plunge"; "Two Inspectors at Border Charged in Drug Probe"; "Drug Czar: 'It Is Time to Sound Alarm' "; "Jury Convicts Two in Probe of Deputies' Drug-Money Skimming"; "Border Crackdown on Drugs Launched"; "Entrepreneurs of Crack"; "White House Readies New Drug Strategy", "U.S Says Colombia Refuses to Cooperate in Drug War"; "$29 Million of Cocaine Uncovered in Raid"; "Mexican Drug Lord Added to FBI List"; "Mexico Vows to Wage War on Drug Smuggling Syndicate"; "Police Arrest 35 People in 5½-Hour Drug Sting"; "Five Convicted in $40 Billion Cocaine Drug Ring"; "U.S., Mexico Join Forces Against Drug Cartels"; "Drug Smugglers Use Canada's West Coast as Gateway to U.S."; "Undercover Officers Report Rise in Drug Sales at Schools"; "Defying U.S. Threat, Bolivians Plants More Coca"; "Pot Farm Raid Yields $24 Million Record Seizure"; "Ex-Prosecutors Charged with Aiding Drug Bosses"; "Experts Question Effect of School's Anti-Drug Programs"; "DEA Arrests Shut Down Heroin Ring"; "The Drug Web that Entangles Mexico"; "Three Charged in Killings over Cocaine Dealing"; "Drug Gang Busted, DA Indicts 22, Ends Terror Wave"; "Colombian Drug Lord Is Captured."

And the game goes on. These headlines over the past four years are virtually identical to those of the previous four years and on back. Can anyone be naive enough to believe that any of these headlines will read differently in the ensuing years if we continue to refuse to take the action necessary to finally bring the drug monster to its knees?

This book was never intended by me—nor, because of its nature, could it ever expect to be—a commercial venture. For this reason, I want to express my deepest appreciation to the book's publisher, Mr. Michael Viner, for caring enough about the future of this country to make the significant financial contribution he has made to disseminate this book and its message to our nation's leaders and all concerned citizens.

Prologue

This book was written with the full realization that the recommendations contained herein may receive as much attention from the federal government as a new fly in the
forest. They are nonetheless set forth in the following spirit:
"Whoever becomes imbued with a grand idea kindles a flame from
which other torches are lit, and influences those with whom he
comes in contact, be they few or many" (Henry George: *Social Problems*).

I believe the federal government will not adopt the measures recommended because for some unfathomable reason, in the area of
fighting drugs, otherwise perfectly intelligent human beings have become virtual automatons who have unconsciously surrendered and
forfeited their right to think in mindless obeisance to existing policies, as pathetically inept as they are. After a seventy-year fight, if the
war on drugs were suspended at this very moment, the consensus of
most knowledgeable observers would be that we have lost the war,
badly. In fact, we've virtually conceded defeat by no longer even trying to win.

Former President Bush's utterances in 1991 that things were looking better in the nation's battle against drug use and that we had
"turned in the right direction," was sadly remindful of President Nixon's announcement to the nation way back in 1973 that we had
"turned the corner on drug use." In any losing war there are rays of
sunlight, and admittedly, in the early 1990s, when President Bush
said this, the use of cocaine (the nation's biggest problem drug) was
down in many segments of our society. But what the Bush Administration failed to note was that the uses of the various illicit drugs
have always been cyclical. For instance, there was a previous drop in
cocaine use between 1979 and 1982, at which time it started to rise
again. Marijuana use rose to record highs in the late 1960s and declined sharply until recently, when its use started to increase again.
Likewise with methamphetamines. And after years of stabilization,
heroin use is again on the rise throughout the nation. So while there

are cycles and dips, the clear, unmistakable trend throughout the years has been dramatically up.

Drug statistics in America that reflect the situation on or even near the date of their promulgation are virtually nonexistent. More often than not, they refer back one, two, sometimes even three years. These statistics demonstrate that illicit drug use is still of epidemic and extremely destructive proportions in America. The most recent National Household Survey on Drug Abuse (NHSDA) is for the year 1994 (published in September of 1995), and reflects that an astonishing 21.8 million Americans used illicit drugs in 1994. Although casual users of cocaine have decreased from 6,247,000 in 1990, 3,889,000 Americans, an enormous number, still use cocaine, and the precipitous drop has stabilized, not changing since 1992. Moreover, the number of hardcore users of cocaine and heroin has remained about the same since 1985 and actually rose slightly in 1994.* And according to the Drug Abuse Warning Network, in 1993, the latest year for which these data are available, drug-related emergency room admissions, long considered a reliable indicator of drug use, are on the increase once again for cocaine, heroin, and marijuana.

More ominously, drug use by the nation's youth is again on the increase. A 1994 national "Monitoring the Future" survey by the Institute for Social Research at the University of Michigan (funded by the federal government's National Institute on Drug Abuse) found that cocaine and marijuana use among eighth and tenth graders doubled since 1991 and had gone up slightly among twelfth graders. "Drug use among American young people has been making a clear comeback in the past two years," Lloyd Johnston, the University of Michigan research scientist said. A December 15, 1995, press release on the 1995 University of Michigan survey reflects a continuing rise among America's youth in the use of all illicit drugs, including LSD, but at the time this book went to press, the report had not yet been released. The very latest 1995 data from PRIDE, the National Parents' Resource Institute for Drug Education, show that marijuana use among junior high school students in America more than dou-

---

*The NHSDA report laid to rest a myth never embraced by law enforcement, but which has nevertheless gained currency among the general population: that drug use in recent years has primarily become a problem among blacks. Although a slightly higher percentage of blacks than whites used illicit drugs in 1994 (7.3 percent to 6 percent; Hispanic use was 5.4 percent), since the vast majority of Americans are white (only 12 percent are black), the NHSDA report estimated that 76 percent of illicit drug users in America in 1994 were white.

bled between 1990–1991 and 1995, and rose 83 percent among high school students. Cocaine use rose one-third. Every survey shows that drug use of all kinds, including LSD and inhalants, is on the increase in high schools throughout the land. What happened in Los Angeles in December of 1994 is typical. Undercover police officers posing as students at Los Angeles high schools arrested the largest number of suspected drug dealers in any semester since 1988. And, of course, property as well as violent crimes continue to be driven by drugs. A 1995 U.S. Department of Justice survey of state prison inmates showed that 40 percent of those incarcerated for burglary were under the influence of an illicit drug at the time of the crime; 30 percent of these committed the burglary to get money to purchase drugs. The figures were 38 percent and 27 percent for robbery, 38 percent and 31 percent for larceny, 28 percent and 5 percent for homicide, and 23 percent and 6 percent for assault. Perhaps most tellingly, in a January, 1995, survey of 382 mayors and other public officials conducted by the National League of Cities, 48.8 percent reported that the problem of drugs and drug-related crime was worsening in their cities. Only 9.1 percent reported an improvement. The balance noticed no difference.

For those who refuse to accept the unassailable reality that we are losing the war on drugs, Robert Silbering, the special narcotics prosecutor for New York City, says: "In no way is the war being won. In fact, all we're doing is fighting a battle of containment, holding the line. We've been reduced to trying to take back streets and apartment houses in the major cities of the nation. Without a real federal leadership and a national commitment, the next generation will be plagued by the same problem." His predecessor, Sterling Johnson, upon hearing some say in 1991 that we were winning the war, replied, "If we are winning the war on drugs, every American better just pray each night that we don't lose. They're kicking our butts. If it was a prize fight, they'd call it." Senior Federal Judge William Knapp of New York jokes that compared to our war on drugs, "the Vietnam War was a brilliant success."

Since the drug crisis in this nation is primarily caused by cocaine and its powerful derivative, crack, the focus of this book will be how to solve the crisis caused by the importation of that drug into this country from the source countries of Peru, Bolivia, and Colombia. However, virtually all of the strategies and tactics recommended herein are equally applicable to every other illicit drug, including marijuana—which comes mostly from Mexico, with domestic and

Colombian production second and third—and heroin, from the opium poppy, which comes primarily from the "Golden Triangle" (Burma, Laos, and Thailand, referred to as "Southeast Asian heroin"), with Colombia second and Mexico and the "Golden Crescent" (Afghanistan, Iran, Lebanon, and Pakistan, called "Southwest Asian heroin"), third.

With necessary exceptions, this will not be a book bursting with statistics and figures. Statistics and figures are for those who are trying to prove a point. Unless one has been living in a bank vault (more about banks later), the point has already been made. The two realities are that drugs are the greatest scourge yet to hit this youthful nation, and that all efforts to curb the importation and abuse of drugs have failed. The estimated $50 *billion* of illicit drugs Americans buy annually are not just destroying the metaphorical *moral* fabric of our nation but, with the thousands upon thousands of drug-related deaths and murders—as well as incalculable human suffering, illness, and lost productivity*—they are, in every sense of the word, knifing the tendons of its *physical* fabric. This book was written pursuant to the above realities.

---

* Estimated by the National Institute of Drug Abuse as costing this country $33 billion annually, due to absenteeism, tardiness, illness, accidents, etc.; the National Public Services Research Institute estimates the overall societal cost of drug abuse at $122 billion per year.

PART ONE

THE DRUG SCOURGE

I n every other area of human endeavor, and routinely in our private lives, when existing methods to solve a problem prove to be ineffectual, we automatically change our methods and technique, i.e., we try something new to achieve our goal. But when it comes to the war on drugs, our nation and its drug-fighting agencies seem determined to give the lie to Longfellow's dictum that "all things must change" by turning their thinking caps to the "off" position and mulishly insisting on combating the drug problem by pursuing policies which have proven to be, over and over again, completely impotent. Never mind, for instance, that ten years ago a kilogram of cocaine sold wholesale for around $60,000 and that today, after billions upon billions of dollars spent in the drug war (at least $30 billion in 1995* alone by federal, state, and local law enforcement), because of the increased availability of the drug, it's around $20,000, dramatic evidence that our efforts have been completely futile. The drug-fighting agencies, each of which is doing a valiant job fighting a war it cannot win, meet this conclusive evidence of failure by a virtually unanimous cry—for what? More money, and more manpower to pursue the same, identical policies. And the fed-

---

* The 1995 *federal* drug budget was $13,264.9 billion. The last available figure for *state* and *local* law enforcement in the drug war, per the 1995 National Drug Control Strategy Report, was $15,907 billion in 1991. (The Clinton Administration's *requested* 1996 drug budget is $14.6 billion.)

eral government, the architect of these policies, obliges, pouring more resources into a bottomless pit.

For instance, the 1988 Anti-Drug Abuse Act, signed amidst much fanfare by President Reagan on November 18, 1988, was called by the president a "*new* sword and shield"* in the nation's battle against the drug epidemic. The act grandly states: "It is the declared policy of the United States Government to create a drug-free America by 1995." But when one cuts through the act's 107 pages, its close to 150,000 words, and its horrendous blizzard of bureaucratic provisions, it is nothing more than a monument to minutiae,** merely providing more of the same, and more funding and manpower to carry it out. The only new measures of any substance whatsoever to bring about this drug-free America were the creation of a "drug czar" to develop and coordinate federal drug efforts; the death penalty for drug-related killings; and a new law that anyone who "knowingly possesses" any drug, even marijuana, in an amount sufficient for personal use, no matter how small, can be fined up to $10,000 and incur other civil penalties, such as a temporary denial of some federal benefits. The drug czar—the actual title is Director of the Office of National Drug Control Policy—in reality is a toothless tiger. The "czar" has no authority to dictate the policies or operations of the various federal agencies in the anti-drug effort. His power, if any, comes from his use of the bully pulpit as a cheerleader for the administration's drug policies, and from his access to the president. The death penalty provision was essentially impotent, since the act provided no death penalty for being a big drug trafficker *per se*; a killing *also* had to be involved, which in many states would *already* carry a possible sentence of death. No one who was in the least familiar with the monumental drug problem this nation faced at the time could have possibly believed that these meager and uninnovative measures could have any effect whatsoever on the problem. And they, of course, didn't.

No American president made the elimination of the drug crisis such a major priority as President Bush. In his inaugural address of

---

*Throughout this book, the author has italicized certain words he wishes to emphasize within quoted passages. Unless indicated otherwise, italics in this book are supplied by the author for emphasis.

**The act also contains delightful gems such as this: Section 487 is titled "Prohibition on Assistance to Drug Traffickers," and actually provides that the president "shall take all reasonable steps to ensure that assistance under this Act" is not provided to drug traffickers.

1989—the year Americans cited drug abuse as the nation's number one problem—he confidently asserted, "Take my word for it, this scourge will stop." In fact, the president's very first televised address to the nation dealt exclusively with the drug problem. Therefore, one would like to be more magnanimous toward the Bush Administration's 1989 National Drug Control Strategy—formulated by former drug czar William Bennett and unveiled by President Bush on September 5, 1989, which provided for a 1990 anti-drug budget of $7.864 billion, later increased to $9.483 billion—but this is not possible. It is nothing short of remarkable that Bennett—supported by a large staff of experts and traveling the breadth and width of the nation the previous half year to speak to large numbers of diverse people and groups (ranging from chiefs of police and district attorneys to mayors and governors; from members of Congress to drug experts and business leaders in the private sector) to hear their ideas on how to solve the drug crisis—would devise a plan which, in terms of innovation, was as empty as a bird's nest in winter.

The centerpiece of the Bennett plan was simply more and tougher law enforcement; namely, more police, more prosecutors, more judges, and more prisons. But *that* has been our answer to the drug problem for the past seventy years. And that answer, we know, hasn't worked. It was as if Bennett and his staff were oblivious to the history of the drug war this nation has waged, offering absolutely nothing new of any real substance and simply recycling, with different ornamentation, old, tired nostrums that have failed miserably throughout the years. It was almost as if Bennett and his staff believed that if it rains long and hard enough, maybe the rain will stop being wet. Instead of becoming a dynamic force for innovative methods to finally bring the drug monster to its knees, Bennett unfortunately seemed satisfied with being the first violin in the orchestra of the status quo. The gruff, peripatetic drug czar, who compared himself to General George S. Patton, was content to simply travel around the country talking about "the good guys and the bad guys" and championing prisons over education. He made such recommendations as taking young black children from drug-infested neighborhoods away from their parents and putting them in orphanages, and pandering to the Yahoo element by declaring, "it would not be immoral to behead" anyone who sells drugs to a minor. To the shouts of Southern Baptist ministers in New Orleans shouting "Amen," Bennett blamed Satan for the national epidemic of drug abuse. Openly partisan, he remarked that "Republicans and *some* Democrats" are really serious about solving the drug problem.*

Bennett, unquestionably a dedicated public servant, also proposed stiffer penalties for casual users of all drugs, including marijuana,** such as incarceration in "boot camps" (already in existence in Georgia, Oklahoma, and Mississippi since the mid-1980s) to make non-users of them. The Bennett plan didn't indicate how the users' mental and emotional makeup, or the environment to which they would eventually be returning—factors that led them to use drugs in the first place—would be reversed in a few weeks of boot camp. Whatever this miracle formula to reshape errant behavioral patterns was, our entire penal system would like to know of it. In view of the very high recidivism rate, penologists readily confess that rehabilitation doesn't normally work, even when the attempt continues for much longer periods.

Among President Bush's opening words in his September 5, 1989, televised address on his drug plan were these: "Our courts, our prisons, our legal system are stretched to the breaking point." He then unabashedly proceeded to reveal how he intended to stretch them further—by far more arrests of drug dealers and users. Bennett's answer to the further stretching? The allocation of $1.477 billion for the construction of new *federal* prison space. But since most drug offenders are prosecuted in the state, not federal, court system, Bennett was forced to acknowledge two days later that in order to meet these goals, state and local governments would have to spend perhaps as much as $5 billion–$10 billion of their *own* money, money they did not have, for new prisons alone.

This cosmetic approach was also evident in foreign aid to the cocaine source countries of Colombia, Peru, and Bolivia. The total economic, military, and law enforcement aid to these three nations in

---

* When he slammed New York Governor Mario Cuomo's drug-fighting record and challenged the Democrat to run for president by saying, "Nobody's afraid of this guy," Senator Daniel Patrick Moynihan (D–N.Y.) felt constrained to reply: "How does such a man come to refer to the Governor of the State of New York as "this guy?" There undoubtedly is a place in the drug fight for someone like Mr. Bennett, but it did not seem to be in the position he occupied. He appeared to be a perfect example of an impressive I.Q. not translating into common sense and effectiveness.

** The high-water mark for marijuana use in America was the late sixties and early seventies—when punishment for the drug's use was much stiffer than that recommended by Bennett, six-month and even one- and two-year sentences not being uncommon in some states. The epitome of irrational punishment was Virginia's Uniform Drug Act, which provided for imprisonment of not less than twenty years for simple possession.

fiscal year 1990 was only $217 million* (up from $61 million in 1989). Did anyone sincerely believe that sending an additional $156 million to these Andean nations (which included the costs of a small contingent of American military advisers in Colombia and Bolivia to train their armed forces and police in combating drug trafficking) was going to have any measurable effect on the problem? "The additional money is spit-in-the-ocean tokenism, that's what it is," opined Florida Congressman Lawrence Smith, chairman of the House Foreign Affairs Committee Task Force on International Narcotics.

The plan, in a nutshell, was an embarrassment to any serious student of our nation's drug problem. Though trumpeted as a "new" strategy, no matter how you sliced it the essence of the plan was simply to spend more money (and very little more at that) to carry out old and already failed policies, reshifting emphasis here and there. "I have a feeling of time warp," said Jack A. Blum, a former special counsel on narcotics for the Senate Foreign Relations Committee. "There is nothing radically new. The Bennett plan calls for a little more of everything," wrote syndicated columnist Charles Krauthammer. "Simply more of the same. Presidents Nixon, Ford, Carter, and Reagan used much the same words—and techniques," agreed *Atlanta Journal-Constitution* columnist Jim Fain. "While Bush proposes some new money, he is mainly relying on old ideas," said the *Los Angeles Times*.

In a tacit acknowledgment by Bennett and his staff of the plan's lack of virility, its vest-pocket goal was to reduce drug consumption in the United States by 50 percent within the next decade. "A program that would bring progress measured in inches," the *New York Times* editorialized. "Extraordinarily modest," opined Mathca Falco, former assistant secretary of state for international narcotics matters.

It's one thing to devise a strategy that at least has the theoretical potential to substantially solve the drug curse soon, but fails. But to propose a strategy which, by the proponent's own admission, will take ten years, and even then, only reduce drug consumption by one-half, is clearly unacceptable. This nation obviously should never, in effect, give its consent to endure many more years of tragedy and carnage.

In 1992, after four years of "Bush's drug war," *New York Times'* reporter Joseph B. Treaster wrote that little had been achieved. "Since taking office," Mr. Treaster observed, "Mr. Bush has poured more

---

* The 1996 requested budget for the three Andean nations is only $137 million.

and more money into . . . trying to stop drugs at the borders, cajoling and threatening drug-producing nations, and jailing thousands of Americans for ever longer terms. Yet emergency room statistics, often regarded as a barometer of drug use, are worse now than when the President launched the most expensive anti-drug crusade in American history . . . grabbing the issue when public opinion surveys showed an extraordinary level of national concern. And each year farmers in Latin America have been producing ever-larger crops of coca . . . and smugglers daily dart through the ever-more elaborate American mazes of patrol boats, planes, and electronic barriers."

Bush, during his campaign for the presidency and throughout his term in office, publicly hammered away at the evils of drugs and vowed to "win the drug war." Yet what he actually did really only constituted the most token of efforts. While the former president, in the abstract, undoubtedly wanted to win the drug war, the reality is that he and his predecessors weren't really willing to cross the street in the rain without an umbrella to do so. As will be gleaned from facts and evidence presented throughout this book, this nation has never been truly serious about ending the drug crisis, and Bush's efforts and public pronouncements were, for the most part, more of the same: perfunctory and simply public posturing.

For the past several years, unlike the 1989 polls citing drug abuse as the nation's number one problem (a fact that, together with the harsh reality it represented, prompted the original writing of this book), drug abuse has not been viewed by the American people as the most serious problem facing the nation. Crime has been. In September of 1989, when the media was focusing on drugs, a Gallup poll showed that 63 percent of the American people believed drug abuse was "the most important problem facing this country today." Only 3 percent said crime. In a July, 1995, Gallup poll, Americans said crime was the number one problem facing this country. Drug abuse was number four. There seems to be only one explanation for this. Despite the fact that virtually everyone knows that drugs fuel crime (a 1995 survey by Peter D. Hart Associates of 386 American police chiefs and sheriffs cited reducing drug abuse as the number one way to reduce crime), and although the empirical evidence remains the same that drugs and crime are irrevocably related, for unknown reasons, the electronic media in particular has started treating the two as separate. In Ayn Rand's book *The Fountainhead*, a big-city newspaper publisher proclaims that "public opinion is what I make it."

Drug Czar Lee P. Brown, alluding to this phenomenon, said in a May 21, 1995, interview with the *Dallas Morning News*: "In 1989, the three major television networks covered drugs about 500 times on the evening news, and crime around 500 times. In 1993, they covered drugs 60 times and crime 1,600 times. [Per Dan Amundson, research director at the Center for Media and Public Affairs, in 1994 there were only seventy-eight drug stories, as opposed to 1,949 crime stories. Complete 1995 statistics are not yet available, but the ratio is reportedly the same.] The irony is that they're not making the linkage that the drug problem pushes the crime and violence problem." Long Island University Professor Micah Fink, in his article "Don't Forget the Hype: Media, Drugs and Public Opinion," in the periodical *Extra*, writes that "public anxiety about drugs subsides after media attention to the drug issue fades . . . but it remains a small matter for the media or [a presidential] administration to bring the issue back to life." However, between July and December of 1995, something curious happened. Although the media has continued to separate crime and drug stories, and to present a far greater number of crime than drug pieces, the latest Gallup poll, released on December 11, 1995, shows that 88 percent of Americans now rate the drug problem a close second to crime (94 percent) as this country's most serious problem.

President Bill Clinton, unlike former President Bush, has had the good taste not to posture as much in the drug arena, nor publicly make the drug war a nominal, yet nonexistent, centerpiece of his administration. However, the quiet, official declarations of the Clinton Administration have continued the charade—acknowledging the severity of the drug problem, yet doing nothing meaningful to end it. In President Clinton's "Message from the President," which introduced his 1995 National Drug Control Strategy report, he proclaimed: "We cannot keep the American dream alive for working families if our youth are turning to illegal drug use and trafficking continues unabated. We cannot compete in the new world economy . . . while international drug trafficking is rampant. We cannot enter the new millennium as the strongest country in the world unless we . . . lead the way against illegal drugs and the terror they bring—both here and abroad. . . . Drug use drains our economy of billions of dollars and prevents *millions of Americans* from achieving their full potential. . . ." Asserting that drugs are "destroying our children's futures," the president said that our "solutions [to the drug problem] must be more creative and flexible, and the 1995 strategy starts us down this path."

But the Clinton Administration's conduct speaks so loudly that I, for one, can't hear a word it is saying. How is it possible that President Clinton could utter these words, yet put his stamp of approval on a "strategy" that not only gives creativity (which the president says we need) a bad name, but is identical to the policies and techniques for solving the drug problem that this nation has been ineffectively employing for decades? In his campaign for the presidency, Clinton, in a different context, defined insanity as "doing the same thing over and over again and expecting a different result." Surely, deep down, the president, like his predecessors with their programs, has to know that that is precisely what he is doing now in attempting to combat this nation's current drug problem.

When President Clinton took office, he appointed Dr. Lee Brown,* a former New York City police commissioner with a doctorate in criminology from the University of California at Berkeley, to replace Bob Martinez, Bush's last drug czar, as the nation's drug czar, and elevated the post to Cabinet level (although reducing the drug czar office's staff from 146 to 40 in a budget-cutting move). Brown, unlike Bennett, has not offended the sensibilities with insufferable statements and positions. But like Bennett, he has been equally ineffective and almost irrelevant.

Clinton and Brown looked at the statistics and saw that although $20 billion had been spent in the previous fourteen years on interdicting the flow of drugs into this country, more drugs than ever were reaching our shores, as attested to by the decreasing cost and increasing cocaine and heroin on the streets of our cities. "I really hope they will push drug reduction," said Jim Fox, head of the FBI office in New York City, about the new administration. "We've been concentrating on supply, and each year we seize more and more tons of hard drugs. But each year they get cheaper on the street. It hasn't been very effective." Also, a 1993 National Security Council report recommended cutting the military's anti-smuggling role, finding that despite the use of military aircraft, Coast Guard ships, and radar bal-

---

* Brown resigned as drug czar in December of 1995. On January 23, 1996, two days before the final draft of this book was submitted for publication, President Clinton nominated Army General Barry McCaffrey to be the new drug czar. McCaffrey has been commander-in-chief of the U.S. Southern Command in Panama City, Panama, where he has overseen a substantial percentage (excluding Mexico) of the military's drug interdiction efforts.

loons, most cocaine was getting through the costly net uninterrupted.

The Clinton Administration responded in its first national drug
control strategy budget (prepared in the president's first year, 1993,
for the 1994 fiscal year) by starting to shift anti-drug efforts away
from supply reduction (law enforcement, interdiction, etc.) to demand reduction (education, treatment, etc.). However, the highly
publicized shift was actually negligible. Instead of the previous year's
split by the Bush Administration in anti-drug spending of 65 percent
for supply reduction and 35 percent for demand reduction (in 1991–
1993 it was the same, in 1990, the split was 67–00 percent), the
1994 Clinton budget altered the percentages to 63–37 percent. In
1995, education and treatment expenditures increased even further,
bringing the split to 62–38 percent. But the Clinton Administration's
proposed 1996 budget is heading in the opposite direction again, with
a 64–36 percent division of anti-drug resources.

The problem, of course, is that anti-drug money and efforts continue to be spent on the same policies that have ineffectually been
in force for years. Though the percentages vary slightly each year,
everything (methodology) remains exactly in place. For political reasons, each succeeding administration (and for each year within the
four-year term) is compelled to come up with what it denominates
"new initiatives" to combat the drug scourge. *But without exception
these initiatives are never anything more than a slight and marginal
increase or decrease in emphasis on initiatives and policies already
in place.* For instance, the Clinton Administration, as evidence of the
president's mandate to be "creative," sets forth four initiatives for
drug control in its proposed fiscal year 1996 drug strategy (pages
114–116 of the 1995 National Drug Control Strategy): empowering
communities with more discretion in the use of drug money grants;
improving drug treatment and prevention; reducing chronic, hardcore drug use; and increasing the drug-fighting effectiveness of the
source countries (mostly, Colombia, Peru, and Bolivia). Is there anyone in the Clinton Administration who blushes over calling these
initiatives "new and creative" when the four proposed 1995 initiatives (pages 78–81 of 1994 National Drug Control Strategy) were:
empowering communities with more discretion to combat drug-
related violence and crime; reducing hardcore drug use through treatment; ensuring safe and drug-free schools by improving prevention
efficiency; and increasing international (i.e., source country) anti-
drug program efforts? And when absolutely no *new* techniques and

strategies are set forth—other than the inevitable and obligatory yearly decrease or increase in money and/or manpower in various areas of the drug war such as interdiction, law enforcement, education, etc.?

We are told (pages 149–150 of the 1995 National Drug Control Strategy) that this magical document had the input from four regional strategy development conferences across the country, six focus groups, fact-finding trips by Mr. Brown to many countries, and perhaps most importantly, consultation with 1,100 people, including every member of Congress, senior federal officials, drug experts, and over 200 mayors and state and local law enforcement officials. But just one reasonably intelligent individual with a facility for the English language and a modicum of expertise in the drug war could write and publish a similar document, overflowing with platitudes and generalities, with the recurrent motif of "business as usual." The document articulates, in an adolescent way, that "drug use threatens the American way of life and things *must* change," and "the drug problem affects everyone. All Americans *must* be involved in its solution," yet offers not one tiny morsel of innovative and realistic technique to bring these objectives about, as if the mere uttering of the words will, miraculously, make these things happen. In its surrealism, the document conjures up the image of Adolf Hitler, in physical and mental decline, stooped over a conference table map with his generals in his Berlin bunker in April, 1945, as the Russian army tightened its vise-like grip on the city, moving imaginary divisions around to change the course of the war.

The fact that no real "war" on drugs has ever been waged by our federal government has been revealed in many and diverse ways. One incident, referred to in the Introduction to this work, was President Bush's mere request to the Andean nation leaders at the 1992 San Antonio drug summit that the leaders reduce narcotic production in their countries. Another (among many that will be set forth in this book) is contained within the very pages of the aforementioned Clinton Administration's own 1995 National Drug Control Strategy report. Unwittingly conceding that the drug "war" is not one to win, but a fact of life—a maleficent staple, if you will, of America's culture—the document casually refers (on page 119) to the funding priorities through 1999, *the very end of the millennium.* The priorities are for the same, identical programs we have implemented for decades, all to virtually no avail, namely: "expand drug treatment capacity; target youth to reduce their use of illicit drugs; reduce drug-related crime and violence; reduce all domestic drug production and continue to target for investigation and prosecution those who illegally manufacture and distribute drugs; strengthen international cooperation and actions against narcotics production, trafficking and use," and so on.

As surely as I am now sitting at my kitchen table writing these words on my yellow legal pad, come the end of this century the drug situation and game will not be dramatically different than it is right now. Only the names of the participants will have changed.

As a former member of law enforcement myself, I feel uncomfortable reading about and watching the chiefs of police, sheriffs, and U.S. attorneys, etc., who, like clockwork, grace the daily newspapers and evening television news every week or so standing behind millions of dollars in seized drug money alongside hundreds of pounds of cocaine. The accompanying article and news report nearly always states that the seizure set some type of record (or was second or third) in the city, county, state, or nation, and often compares the amount of money and drugs seized with seizures in other parts of the country, almost as if it has become some type of game among law enforcement agencies as to "who can put the most powder on the table."

In fact, the world's largest seizure of cocaine was on September 28, 1989, in Sylmar, California (a community about twenty miles northwest of Los Angeles), where federal and local law enforcement agents seized the incredible amount of 21.4 tons of the drug in a single warehouse, with an estimated street value of close to $6 *billion*. That's just $300,000 less than the entire 1989 U.S. federal budget to fight drugs! The previous record was on March 10, 1984, when Colombian police seized and destroyed 13.8 metric tons (15.2 tons) of cocaine at a complex of cocaine laboratories located in a remote jungle area 350 miles southeast of Bogota called Tranquilandia (Quiet Village). The domestic record for a heroin seizure is 1,071 pounds in Oakland, California, on May 20, 1991. The marijuana record seizure is 389,113 pounds in Miami, Florida, on August 8, 1988. Photographs of large seizures of drugs and cash have been taken thousands of times around the country throughout the years, dating as far back as 1916, when federal agents are shown standing behind a table with a large stack of money and heroin on it.

The large seizures of drugs and cash are, for the most part, valueless. Law enforcement has already learned that where the drugs and money come from, there is, has always been, and will always continue to be much more to follow, and that trying to stop the importation and use of drugs in this country under existing techniques is no more effective than trying to stop a gust of wind with a net. We have new, get-tough legislation, police sweeps and "crackdowns" on users, pushers, and gangs, law enforcement symposiums, news conferences, blue-ribbon task forces and studies, TV and Hollywood movies, national polls and cover stories, and the drug crisis goes on. The latest game plan of major metropolitan police departments throughout the country? "A reverse sting operation" against users. The police set up, mind you, their own "crack houses," in which they lure buyers, sell them drugs, then arrest them. Not only is it distasteful on its face to have the police go out and peddle narcotics, but the lesson of its futility has been ignored: Miami did the same thing back in 1986, and other than resulting in over 3,000 arrests and increasing the already heavy burden on Miami's criminal justice system, the effort predictably had no effect whatsoever on the city's raging drug problem.

As Miami's Metro-Dade narcotics detective Preston Lucas (with Luis Fernandez, often referred to as the real-life counterparts of "Miami Vice's" Sonny Crockett and Richard Tubbs) sums it up: "It's just a big fat game, and we're losing."

The official history of our *national* effort to fight drugs dates back to the Harrison Narcotic Drug Act of 1914. Although the Pure Food and Drug Act of 1906 also regulated narcotics, its purview was limited to prohibiting the adulteration and mislabeling of drugs contained in patent medicines shipped in interstate commerce. Actually, the Harrison Narcotics Act was not even a criminal statute, and possession and use of opiates (opium, heroin, and morphine) and cocaine were not, per se, prohibited. It was a revenue measure providing for the registration and taxation of those who manufactured, sold, or dispensed opiates and cocaine, and the only criminal violations specified were for failure to keep honest records, or for possession of these drugs without having "registered under the provisions" of the act, or having "paid the special tax provided for" by the act. Before the Harrison Narcotics Act, because of almost nonexistent enforcement of state laws, narcotics were freely sold in the nation's drugstores. Around the turn of the century, narcotics were an ingredient in many commercial products. Examples include not only the more famous Coca-Cola soft drink, which until 1906 contained cocaine, but also products like Dr. Agnew's Catarrah Powder, a cure for the common chest cold that also contained cocaine. Adamson's Botanic Cough Balsam contained heroin. Kohler's One-Night Cough Cure contained morphine. In the mid-1880s, Parke, Davis & Co. was selling cocaine and coca in fifteen forms, including coca-leaf cigarettes and cheroots, cocaine inhalant, a coca cordial, cocaine crystals, and even cocaine in solution for hypodermic injection. This continued after the Harrison Narcotics Act, although under Section 6 of the act the products now could not contain more than a specified amount of the drug, e.g., "one-eighth of a grain of heroin."

Since the Harrison Act was only a tax law, responsibility for enforcing it was left to the Bureau of Internal Revenue in the Department of the Treasury. However, the act contained an open-to-interpretation clause, which provided that a physician should dispense narcotics "in the course of his professional practice only," and federal agents began to arrest physicians who were supplying addicts in violation of this provision. Thus the bureau, the original predecessor to today's Drug Enforcement Administration (DEA—the leading federal anti-drug agency) became the first federal drug law-enforcement agency. The bureau was followed by a succession of agencies, including the Bureau of Narcotics and Dangerous Drugs (BNDD). The BNDD, created in 1968, was under the aegis of the Department of Justice, the first time in half a century that drug enforcement was no longer managed through the Treasury Department. BNDD's successor in 1973, today's Drug Enforcement Administration, also operates through the Department of Justice.

Headquartered in Arlington, Virginia, the DEA is the only federal agency in the drug-fighting effort whose sole mission is combating drugs. "Like all the other agencies," says Miami DEA agent John Fernandez, "we also have multiple jurisdictions. Ours is drugs, drugs, and drugs." The DEA, with 2,775 agents (3,648 agents are authorized), has 142 offices in the United States and 71 offices in 49 countries around the world. The foreign offices coordinate their efforts with the U.S. Department of State and foreign law enforcement officials to stop the flow of drugs destined for the United States. No job in U.S. law enforcement is more dangerous yet receives less public recognition for itself (as well as for the superior and courageous job it has done fighting a hopeless battle in the drug war) than the DEA. Most agents carry two or three handguns on assignment; many even carry knives. Currently, the DEA is the only federal law enforcement agency authorized to routinely carry fully automatic submachine guns. In other federal law enforcement agencies, only certain special squads within the agency are so authorized. Ralph Lochridge, DEA spokesman for the Los Angeles office, who himself has been shot and wounded twice, says that there's a rule of thumb in the DEA that if you've been in the agency ten years, you've "probably been shot at at least once," an uncommonly high risk. Since 1973, forty-three DEA agents and employees have been killed in the line of duty.

In 1982, the FBI received concurrent jurisdiction with the DEA to investigate violations of federal criminal drug laws. Though relatively new to the drug fight, the FBI has already made its presence felt, conducting a great number of successful narcotics investigations. Although a 1982 order of the attorney general placed the DEA under the general supervision of the FBI, this is not the reality. As a March, 1990, report of the U.S. General Accounting Office to the Senate Committee on Governmental Affairs stated, "For the most part, the two agencies operate independently." An August, 1993, recommendation by Vice President Al Gore to merge the DEA into the FBI for cost-cutting purposes was not adopted.

Since 1914, our country's efforts to combat drug abuse clearly and unequivocally reveal that along with the consistent and whopping increases in manpower and money poured into the fight by the federal coffers (e.g., in 1919, only $250,000 was allotted by the federal government to drug enforcement, the requested 1996 fiscal year drug budget is $14.6 billion), the nation's quenchless appetite for narcotics has dramatically increased. This is not to suggest, obviously, that the increased use of drugs is due to, or in any way induced by, the efforts to stop it. What it does mean—and this is not open to debate—is that our nation's efforts to stop the drug scourge have been completely ineffective.

What the history of the country's fight against drugs also reveals is that the nature of the war fought, and the game waged, have changed precious little. As far back as the 1920s and 1930s, narcotics agents were using informants, buying drugs with marked money in an undercover capacity, conducting raids and "record" seizures of narcotics, etc.; smugglers, in waters off our shores, were using smoke screens, decoy vessels, and all types of elaborate evasive tactics to avoid the interdiction of the U.S. Coast Guard; narcotics were concealed, as today, in large quantities on incoming ships (e.g., 650 pounds of cocaine and opium on the S.S. *King Alexander* in 1927;

1,000 pounds of morphine on the S.S. *Alesia* in 1930); opium and marijuana were being smuggled across the Mexican border in a variety of ways, including inside the gasoline tanks of motor vehicles, etc. And the hand-wringing and dire headlines of the day were virtually interchangeable with those of today.

We tend to think the situation today is somehow new. This is because we are unaware of the past. Only the degree of the problem has changed. We read today about "strawberries" (usually black prostitutes) selling themselves for cocaine; then we learn that in 1903, the state of Georgia reported that "almost every negro prostitute in the state is addicted to cocaine." A committee report to the New York legislature in 1917 stated: "The problem of narcotic drug addiction has passed all the bounds of reasonable comprehension in the State of New York and in the United States, and has become the greatest evil with which the Commonwealth has to contend."

In 1925, California Congressman Walter F. Lineberger, in an effort to curb the growing use of drugs by teenagers, sent letters to 5,000 city and county superintendents of education throughout the country, calling for their support in bringing before school boards, teachers, and parents a document titled "The Peril of Narcotic Drugs." Richard P. Hobson, the chief anti-narcotic crusader of the day, in a nationwide radio broadcast on March 1, 1928, warned: "Upon this issue hangs the perpetuation of civilization, the future of the human race."

This, from the February 16, 1929, edition of the *Saturday Evening Post:* "The wholesale smuggling of narcotic drugs into the country is a grave menace to our national well-being." Referring to the estimated 100,000 addicts* in the land (the U.S. Senate Judiciary Committee estimates the present figure to be 5.6 million), the article stated that "if Congress would attack the evil aggressively it would be largely abated." Noting that the "present budget and personnel of the Narcotics Bureau" were inadequate, the *Post* called for "a much larger force to seriously cripple the dope-selling industry." The *Post*

---

*Early figures of drug use and addiction were very sporadic and wildly divergent. The statistics were unscientific estimates and almost always dealt only with addicts, not mere users. An example of divergence: There were two New York State estimates of drug addiction in 1917, one of 39,000, the other 200,000, the latter almost surely wrong. Throughout the 1920s, one finds this same type of disparity. The most consistent figure once reads, however, is around 100,000 addicts in the land in the 1920s. The main drug was opium, and its derivatives of morphine and heroin. Cocaine was second in preference, and marijuana a distant third.

also called for "heavier penalties" for drug sellers and users to stem the use of narcotics.

On July 9, 1933, a League of Nations treaty (one of many in a succession of effete international anti-narcotic agreements—the first one resulting from the thirteen-nation Shanghai Convention in 1909) went into effect. The fifty-seven-nation treaty laid down the guidelines for a concerted multinational effort to fight the production, distribution, and sale of illicit narcotics. On July 10, 1933, the *New York Times* quoted President Roosevelt hailing the treaty as "a wonderful achievement." The head of the World Narcotics Defense Association said that the treaty "placed in operation the majestic power of the civilized world to strike down the illicit narcotic drug traffic. It is a signal victory in the war against the narcotic evil." A local judge told the *Times* that in his Manhattan court alone in 1932, 1,188 defendants had been arraigned for the possession or sale of narcotics. Referring to the new treaty, the judge said, "There is only one possible solution to this problem, and that solution is now in sight."

The *Literary Digest*'s July 29, 1933, edition referred to the "thirty years of struggle [*taking the war on drugs back to 1903*] to end one of the most insidious perils to mankind." Louis Ruppel, deputy commissioner of the Bureau of Narcotics, wrote in the May, 1934, edition of *Current History*, "The Federal Government is confronted with a titanic and apparently endless job in fighting dope peddling," and referred to the "long and bitter fight against the illicit drug trade."

On February 2, 1939, the *New York Times* reported that "forty U.S. Treasury agents invaded the San Juan Hill section yesterday and arrested twelve narcotic dealers. Before descending on the scores of tenement houses, the agents blocked off exits by placing their automobiles across the thoroughfare. Garland Williams, district supervisor of the Treasury narcotics agents, said, 'For more than twenty-five years San Juan Hill has resisted every effort by law enforcement agencies to clean it up. In recent years, seven policemen have been killed and in the past two years more than 200 arrests have been made, but the narcotic trade has gone on unimpaired.' "

Due to the increased availability of opium in this country, on July 3, 1944, President Roosevelt approved a joint resolution by Congress urging the opium-producing countries of the world to take steps to control the production and trafficking of the drug.

The July 31, 1948, edition of *Colliers* wrote of the "War against

Dope Runners": "Heroin, morphine, opium—products of Mexico's red poppy—are today moving in a hundred cunning ways across the Mexican border into the United States. A determined effort to stop this traffic is engaging the full time of hundreds of American and Mexican customs officers and narcotics agents." And, quoting one narcotics agent: "It's mighty serious when that stuff coming up from below the border finds it way into high schools. That's why this war is an *all-out war*." That was in 1948, forty-seven years ago! As indicated, such headlines and stories are interchangeable with those of today.

(Most people, in fact, believe that the term and notion of a "war on drugs" is of recent origin. But the affinity for the war metaphor goes way back. As early as July 21, 1929, a *New York Times* article was captioned, "Waging the War upon Narcotics." Actually, the first presidential administration to formally declare a war on drugs was that of Richard M. Nixon. In a speech on September 18, 1972, Nixon said, "We are living in an age . . . when there are times that a great nation must engage in what is called a limited war. I have rejected that principle in declaring a total war against dangerous drugs. Our goal is the total banishment of drug abuse from the American life." That was twenty-three years ago, more than twice as long as World Wars I and II combined. Earlier, on June 17, 1971, Nixon had told Congress that the drug problem in America had become a "national emergency." Calling it "public enemy number one," he promised "a total offensive.")

With this mildewed history, the 1950s begin to sound modern, until we remind ourselves that 1950 was forty-six years ago, close to half a century. No "war" in American history has lasted anywhere near that long, and not only have we made no progress since then, the situation has gotten much worse. *Reader's Digest*, in its April, 1950, edition, wrote of "Our Global War on Narcotics." The *Digest* noted that "drug trafficking and addiction are contributing more and more to crime of all kinds—from gang warfare and murder, to prostitution and larceny by addicts in need of money to satisfy their expensive craving." The article referred to "a single shipment which U.S. Customs inspectors recently found in the tail assembly of an airplane at LaGuardia Airport" worth "over a million dollars in the retail trade."

In *Newsweek*, June 11, 1951, a U.S. Customs officer is quoted as saying that "it's a physical impossibility" to stop the flow of drugs into this country. William Jennings Bryan, Jr., the collector of customs in Los Angeles, added that seizures were up 35 percent from the previous year, but that nearly every ship was bringing in narcotics. "Both the League of Nations and the U.N. have tried in vain to stop the traffic at its source by getting drug-producing countries to cut production down to a level where it meets only medical and scientific needs," the article reported. *Time*, June 25, 1951, referred to New York City as "a city where pushers peddle their wares almost as casually as sidewalk vendors, where children sniff heroin even in classrooms, where an innocent-looking drugstore or cafeteria may be an addict's hangout." *Time* spoke of New York City's traffic in drugs—$100 million a year in street sales—as the nation's worst, but spoke of the "alarming increases in dope consumption" throughout the nation's cities.

The August 4, 1951, edition of *Colliers* warned: "Heavy as the federal tax burden is today, it is not possible to talk of economy in this matter when one has read the pathetically tragic stories of teenage, and sometimes less-than-teen-age, drug users." The article goes on to refer to "the life-wrecking torture of physical and moral degeneration and almost inevitable commission of crime which the drug habit inflicts upon the pitiful youngsters. It will take a *total war* on all fronts to stamp it out."

Need we trace the progression of the drug problem up to the present time any further? What this brief history proves is that if we continue to fight the drug war as we have for more than seventy years, and do not employ completely new, revolutionary, and draconian measures, writers in the twenty-first century, lamenting the cataclysmic dimensions of the narcotics problem of the times, will be writing about us as we do today about our predecessors. To think otherwise is to deny reality and engage in a national self-delusion. And if the alarming progression of drug abuse with its attendant horrors is any guide, by extrapolation, our nation's streets could be on the brink of anarchy even before the dawn of the twenty-first century.

The philosopher George Santayana said that those who cannot remember the past are condemned to repeat it. Our fight to stop drugs today, and the toll it has taken on our society, is a darker photostatic copy of our past, and if we don't change our methods of fighting the war, we can only expect more and worse of the same in the future.

Cocaine (although a drug, cocaine is technically not a narcotic, since it is a stimulant, not a depressant) is widely acknowledged by American authorities to be by far the most serious problem drug facing this nation today. According to the most recent (1994) National Household Survey on Drug Abuse (NHSDA) report, for every user of heroin in 1994, the other major addictive drug, there were approximately thirteen users of cocaine. As opposed to cocaine, heroin, in fact, has never been a prevalent drug of choice. The 1994 NHSDA survey estimated that while 21,821,000 Americans have at one time used cocaine, only 2,083,000 have used heroin. As mentioned earlier, however, heroin use is on the rise. Although still not chic, nor attaining, like cocaine in the eighties, *de rigueur* status among some segments of "yuppicdom" and the entertainment industry, heroin, traditionally a drug of street people, has expanded its constituency and is starting to invade suburbia. One indication among many: The number of people treated for heroin addiction at the upscale Betty Ford Center in Rancho Mirage, California, doubled in 1995 from 1994.

Unlike heroin, which is a true narcotic, producing a dreamlike state of well-being and lethargy, cocaine can produce violent behavior. And cocaine is the source of the highly addictive "crack" ("I hit it once and I've been strung out on it ever since," one continually hears from crack addicts), which produces even more aggressive, paranoid behavior and is at the root of the orgy of violence, blood, and despair engulfing the nation's inner cities. Because crack, first introduced into this country in 1981, induces aggression and paranoia, murder rates have risen sharply in the nation's major cities since its use became widespread in 1986. Crack is made by mixing the cocaine powder with baking soda and water and then heating it. This produces a solid product, which is "cracked" into salable rocklike fragments usually sold in a vial for five to ten dollars. *Los Angeles Times* staff writer David Ferrell, reporting in December, 1994, on the scourge of crack on Los Angeles's inner city, tells a story that is repeated in virtually every major city in the land: "Crack is everywhere, a fiercely dominating drug that has eroded much of the city's beleaguered core while scattering 'mini-Skid Rows' throughout poorer outlying neighborhoods. . . . For the sake of a hit, guns blaze, people die, apartments are ransacked, windows are smashed. Driven by their cravings, men steal from their families. Young mothers forsake baby food and diapers . . . and walk the streets as prostitutes, trading sex for [crack] . . . Teenagers drop out of school, employees quit their jobs or get fired for theft or absenteeism. In the crass street ethic of the drug, all other rules and priorities submit to a single, overriding aim: to obtain that next rock."

In attempting to suppress cocaine use, it must be recognized that the drug is a very formidable opponent. Says an everyday user: "The silver bullet reaches your brain with such an impact, sometimes you forget your own name, but you don't care. The euphoria is so intense, nothing else matters except the feeling." Monkeys taught to press a lever to receive a cocaine injection have repeatedly done so until they died, stopping neither to eat nor to sleep. And cocaine use has a rather distinguished ancestry. For example, Ulysses S. Grant, in failing health, reportedly wrote his memoirs sustained by the drug. Scottish novelist and poet Robert Louis Stevenson used cocaine. Sigmund Freud was particularly taken with the drug, writing in a letter to his fiancée, Martha Bernays, in 1884 that a dose of cocaine "lifted me to the heights in a wonderful fashion. I am just now busy collecting the literature for a song of praise to this magical substance." In his subsequent "Song of Praise" to cocaine published in the July, 1884, issue of the medical journal *Centralblatt für die gesammte Therapie*, he endorsed the mythical saga of how Manco Capac, the first Inca emperor and Royal Son of the Sun-God, had brought cocaine from heaven as "a gift from the gods to satisfy the hungry, fortify the weary, and make the unfortunate forget their sorrows."

But this unlettered poem captures cocaine's formidable nature even more:

I am the King of crime and the prince of destruction,
I'll cause the organs of your body to malfunction.
I'll cause babies to be born hooked,
I'll turn honest men to crooks.
I'll make you rob, steal and kill,
When you're under my power, you have no will.

Cocaine has been available in this country since approximately 1870 (an Austrian chemist, Albert Nieman, first extracted pure cocaine from the coca plant in 1861), but the first heavy influx of the drug into the United States occurred in South Florida in the late 1970s. It wasn't until 1980 and 1981, with the "cocaine wars"—a bloody eruption of murders and shootings in Miami between rival cocaine trafficking organizations fighting for control of the cocaine market—that the public's attention became focused on the expanding cocaine trade in America. "Up until the early 1990s, Miami was the focal point for [Colombian cocaine] cartel activities in the United States," says Charles Gutensohn, former chief of cocaine investigations for the DEA. "For the first time," added Salvatore R. Marloche (then the assistant secretary of the Treasury for Enforcement) in 1991, "it's become a horse race between Miami and L.A., but Big Daddy is still Miami." In fact, even to this day, illegal drugs, primarily cocaine, are a mainstay of the Sunshine State's economy, pumping more than $6 billion in 1994 into the South Florida economy alone. That is almost $1 billion more than all the revenues produced by Florida's agriculture industry, including citrus.*

When Florida's dealers and traffickers are caught and prosecuted, who represents them? Very frequently, as is the case throughout the country, former prosecutors with the U.S. Attorney's office who, before they switched sides, specialized in prosecuting major drug cases, i.e., they are now defending the very types of drug traffickers they once vigorously prosecuted. And what is the source of their six- and sometimes seven-figure fees, which allows them to live regally in places such as Bay Point, an elegant walled and gated enclave off Biscayne Boulevard in Miami? Their clients' drug profits. And the game goes on.

Approximately 80 to 85 percent of the cocaine reaching the United States is produced in Colombia for commercial consumption. Peru and Bolivia are responsible for most of the remainder. While the coca plant is grown predominantly in Peru and Bolivia, and the coca leaves converted into a thick paste and then coca base there, most of the semi-refined cocaine base is sent to Colombia, where processing laboratories refine it into cocaine powder (cocaine hydrochloride), the form it is in when ultimately used. To make the cocaine powder good for inhaling, the base has to be dissolved in the chemical ether, or an emerging substitute for ether, the chemical methyl ethyl ketone (MEK). Each kilo of base requires seventeen liters of ether. Prior to the 1989 Chemical Diversion and Trafficking Act, which empowers U.S. officials to halt shipments of precursor chemicals out of this country that they believe are likely to be utilized for the production of cocaine, 90 percent of ether, acetone, and other cocaine chemicals came from U.S. companies. Since the new law reduced American shipments of the chemicals markedly, West Germany has taken up

---

*Sometimes, even the good guys prosper. Florida's conservative former Governor Bob Martinez (who went on to become drug czar under President Bush), for example, frequently traveled in a $600,000 twin-engine plane confiscated from Pinellas County smuggler Joseph Valverde. Even drug informants are prospering. According to a 1992 House Government Operations Committee report, several informants made more than $500,000 a year in 1990 and 1991. Sixty-five made more than $100,000 a year. The DEA pays informers up to 25 percent of the street value of the drugs seized.

the slack, now providing Colombia with two-thirds of the needed chemicals.

It is the consensus of federal drug officials that even if the nation were unable to solve the problems of all the other illicit drugs,* such as marijuana (considered by many a harmless, recreational drug) and heroin (as we have seen, not nearly as popular a drug as cocaine is today—nor was it even during the Turkish heroin days of the "French Connection" in 1967–1971—and which doesn't produce aggressive behavior), the nation's vitals would in no way be threatened. Not so with cocaine and its derivative crack, which, as *Time* put it succinctly, is "tearing the heart out of U.S. cities." A February 27, 1995, staff report of the U.S. Senate Committee on Foreign Relations said: "Cocaine remains the primary drug threat to the United States."

Although drug abuse is a global concern, the United States is by far the world's biggest market for narcotics. Comprising only 5 percent of the world's population, it is estimated that we consume nearly 75 percent of the world's cocaine supply. The drug problem is so pervasive that virtually every family in America has been touched in some way by its tentacles, always adversely, and many times tragically.

And in almost every major city in the nation, well over 50 percent of *all* criminal prosecutions are drug cases. Of the remaining prosecutions, a great number—particularly those for burglary, theft, and robbery to support the drug habit—are drug related. A 1992 Bureau of Justice Statistics survey of male arrestees in twenty-four cities showed the percentage testing positive for an illicit drug ranged from 42 to 79 percent across the nation. For females, it was 38–85 percent. A 1993 BJS survey found that 59.8 percent of all federal prisoners were serving a sentence for a drug offense. In 1993, the latest year for which data are available, the FBI reported that state and local police made an estimated 1,126,300 arrests for drug violations.

---

*Methamphetamine use is becoming an increasing problem. For many years confined mostly to the West and Southwest and to certain distinct groups of users (motorcycle gangs, older polydrug users), the synthetic stimulant, which is also known as "speed" and "crank," is becoming more attractive to younger users and is expanding into areas of the country not previously involved with its use. When used to excess, the drug can induce irrational, bizarre, even homicidal behavior. In the past three years, Mexican drug organizations with ties to illegal aliens residing in this country have replaced outlaw motorcycle gangs as the predominant meth producers and traffickers. In 1994, the DEA seized 263 clandestine meth laboratories located in isolated rural areas, mostly in the state of California. Much of the meth seen in the United States, however, is manufactured in Mexico.

Hospital emergency rooms are overflowing with drug overdose cases. In 1993, the Substance Abuse and Mental Health Services Drug Abuse Warning Network reported a staggering 466,900 admissions in hospital emergency rooms nationwide involving drug abuse. A total of 8,541 drug-abuse deaths were reported by 145 medical examiners in 43 metropolitan areas. Drug-related murders are becoming so common that most are not even reported in the major dailies. Vicious teenage street gangs are armed with semiautomatics and, high on crack, are warring over their drug "turf," in the process terrorizing and ravaging inner cities and routinely killing innocent victims in the crossfire or in random "drive by" shootings. The latest year for which statistics are available is 1993, when, per the FBI, there were 23,271 homicides in America. Although the FBI only found 1,280 (5.5 percent) to be drug-related, everyone, including the FBI, knows this number is not accurate: The FBI does *not* include as drug-related a murder that occurs during a robbery or burglary committed by someone under the influence of drugs, or even murders that occur during robberies or burglaries committed to obtain money to buy drugs. In these cases, the homicide is recorded in terms of its relationship to the most serious offense only, and robbery and burglary are more serious than narcotic offenses in the FBI offense classifications, as well as under most state laws.

Infants are born addicted and physically deformed. It is estimated that upward of 225,000 infants are born each year with cocaine-induced damage due to a reduced amount of oxygen and blood reaching the uterus, and many others are abandoned on doorsteps and in alleys. "With cocaine, the mothers don't care about anything or anybody," a social worker says. Jails and courtrooms are teeming with drug offenders. Drugs are even infecting the nation's elementary schools. All of this—and much more—attest to the fact that other than the Civil War, America has never been faced with an internal crisis of this magnitude and gravity. Even the Great Depression pales next to it: Though an economic crisis, people at least ate, and of course there wasn't the endemic violence and destruction of millions of lives.

The emerging consensus in the country is that we are dealing with a hopeless situation, a war that cannot be won. According to Peter Reuter, chief drug policy expert for the Rand Corporation who has headed up comprehensive studies of the drug problem in America for the U.S. Department of Defense: "The conventional wisdom is that nothing works. It's a view that comes out of despair." The *New York*

Times editorialized on February 25, 1990, that "if the task is to win the war on drugs, America is doomed to lose."

I do not believe this for a moment. I firmly believe we can solve the problem to an appreciable degree. The only question is whether we really want to badly enough, or if, in the last analysis, we find more security in our insecurity, wringing our hands in despair as we undeniably continue to let a handful of foreign drug lords determine our nation's destiny. If the suggestions contained in this book are rejected out of hand, I maintain that other equally extreme measures will ultimately have to be employed if we are ever to rid this nation of a plague of nearly biblical proportions.

Virtually the only recommended solution to the drug problem that one reads about over and over again is legalization. Legalization, of course, is not a solution, only a different approach whose advantages may or may not outweigh the disadvantages (more on that later). In either event, with legalization, the problem of people using drugs will remain, although it will take on a new complexion.

On those occasions when there is any recommended "solution" to the drug problem other than legalization, the proposals range from the ludicrous and silly (e.g., declare war on Colombia, Bolivia, and Peru and have our military bomb and/or invade these countries; mandatory jail time for everyone who uses drugs—i.e., incarcerate over 20 million Americans) to the sane but inefficacious attempt to interdict all drugs entering our borders, or eradicate all drug crops.

The predicate of this book is a simple one: Since the drug problem is an extreme one, equally extreme, revolutionary measures have to be employed to solve it or at least make a significant dent. *In other words, either we are serious about solving this terrible curse, or we are not.* This book will set forth two separate and independent prescriptions for handling the problem.

There *is* an answer to the drug problem. We simply have to find it and then have the courage to carry it out. But first, let's examine, in depth, the solutions our nation has been using.

Interdiction

T he job of keeping narcotics from entering this country falls mostly on U.S. Customs, the "lead agency" for drug inter- diction efforts within the federal government, though many other federal* agencies, such as the U.S. Border Patrol and the U.S. Coast Guard, are actively involved in the process.

Although the interdiction effort has been a vigorous and reasonably coordinated one, and seizures are high (e.g., in fiscal year 1994, U.S. Customs seized 204,392 pounds of cocaine, and 2,577 pounds of heroin, some of which, however, resulted from joint efforts with other federal agencies, such as the DEA), the seizures are almost meaningless, since it is estimated that for every seizure of a narcotic shipment of any kind (air, boat, vehicle), ten others get through. The traffickers know the odds are on their side and recognize the seizures for what they really are, simply a necessary cost of doing business.

Originally, the greatest percentage of cocaine entering South Flor- ida, for years the main entry point in the United States, was flown in

---

* The National Guard, a *state* organization under the authority of individual state gover- nors, is also heavily involved in the drug interdiction effort. Since 1989 (under 32 U.S.C. §112), the secretary of defense has provided states with funds for the guard to assist in drug interdiction and other counter-drug activities, including assisting in cargo inspection at sea ports, helping to operate ground radar sites, and, through its Air National Guard, assisting U.S. Customs in aerial interdiction. Perhaps the guard's biggest counter-narcotic effort, however, is in domestic marijuana eradication, dating back to "Operation Green Harvest" in Hawaii in 1977.

by private aircraft landing on private airstrips. Our interdiction effort responded with radar and interceptor aircraft, and although aircraft continued to penetrate, the smugglers shifted their emphasis in the early 1980s to flying the cocaine to a transshipment point, usually the Bahamas (and, to a lesser extent, Panama), and shuttling the packaged powder from there to Florida in high-speed boats. In response, Customs beefed up its marine interdiction capabilities with the famed "Blue Lightning Strike Force," which featured the super-fast catamarans called "Blue Thunder," and were designed especially for the U.S. Customs Service by the late Don Aronow, the famous racing boat designer (murdered in 1987). Even the Blue Thunders couldn't stop the smugglers, although they were successful enough to force the smugglers into a variation of the air and sea operations. Private aircraft were used to get loads of bundled drugs relatively close to Florida shores, where they were dropped into the sea. Smuggler boats waiting in the vicinity of the drop would pick up the floating bundles and speed with them to shore. Per James Shedd, DEA spokesman in Miami, this practice, though no longer the principal technique of the smugglers, continues to the present time.

The flow of drugs into this country has proved to be as resistless as the force of gravity. As writer Jessica Speart pointed out in the June 11, 1995, *New York Times Magazine*, the methods used to transport drugs into this country are limited only by the fertility of the smuggler's imagination. For example, in the past several years, cocaine-filled condoms were found in the stomachs of horses; an oily sludge on the bottoms of several bags of tropical fish turned out to be liquid cocaine, which doesn't dissolve in water; parrots were found dead, eviscerated and stuffed with cocaine, their carcasses mixed in with a shipment of live parrots; a bust of Jesus, spray-painted a light gray, was found to be molded of cocaine; half-pound packets of cocaine were found surgically implanted into a man's thighs; cocaine has frequently been found beneath ice cream on cones that are licked very slowly as the smuggler strolls across the border, and so on.

The conclusive proof that the interdiction effort is failing, despite the infusion of more money, manpower, and technological advances, is that the cost of cocaine on the street today is much less than it was ten years ago, reflecting the economic principle of supply and demand at work. Wherever one looks, one finds confirmation. For instance, on January 30, 1982, President Reagan formally declared his administration's "War on Drugs." Since 85–90 percent of the nation's cocaine at the time was entering through South Florida, 10–15 percent through Southern California and the rest of the Southwest border, the federal government met the challenge head-on, establishing the South Florida Task Force and placing then–Vice President George Bush in charge.

The DEA was reinforced in Miami with seventy-three additional agents, the FBI with forty-three more, U.S. Customs with 145 more investigators, and so on down the line with the U.S. Border Patrol, the Bureau of Alcohol, Tobacco and Firearms, etc. The Coast Guard got more and faster cutters, and the U.S. Navy pitched in with its E2C "Hawkeye" surveillance aircraft. Money was no object, and even local and Florida state law enforcement increased their efforts under the supervisory umbrella of the task force. As could be expected, from 1982 on, drug seizures rose consistently and dramatically every year. Yet, more was coming in, unseized, every year also. The proof? In 1982, when the task force commenced operations, one kilo of cocaine cost $47,000–$60,000 in Miami. Today, the cost has dropped (and the purity of the cocaine has even increased) to $20,000–$25,000.

Due to the massive law enforcement interdiction efforts during the eighties in South Florida (as well as on seagoing and air routes to South Florida across the Caribbean), there's been a considerable shift from the Southeast region of the country to the Southwest as a point of entry of Colombian cocaine. However, as late as early 1991, Con Dougherty, veteran spokesman for the DEA in Washington, said: "Though the definite trend is to the Southwest border, most of the cocaine that we can quantify is still coming through the Southeast region of the country." Referring to the proximity of Colombia to South Florida and the Gulf states, Dougherty noted that the cartels continued primarily to take "the path of least geographic resistance." And South Florida remains to this day a key entry point for Colombian cocaine, with the Caribbean island of Puerto Rico as a primary transshipment point. Because of its distance from the United States, Puerto Rico is not a point from which cocaine is transported to the continental United States via high-speed boats. Rather, once reaching Puerto Rico (via air drops to waiting speed boats; via wood and fiberglass "stealth" boats that can evade radar detection; inside ship cargo containers; etc.), the cocaine is loaded in bindles onto ships bearing U.S. flags and destined primarily for South Florida, but also the eastern seaboard.

Puerto Rico is attractive as a transshipment point due to its proximity to the north coast of Colombia (only 500 miles) and because, as an island surrounded by ocean, it gives the drug smugglers a lot of coastline to work with. It has been repeatedly reported in the media and even asserted in law enforcement publications that once cocaine is loaded onto ships in Puerto Rico, since Puerto Rico is a commonwealth of the United States, the cocaine is effectively in the United States. That is, there cannot be any further customs check on the mainland because the shipment is considered "domestic to domestic." However, a check with U.S. Customs at the Port of Miami reveals that although they don't routinely search vessels from Puerto Rico, they do so whenever there is any suspicion that they may contain drugs or other illicit contraband. According to Jim Moster, regional counsel for U.S. Customs in Miami, several federal cases hold that whenever a vessel enters international waters—which is the case with vessels from Puerto Rico en route to South Florida or other mainland destinations—it may be searched once it crosses the border into this country. The rationale, he explains, is the "border search" exception to the Fourth Amendment to the U.S. Constitution, as well as the fact that once in international waters, a vessel may surreptitiously take on contraband from another vessel or source.

Responding to the increasing use of Puerto Rico by Colombian cartels, the Puerto Rico office of the DEA, formerly under the Miami field division's jurisdiction, was upgraded in 1995 from a district office to a field division with a larger staff reporting directly to Washington. Also, in November, 1994, Puerto Rico and the three U.S. Virgin Islands were designated "a high-intensity drug-trafficking area" by the drug czar's office, entitling it to additional federal money ($9 million in 1995) to combat drug trafficking. The other areas are Miami, New York, Washington, D.C., Houston, Los Angeles, and the Southwest border region.

Per Jim McGivney, chief of public affairs for the DEA in Washington, 70 percent of the cocaine reaching the United States today enters through the Southwest border from Mexico. The remaining 30 percent, he says, continues to enter mostly through South Florida, its transshipment points being Puerto Rico, as indicated, and to a much lesser extent, the Bahamas and the Dominican Republic. This 70–30 percent breakdown, of course, can only be a rough estimate, but virtually all experts, including the Office of National Drug Control Policy and the DEA's El Paso Intelligence Center, have endorsed the percentages. However, the 1995 International Narcotics Control Strategy Report merely says that "over half" of all cocaine enters the United States through the Southwest border. And if total cocaine seizures are an indication of the amount of cocaine entering the respective Southwest and Southeast regions of the country, the 70–30 percent breakdown may be too high a disparity. Although 1995 figures were not yet available at the time this book went to press, according to the Federal-Wide Drug Seizure System, 52,310 kilograms of cocaine were seized in 1993 by federal authorities in Florida, Puerto Rico, and the Atlantic/Caribbean area, and 44,461 along the Southwest border. In 1994, 44,903 kilos were seized in the Southeast region, and 51,533 along the Southwest border.

The cocaine entering the country through the Southwest border is mostly transshipped by air by Colombia's drug lords from Colombia to South America and then to Mexico in converted Boeing 727s, McDonnell Douglas DC-8s, and French-made Caravelle passenger jets. As much as six tons or more of cocaine are carried on a single flight. In the late eighties and early nineties, most of the planes landed in northern Mexico close to the U.S. border, where the cocaine was then transferred to cars, trucks, or other planes for the first leg across the porous border into the United States. This produced, in April, 1990, a joint U.S.-Mexico interdiction effort originally called the Northern Border Response Force, now known as Operation Halcon, whose purpose was to intercept cocaine in Mexico before it ever got to the U.S. border. The heart of the Response Force (guided by a U.S. Customs and Department of Defense radar net)* was four U.S. Cessna interceptor planes, two jointly operated by U.S. Customs and Mexican pilots, the other two purchased by Mexico from the United States and operated by U.S.-trained Mexican pilots; also, twenty-one UH-1H Huey helicopters, loaned by the U.S. to Mexico in 1991 and 1992 to transport Mexican federal judicial police agents to suspected landing sites.** In October, 1995, we loaned Mexico twelve additional

---

*This net, however, can only pick up air traffic up to 150 miles south of the U.S.-Mexico border. On its southern border, Mexico relies on a single radar station in the southern state of Chiapas to detect and monitor jets used by the Colombian cartels to transport cocaine into Mexico.

**Permitting U.S. Customs planes and pilots to conduct surveillance flights over Mexican territory, which commenced on January 25, 1991, and is still taking place, was a significant first step by then-President Carlos Salinas de Gotari in carrying out his pledge to cooperate more fully with the United States in the anti-drug effort. In 1991 and 1992, we gave Mexico $70 million for their counter-narcotics effort and loaned them the aforementioned 21 helicopters. Shortly thereafter, Mexican officials discovered that the DEA

UH-1H Huey helicopters (we will soon furnish them with some Blackhawk UH-60 helicopters, which are faster and have a greater operating range.) And in May, 1995, Mexico's president, Ernesto Zedillo, ordered the Mexican military to start deploying some of its F-5 jet fighters and T-33 trainers in pursuit of the Colombian planes laden with cocaine.

Because of the success of Operation Halcon, most of the planes today land in central or southern Mexico, even Guatemala, El Salvador, Belize, and Honduras. Before Operation Halcon, 90 percent of the Colombian cocaine reached Mexico by air. Today, U.S. Customs officials believe that approximately 60 percent is coming in by air and 40 percent inside ship containers docked in Mexican ports like Veracruz, Acapulco, and Ensenada. In many cases, DEA agents now find themselves trying to chase flies in the dark all over South America in pursuit of the Colombian cocaine trail—from Colombia south to Paraguay and Argentina, east to Brazil, northwest to Ecuador and northeast to Venezuela, as virtually every South American country is sucked into the cocaine vortex.

Eventually, the cocaine crosses the border into Southern California, Arizona, New Mexico, and Texas mostly by trucks, but also by passenger vehicles, small aircraft, ship containers, horseback, "mules" (human couriers), and, a few years ago, even via a 270-foot tunnel built underground between a home in Agua Prieta, Mexico, and a warehouse in Douglas, Arizona. Since then, two other tunnels, uncompleted, have been discovered along the border; one in September, 1995, stretched from an abandoned church in Nogales, Arizona (and within yards of a U.S. Customs Service office), into Mexico. Then there are the "port runners," drivers who simply step on the gas into U.S. territory when it appears that U.S. border inspectors are about to search them and their vehicles.

Desperate to plug up the sieve-like border, in 1989 the U.S. Border Patrol actually constructed a ten-foot-high, one-inch-thick steel fence from the Pacific Ocean extending eastward fourteen miles over rough terrain along the international border. (By the end of 1996, the Border Patrol expects to install a total of twenty-six miles of steel fence at various places along the 1,933 mile Southwest border.) According

---

had paid for the 1990 kidnapping of a Mexican doctor (see page 123 et seq.), and although they continued to cooperate with Washington in the counter-narcotics fight, they refused all monetary aid from us until October 5, 1995, when they accepted $6 million and the additional twelve Huey helicopters.

to Marco Ramirez, San Diego spokesman for the Immigration and Naturalization Service (INS), the fence, which is still there, has lowered the number of vehicles and individuals crossing the border, although it has not proven to be impenetrable. For those smugglers who don't want to bother crossing the border farther inland where there is no fence, many, Ramirez asserts, have used torches to burn holes through the wall. And recently, the smugglers, who don't suffer from a lack of ingenuity, have taken to loading up narcotic-laden trucks on top of the type of 18-wheelers used to transport new cars from the factory, raising the rack up to the fence, and then just rolling off the trucks onto U.S. territory. And the game goes on.

Today, the greatly predominant method of cocaine smuggling across the Southwest border is by land—believed to be 80–90 percent, with 10–20 percent by air and sea. (Along the Southeast border, U.S. Customs estimates that upward of 75 percent of cocaine is smuggled into the United States by ship container, with the remainder by air and land.) Some attribute this to NAFTA (the North American Free Trade Agreement Implementation Act), which became law on January 1, 1994. The purpose of NAFTA, of course, is to facilitate and promote commerce and trade between the United States and Mexico, as well as Canada, by the reduction of tariffs and the relaxation of other trade barriers. Since NAFTA went into effect, there has been a dramatic increase in the number of trucks crossing the Southwest border. U.S. Customs reports that in 1994, trucks carrying cargo across the border increased 47 percent over 1993, yet truck cocaine seizures declined 77 percent. And U.S. Customs finds itself in a schizophrenic and inherently incompatible dual role: helping to ensure that NAFTA's goal (to free up trade between the United States and Mexico) is carried out, while at the same time protecting our borders from the importation of drugs.

Other observers attribute the tremendous influx of cocaine by truck across the border to the "Line Release" program instituted by U.S. Customs in 1989. Under Line Release, American importers and Mexican exporters—sometimes the same company—that pass a U.S. Customs background check can truck their goods across the border without the likelihood of inspection. Their truck drivers carry manifest sheets authorizing them to enter the United States via bar codes that are checked by computer at the border. But Customs does not subject drivers and trucking companies to the same background checks as the importers and exporters. A veteran U.S. Customs investigator told *Los Angeles Times* staff writer H. G. Reza that "you can have the biggest drug dealer in Mexico drive a truck through the compound [at Otay Mesa, near San Diego] and the computer would never tell you who he was, even if he used his real name." [This loophole will be plugged up starting July 1, 1996, when, as announced by U.S. Customs Commissioner George Weise on September 6, 1995, every American importer wishing to participate in the Line Release program will be required to use Customs-approved carriers and drivers. But is this the way one acts when one is at "war"—wait almost an entire year to start plugging up a major hole in your front line through which the enemy is moving every day?] Additionally, Mexican drug dealers have been purchasing otherwise legitimate trucking companies that transport goods into the United States. Using the bar codes on the manifest sheets, they take the commercial lanes (or, as they are called by some, "the cocaine lanes") across the border.

A Los Angeles DEA agent says: "The traffickers used to have to figure out all types of ingenious ways to get the cocaine across the border. Now, with NAFTA and Line Release, all they have to do is put it on trucks and truck it across." U.S. Customs in San Diego says this is not so. "NAFTA isn't responsible for the increased amount of cocaine coming across the border by truck. And even sellers and buyers who are under the Line Release program can and frequently do have their trucks inspected," maintains Bobby Cassady, chief spokesperson for U.S. Customs in San Diego. According to Cassady, although only 3.7 percent of trucks are thoroughly inspected from front to back, there is "some sort of examination" on 34 percent of the trucks. This includes cocaine sniffing dogs, hand-held, laser-guided range finders, and an X-ray scanner, although the $3.2 million scanner, commercially known as Cargosearch—the newest addition to U.S. Custom's drug-detecting arsenal and the one for which they hold the greatest hope—has yet to detect one grain of cocaine in one year of operation. The problem? "If we had a truckload of jalapeño pepper cans, for example, the machine could see the cans, but it couldn't see what was inside the cans," a San Diego Customs supervisor explained. Nonetheless, whether it's NAFTA, Line Release, or both, the cocaine-seizure figures at the border do not look good. In fact, they are so bad they wouldn't sound believable were it not for the fact that the source of the figures is none other than the U.S. Customs Service, which, together with the INS, operates the many ports of entry along the Southwest border. Although trucks are believed to be the main conveyance of cocaine at the four major ports of entry along the Southwest border, in 1994 not one pound of cocaine was seized from trucks at Laredo, not one pound at El Paso, not one pound at Nogales, and there was just one seizure of 1,765 pounds from a truck at the Calexico branch of the San Diego port of entry. *So not a single pound of cocaine was seized in 1994 from over 2 million trucks that passed through three of the busiest ports of entry at the Southwest border,* where U.S. officials say most of the cocaine enters this country. In fact, only 9,845 pounds of cocaine were seized by Customs at these four ports from all sources, mostly cars and human couriers. Responding to criticism that the Southwest border has become so easily penetrable by drug traffickers, Customs Commissioner Weise launched "Operation Hard Line" in February, 1995, promising increased inspections by his Customs inspectors (eighty have been added) of cars as well as Line Release trucks crossing the border. Customs reports that as of June 1, 1995, cocaine seizures are up, although not appreciably.

Apart from Line Release and NAFTA, two other factors militate against the successful seizure of drugs along the Southwest border: the increased corruption of U.S. federal officials at the border who are working in league with Mexican drug traffickers, and the sheer volume of vehicular traffic. In 1994, per the DEA's El Paso Intelligence Center, at four of the ports of entry (San Diego, Nogales, Laredo, and El Paso), an incredible 81,659,575 automobiles and 2,739,728 trucks passed through, and in the San Diego port alone, 108,127,203 persons crossed the border, with 232 million crossing through all the ports combined. With these numbers, it's not just difficult, it's impossible for U.S. Customs, the INS, or anyone else to prevent the drug traffickers from bringing as much cocaine into this country as they want.

In Los Angeles, the main drug-trafficking center in the Southwest, a kilo of cocaine sold for around $15,000–$20,000 in 1991, when this book was first published. Today, it's $13,000–$17,000, and the purity has remained about the same (83 percent). In 1991, in Miami, a kilo of cocaine sold for $20,000–$25,000. Today, it's $16,000–$20,000. Nothing has fundamentally changed, and nothing will, unless completely new techniques to fight the drug war are employed.

As accurate a barometer as any of the futility of the federal anti-drug effort is the DEA's nationwide cocaine seizures from 1981 through 1994. Disraeli said there are three types of lies: lies, damned lies, and statistics. But it is hard to see how these statistics can lie:

Fiscal Year	Seizures in Kilograms[a] (2.2 pounds per kilo)	Federal Spending in War on Drugs[b] (in billions)
1981	1,937.8	$1,138.0
1982	5,587.0	1,310.6
1983	8,434.0	1,536.6
1984	10,985.1	1,844.8
1985	24,654.9	2,145.9
1986	27,500.1	2,269.1
1987	37,404.8	4,026.3
1988	55,896.9	3,822.5
1989	81,762.1	6,302.0
1990	71,599.2	9,483.0
1991	59,320.5	10,957.6
1992	78,802.3	11,910.1
1993	60,666.2	12,265.3
1994	64,425.9	12,184.4

(a) Source: DEA.
(b) Source: 1981–88, Office of Management and Budget; 1989–1994, Office of National Drug Control Strategy.*

Though seizures have *increased* a remarkable 3,320 percent between 1981 and 1994, this is primarily attributable to the vast increase in the amount of cocaine reaching our shores. In 1981, the amount of cocaine entering the United States was believed to be around 30 metric tons; in 1994, it had risen to around 250 metric tons. And because of the considerably increased availability of cocaine in America, the average wholesale cost nationwide of a kilo of cocaine (it varies from region to region, depending on availability) has *decreased* during the same period, plummeting from an average cost of around $70,000 in 1981 to around $20,000 today. *This is what the nation has to show for the expenditure of billions of dollars and nearly fifteen years of death, blood, and trench warfare.*

Looked at from another perspective, the federal drug budget has grown from $1.5 billion in 1981 to $13.2 billion in 1995. Close to $100 billion has been spent on the drug effort during this period alone, yet, even with the recent arrests of the Cali cartel leaders, illicit drugs are cheaper and more readily available today than they

*Since 1991, the Federal-Wide Drug Seizure System (FDSS) reflects the combined drug seizure efforts of the DEA, FBI, U.S. Customs, and U.S. Coast Guard. FDSS eliminates duplicate reporting of a seizure involving more than one federal agency. In fiscal year 1991, FDSS reported a combined seizure by the above federal agencies of 246,324 pounds of cocaine; in 1994, 282,086. In fiscal year 1991, 3,030 pounds of heroin; in 1994, 2,824. In 1991, 499,070 pounds of marijuana; in 1994, 778,715.

were in 1981.* As William Yout, the DEA's spokesman in Miami in 1987, aptly put it: "We win battles while they win the war."

To seal the American border from the invasion of narcotics is an unachievable objective, an attempt to stop the unstoppable. The United States has 11,323 miles facing two oceans and the Gulf coast. Additionally, there are 3,987 miles of shared border with Canada and 1,933 miles of shared border with Mexico. Take, for instance, interdiction of drugs coming in by land only, from San Diego to Miami, a distance of approximately 3,500 miles. With the exception of official ports of entry like San Ysidro, California (south of San Diego), and El Paso and Laredo, Texas, manned by INS and U.S. Customs agents, the sole federal agency physically patrolling this enormous breadth of land in between, where the Southwest border is merely an invisible line in the desert, is the U.S. Border Patrol. And the primary function of the patrol, part of the INS, isn't even to interdict drugs, but to keep illegal aliens from entering the country. Although enlisted into the drug war and receiving drug interdiction training, the patrol presently has only 4,728 agents in the country, 3,843 of which patrol these 3,500 miles (only 885 patrol the rest of the country, which includes the East and West coasts and the 4,000-mile U.S.-Canadian border, which the DEA notes is also starting to be used by drug smugglers, particularly of drug currency). With three eight-hour shifts per day, this means that only 1,280 agents at any given time are trying to cover 3,500 miles of terrain. That's roughly one agent per 2.7 miles. Though the border patrol does an excellent job under the circumstances, seizing 33,051 pounds of cocaine in 1994, their numbers can't begin to handle the problem. But it wouldn't matter if we had 100,000 border patrol agents. William Walls, agent in charge of the FBI office in Miami in 1987 and 1988, put it this way: "We could have people standing a few feet from each other along the entire border, and the drugs would still get in."

To give one a sense of the magnitude of the interdiction problem, the Bureau of Justice Statistics estimated that in 1991, 438 million people entered or reentered the country, along with more than 100 million vehicles, 220 thousand vessels, and 635 thousand aircraft. No current figures are available, but with the advent of NAFTA, the

---

*It should also be kept in mind that this book is about what we, the United States, should do to solve the drug problem. The recent, temporary successes in Colombia (see Chapter 3) were brought about by the efforts of the Colombian government. This nation's efforts to solve the problem through interdiction, eradication, law enforcement, and education have been monumental failures.

1995 figures are undoubtedly substantially higher. And, if sealing our borders is an impossible task, consider the job of the U.S. Coast Guard, the nation's "drug agents at sea," who have drug-interdiction responsibility on the high seas *outside* U.S. territorial waters. The almost prohibitively difficult nature of drug interdiction at sea is obvious when one realizes that the Caribbean and Gulf of Mexico alone comprise 1,664,500 square miles! And every boat traversing these waters, of course, is a potential drug-smuggling vessel. Moreover, the Coast Guard, the smallest of the United States' five armed services, is a multi-missioned organization, and in 1995, only 9.5 percent of the Guard's budget was allocated to support drug interdiction. Although the planes have other missions, 205 Coast Guard aircraft (30 HC-130H Hercules, 41 HU-25 Guardians, 40 HH-60 Jayhawks, and 94 HH-65A Dolphins) are used as drug "spotters" for the guard's 131 vessels (12 High Endurance and 33 Medium Endurance cutters, 86 patrol boats), which make the actual interdiction.

In 1994, the Coast Guard seized 62,126 pounds of cocaine, and on July 25, 1995, the guard made the largest ocean seizure of cocaine in maritime history. A Coast Guard team boarded a Panamanian fishing vessel with a ten-man Colombian crew on the Pacific Ocean 780 miles west of Peru. Twenty-four thousand pounds of cocaine, with an estimated wholesale value of $143 million, were found in hidden compartments on the vessel, which was bound for California. Previously, the highest maritime seizure occurred on October 2, 1989, when 12,000 pounds of cocaine were seized by the guard in the Gulf of Mexico on a ship bound for Tampa, Florida.

The land borders, the air above, and the sea leading up to the shores have proven impossible to patrol effectively, particularly since the traffickers are extremely flexible, changing their routes and methods constantly in their assault on the rich U.S. market. By analogy, in years past, when farmers found rat holes in the concrete floors of their wooden granaries, they often plugged them up with cement. If this tactic kept the rats from even trying to penetrate that particular barley bin, it was only because they had gnawed their way into a new one.

Although the media sometimes prefers to feature the more exciting and glamorous war in the air, federal authorities estimate that today only 5–10 percent of the cocaine entering the country does so by plane. Before NAFTA, the definite trend was toward smuggling cocaine into the country by way of cargo containers in large ships, which remains a significant method used by the drug cartels, particularly, as indicated, in the Southeast region. Many of the containers are as large as $40 \times 8 \times 8 \frac{1}{2}$ feet, and the cocaine is hidden behind false walls, in the I-beams (there are 24 I-beams per container, each of which can contain $4\frac{1}{2}$ kilos), and inside the ribs of the containers. Oftentimes, the cocaine is concealed within the product shipped (furniture, produce, auto parts, etc.) itself. To demonstrate the immensity of the problem, in 1993, the most recent year for which statistics are available, U.S. Customs reports that 4,227,033 containers entered the United States through the nation's ports, only a minuscule percentage of which were checked by Customs.

The Los Angeles port at Terminal Island is a typical case. Jack Pansky, Customs Enforcement Branch Chief at the port, says that approximately 1,470,000 containers per year enter the port, 122,500 per month. Of them, only 275 per month receive a full inspection (a difficult process that involves transporting the containers to an inspection site eight miles away, where it takes about four days to unload the enormous containers, inspect, and reload them), which is less than one-fourth of one percent. An additional one-fourth of one percent are given a very limited inspection dockside. Although U.S. Customs in Los Angeles knows that cocaine is coming in through its port, in 1993, there were only two container cocaine seizures, one of 880 pounds hidden behind a false wall, and one of 77 pounds hidden inside a furniture shipment, both originating in Colombia. There were no seizures in 1994 or thus far in 1995.

Not only doesn't U.S. Customs in Los Angeles and elsewhere have enough personnel to inspect more containers, but if they did have the capacity and inspected each container or even a substantial percentage, commerce would be paralyzed, slowing to a standstill.

David McKinney, Pansky's counterpart at the Port of Miami, says that Miami, a smaller port than Los Angeles, receives about 260,000 containers a year, mostly from South America. Since South America is a "high risk" area, his 48-person team (23 customs inspectors augmented by 25 members of the Florida National Guard and 4 narcotic sniffing dog teams) inspect about 4 percent a year, a higher percentage than the Los Angeles port. Of this 4 percent, however, less than 1 percent result in drug seizures—"about 18–22 seizures per year," McKinney states. Because the Colombia cartels' principal means of importing cocaine into South Florida is by containerized cargo on ships, McKinney's group frequently makes huge seizures. In fact, the largest seizure ever of a single shipment of cocaine (the 1989 Sylmar, California, warehouse seizure mentioned earlier—21.4 tons—was of several accumulated importations of cocaine) resulted from the discovery by U.S. Customs at the Miami port on August 23, 1991, of

31,429 pounds of cocaine found hidden inside the hollow center of ten cement posts on the vessel *Mercandian Continent* from Venezuela. Sent by Colombia's Cali cartel, most of the shipment was surveilled until its ultimate seizure in Longview, Texas, three months later. A spinoff from that record seizure, with the same scheduled recipient, was the confiscation by U.S. Customs on April 15, 1992, at Port Everglades (Fort Lauderdale, Florida, seaport) of 14,821 pounds of cocaine found inside refrigerated containers of frozen broccoli on a vessel from Guatemala. Other large seizures at the Miami port were 13,677 pounds of cocaine found inside containers of coffee on a vessel from Colombia on September 2, 1993; 8,400 pounds of cocaine found inside containers of saltine crackers on a Colombian vessel on February 4, 1994; and 4,000 pounds of cocaine found inside six containers of ferrosilicon (ground-up iron) on a ship from Venezuela on March 23, 1995.*

Although Miami Customs has had substantial seizures, McKinney is aware that they are only a fraction of what's coming in. "Obviously, a lot more cocaine is getting through," he says, a refrain one constantly hears from the men and women on the front lines of America's war on drugs. "They beat you in the numbers," another U.S. Customs agent laments. "You win one, you lose twenty-three," echoes a California Bureau of Narcotics Enforcement special agent.

What is found across the board on a local, state, and federal level are very hard-working and dedicated law enforcement personnel who are members of agencies (DEA, Customs, FBI, IRS, police, etc.) that are woefully understaffed, who are poorly paid, and who are frustrated and resigned to the reality that they cannot win the war on drugs. The interdiction effort continues, but as long as the demand for drugs continues, the drug lords will find a way to satisfy that demand. We already know this from hard experience.**

And it's not as if the federal government is lying down for the smugglers. For instance, in *air* interdiction the very latest, high-tech

---

*On December 6, 1993, 10,000 pounds of cocaine, hidden inside a shipment of 7th Day Adventist bibles on a vessel from Colombia, got by Customs and were discovered by an innocent recipient. Customs is certain that, as is frequently the case, the shipment was supposed to have been opened up by dock workers at the Port of Miami alerted by, and working with, the Cali cartel.

**Even the mail is used, and ingeniously. A typical day at the Customs mail facility in Oakland, California, uncovered drugs concealed inside bags of red pepper, a wooden water pump, a wooden drum, and dozens of broom handles. The mail interdiction effort is obviously a needle-in-the-haystack proposition, since 999 out of 1,000 parcels mailed to this country from the outside are legitimate.

instrumentation is being used in an attempt to create a "radar fence" across the nation's southern border. The U.S. Customs Domestic Air Interdiction Coordination Center (DAICC), located at March Air Force Base near Riverside, California, is responsible for the tactical direction of U.S. government efforts to intercept and apprehend aircraft illegally entering the United States. DAICC controllers monitor the southern border twenty-four hours a day using computer-processed radar images displayed on color television surveillance monitors and wall-mounted screen displays. The system is able to display and manage up to 6,000 radar tracks per twelve-second scan. Additionally, extensive federal and state law enforcement databases at the controller's fingertips provide detailed information, such as registration and criminal history, on aircraft, vehicles, and individuals.

DAICC has nine branches and seven units under its control, and 101 aircraft, including ten UH Blackhawk helicopters, at nine U.S. Customs Air branches throughout the country, twenty-eight of which (twenty Cessna Citations and eight P-A42 Chets) are interceptor aircraft with radar capability. The flagship planes, however, are all at the Corpus Christi Naval Air Station, which has four P-3A Orions and four P-3B AEW (Airborne Early Warning) Orions. All of these planes have a radar capability, but the four P-3B AEWs, with their rotodome-mounted antenna (each plane costs $19.6 million), have a 200-mile radius, 360-degree radar capability. Also enlisted in the air war are eleven tethered balloons (aerostats) with radar capability, each costing $19 million, and positioned in Yuma and Fort Huachuca, Arizona; Deming, New Mexico; Marfa, Eagle Pass, Rio Grande City, and Matagorda, Texas; Morgan City, Louisiana; Horseshoe Beach and Cardjo Key, Florida; and Lejas, Puerto Rico. The aerostats, once operated by U.S. Customs, now are run by the Department of Defense (DoD).*

But the smugglers, who monitor U.S. Customs and military frequencies with voice scanners, and route smuggling planes accordingly, still get through to U.S. territory: by flying slowly and at low

*As a cost-cutting measure, DoD, against U.S. Customs' advice, removed three aerostats in the Bahamas (High Rock, Georgetown, and Andros). Customs believed that these were critical to the counter-drug mission because they were the only radars in that high-threat area, and if any aerostats were to be sacrificed it should be those in the lower-threat Gulf Coast area. DoD replaced the Bahamas aerostats with a relocatable over-the-horizon radar system that bounces a radar signal off the ionosphere. The system is limited in its capabilities, as it cannot "read" an aircraft transponder (IFF code), is impacted by frequent changes in the ionosphere, cannot give aircraft altitude, and has limited total area coverage.

altitudes (some, flying as low as treetop level, have crashed into trees) below the radar screen (the balloon radar capability is effective to as low as 500 feet, where it begins to deteriorate), or sufficiently low for their "radar echoes" to be indistinguishable on the screen from environmental clutter; by flying 95 percent of the time at night, where drug drops from the plane go completely undetected; by blending in with legitimate aircraft traffic; by filing a flight plan with the FAA for a U.S. airport and, at the last minute, deviating from the plan to quickly unload the drugs; even by techniques like "mating," in which two aircraft fly in formation as close together as possible, showing only a single blip on the radar screens, then, just before the planes reach their destination, peeling apart, one with the cocaine, the other with a legitimate flight plan.

The smuggler pilots are also willing to take enormous risks, since they are paid as much as $250,000 per flight. Their planes (they favor turbo Commander 1000s and Cessna 206s) have the latest equipment, including radar detectors that employ the same technology used to warn automobile drivers of police radar. Barry Seal, the most famous cocaine smuggler pilot ever (who was eventually murdered by the Medellin cartel when he cooperated with the DEA by, among other things, filming Medellin cartel leader Pablo Escobar and some top-ranking Sandinista officials loading planes with sacks of cocaine), gave this testimony before Congress: "My smuggling aircraft was outfitted with the most sophisticated of equipment—Loran C, VLF, Omega, long-range navigation equipment, radar altimeters, beacon-interrogating digital radar, communications scramblers, and digital communication equipment for position tracking. I don't believe there is any paramilitary group better equipped than my former associates." Seal testified that he "participated in approximately one hundred smuggling flights without ever being intercepted."

Detecting a suspicious plane on radar isn't enough. Interceptor planes then have to be dispatched, not to bring the plane down, but to identify and follow it without being spotted until the smuggler is about to land, at which point ground law enforcement and helicopters descend on the smuggler and his cargo. Oftentimes, the smuggler sees the interceptor pilot, and the mission on both sides is unsuccessful. Peter Kendig, former deputy director of the Surveillance Support Center at Corpus Christi, and himself a Customs pilot veteran, tells of the many times the smuggler pilot will spot the interceptor, "flip the bird," smile, turn around, and fly back to safety across the Mexican border.

Smuggler planes can frequently outrace the interdiction process by taking off from small dirt airstrips just south of the U.S.-Mexican border, hopping over the border, and either landing on a private road, airstrip, or dry lake bed, or air-dropping their load at predetermined points totally inaccessible by roads.

Whenever a technique or route they use begins to get interdicted, the smugglers simply adapt and get in through some other route or means. As Joe Maxwell, the very knowledgeable director of DAICC, says, "It's like a blown-up balloon. You grab it in one place, and it bulges out in another." Such is the nature of the beast.

To put the matter into a realistic perspective, just a single cargo plane, fully loaded with cocaine, could supply the nation's current demand for one entire year, believed to be approximately 110 metric tons. The only reason, of course, the drug cartels don't do this is that they fear that single plane might be the one out of the twenty or so (the current *air* interdiction ratio) that would be interdicted, and hence would constitute an enormous loss of money.

To put the situation into another realistic perspective: If we couldn't interdict the Vietcong along the Ho Chi Minh Trail, a path for Communist supplies into South Vietnam that was only 50–60 *feet* wide (the Ho Chi Minh Trail, admittedly, was not *one* trail; when we would block off one trail, the Vietcong would simply cut a new path nearby in the jungle), how can we possibly expect to cut off drug supplies to this country over a southern border which alone occupies 3,500 miles, and one that, unlike the Ho Chi Minh Trail, deals with not only land, but the air above it and the waters of the Caribbean and Gulf of Mexico?

The problem of interdiction is so immense that even the entire American military might not be able to do the job. In September, 1986, the House of Representatives passed a bill (later killed by the Senate) ordering the president, as commander-in-chief of the armed forces, to use the military to seal our borders from drugs.

Opposing the bill, then–Secretary of Defense Caspar W. Weinberger told reporters on September 15, 1986: "Let's look at some of the details. You have to have a complete naval and air blockade to do this against anything on the sea or in the air that might be carrying narcotics. That is about 290,000 registered and 4,000 unregistered general aviation aircraft, plus a great many commercial aircraft. Without adequate intelligence, we wouldn't have any idea whether any of these planes were actually carrying narcotics. We would also have to have a continuous 4,000-mile naval blockade off the coastline. We'd have to be able to intercept 160,000 documented, registered vessels which arrive each day at the U.S. ports. In effect, you're ordering the *entire* military to do one nonmilitary task."

The following day, Assistant Secretary of Defense for Force Management and Personnel Chapman B. Cox, said the military "couldn't even do it with what we've got. It's an impossible task."

In testimony before the Senate and House Armed Services Committees on Drug Interdiction on June 15, 1988, U.S. Air Force Gen. Robert T. Herres, vice chairman of the Joint Chiefs of Staff, said that "even a massive dedication of our military capabilities to the interdiction mission as our department's highest priority commitment would not suffice to halt the flow of illegal drugs. The adversary just has too many options at his disposal. *There is no practical way the Armed Forces of the United States can seal our borders.*"

Nonetheless, under the National Defense Authorization Act of 1989, the DoD became a major drug war participant by being designated as the lead federal agency for the detection and monitoring of the transit of illegal drugs into this country by air and sea (not actual interdiction by way of arrest, searches, and seizures, and not by land). The 1988 congressional hearings that resulted in the act of 1989 reflected the belief that giving the military an expanded role in the drug war was a necessary response to the cocaine epidemic threatening the security of the United States. The consensus at the hearings was that the existing strategy of "interrupting and reducing the available supply of illicit drugs was not working."

DoD's detection is mostly achieved by the North American Aerospace Defense Command (NORAD), headquartered at Cheyenne Mountain just outside Colorado Springs, Colorado, with a network of forty fixed and mobile ground radars around the country designed to warn of high-altitude penetrations of U.S. airspace. NORAD coordinates all its radar with the U.S. Customs Air Interdiction Coordination Center near Riverside, California. Though not the primary mission of the aircraft, NORAD can call on their E-3 AWACS and E-26 surveillance aircraft and forty F-15 and F-16 interceptor alert aircrafts to assist U.S. Customs and the U.S. Coast Guard with tracking missions when requested.

Question: Isn't NORAD's vast radar screen coordinated out of Cheyenne Mountain simply duplicative of U.S. Customs' vast radar screen coordinated out of Riverside? Obviously, they both achieve the same purpose and one could operate virtually as efficiently without the other. In July of 1995, a high-level Customs official, speaking for nonattribution, explained what has happened, and it is compatible with the consistently decreasing DoD anti-drug budget of the last few years: "When the American military first got involved in the anti-drug effort, many, though not all, of the brass thought they could prevail—like they do in a typical war—in a year or so and get out. When they found the drug problem was intractable and not amenable to such a quick solution, they lost interest. The will of the military is no longer concentrated on the drug war. NORAD's radar screen is now primarily used for hostile threats to our air sovereignty by foreign governments, always DoD's original objective in war or peace. And DoD considers drug planes as nonhostile threats to our sovereignty."

This DoD posture of no longer seeking a big role in the drug war was made clear recently when U.S. Rep. James A. Trafficant (D–Oh.) introduced legislation to give the attorney general the authority to ask for up to 10,000 military troops to patrol our Southwest border. Brian Sheridan, deputy assistant secretary of defense for drug enforcement policy and support responded on September 9, 1995: "If you want to seal the border, give the Border Patrol the resources to do it. The military is not the Border Patrol, and if someone wants to turn us into it, I think that is a mistake."*

With the end of the Cold War as well as the Persian Gulf War in 1991, the military had become antsy and sought out a new lease on life. For a while, the drug "war" looked like a promising new venture to them. The first public sign that this was not to be was in September of 1993, when the U.S. General Accounting Office (GAO) reported to Congress that since 1989, DoD had spent $3.3 billion on its detection and monitoring mission to interdict drug traffickers in both source and transit countries, but that "DoD's surveillance capabilities are more costly than beneficial to the drug war. . . . In September, 1991, we reported that although DoD had made a strong commitment to its mission and had expanded the nation's surveillance capabilities, its impact on supply reduction goals had been negligible. Two years later, that situation remains unchanged. . . . DoD's flying hours and steaming days (maritime) have contributed to increased cocaine seizures and other limited successes . . . but cocaine production has increased, the estimated flow into the United States

*On January 11, 1996, DoD authorized the use of an additional 200 (bringing the total to 350) troops from the Marines, Army, and National Guard to help the Border Patrol in California and Arizona repel (not by arrests and seizures, but by aerial and ground surveillance) drug smugglers as well as illegal immigrants.

is essentially undiminished, and cocaine remains affordable and available on American streets. . . . Interdiction success at deterring the cocaine flow has been more symbolic than real." The GAO accordingly recommended a scaling back of funding for DoD's anti-drug effort.

In October of 1993, the Clinton Administration, responding to the U.S. government's own statistics as well as to most drug war experts who questioned the cost-effectiveness of interdiction, started to de-emphasize the interdiction effort, particularly by the military.* "Clearly, what we've done in the past hasn't worked," said Represen-tative John Conyers, Jr. (D–Mich.), agreeing with the administra-tion's decision. The overall spending on interdiction was reduced from $1.760 billion in 1993 to $1.312 billion in 1994.** The Penta-gon (DoD) anti-drug budget was slashed by $273 million, a reduction of nearly one-fourth from fiscal year 1993. Not too many at the Pen-tagon complained. DoD's Brian Sheridan said: "Somewhere along the line, people began to think that if the military got involved in the air interdiction effort, we could stop the flow of drugs to the United States. That is not going to happen. The demand for drugs is too high."

As far back as 1988, a Rand Corporation study, prepared for the Office of the Undersecretary of Defense, concluded: "No one seri-ously claims now that interdiction can control the amount of drugs physically able to reach this nation." The belief, by a few diehards, that interdiction at least reduces cocaine availability in the United States by the amount seized, is based on the assumption that all available cocaine is already being shipped to this country. But there is no evidence to support this theory. Cocaine production capacity is much, much greater than actual production. As the GAO said in its 1993 report to Congress: "South American cartels ship to the United States whatever amounts their customers demand, with interdiction losses merely replaced by later shipments. In relation to its enormous profits, cocaine is cheap to produce and smuggle, and losses are rela-tively inconsequential to trafficking."

Peter Reuter, the Rand researcher who has studied interdiction and Andean crop substitution and eradication programs (see Chapter 2) since the early 1980s, opines that they are both a "colossal waste of money."

---

*From a high of $1.22 billion for fiscal year 1991, President Clinton's 1996 funding request for DoD is $812 million.
**The 1995 amount is $1.293 billion.

Eradication

Not only is eradication of the coca crop, like interdiction, simply not feasible, but in addition, unlike the effort to interdict the smuggling of cocaine into this country, the effort to eradicate creates all types of legal and moral problems. This is so because in Peru, the world's foremost producer of the coca plant (54 percent in 1994), whose leaf is the raw material of cocaine, coca cultivation is lawful when licensed by the government. In 1994, the most recent year for which statistics are available, 18,000 hectares (44,460 acres) of coca cultivation were licensed. And in Bolivia, Peru's neighbor to its southeast and the next highest grower (31 percent in 1994) of the coca crop,* coca cultivation in certain regions of the country is lawful. The reasons are historical and cultural. Of Peru's 24 million people, approximately 55 percent are Indian. About 75 percent of Bolivia's 8 million people are Indian. To a considerable number of these Indians, the chewing of coca leaves is an accepted pleasure and cultural tradition dating back to 2,100 B.C. To this very day in some of the Inca tribes, coca is also thought to be magical and divine and is at the center of the tribe's social and religious system.

The Indians in the Andes Mountains chew the coca leaves, which contain small amounts of cocaine, to counter hunger and thirst (the

---

*Colombia accounted for 15 percent in 1994.

juice of the leaf anesthetizes the stomach so hunger and thirst are not felt) and to lessen the physical effects, such as fatigue, of living and working at a high altitude. Additionally, coca tea and leaves are lawfully sold in restaurants and supermarkets throughout Peru and Bolivia. Peru even has a governmental agency, *Empress Nacional de la Coca*, to regulate the legal cultivation (estimated to be only 5–10 percent of the total leaves harvested) and sale of coca leaves. So the coca crop has a valid and legitimate social purpose that we, as a foreign nation, have no legal or moral right to extinguish.

Moreover, there are lawful purposes for cocaine in our own country. Coca leaves from Peru and Bolivia are shipped to the Stepan Chemical Company in Maywood, New Jersey, where the cocaine is extracted for medical use. (A residual flavoring agent from the leaves goes into the Coca-Cola drink enjoyed daily by 300 million people in 170 countries.) Mallinckrodt, Inc., of St. Louis, Missouri; Roxanne Laboratories, Inc., of Columbus, Ohio; and Eli Lilly & Co. of Indianapolis, Indiana, sell the cocaine in different forms to hospital pharmacies throughout the country. The drug is extensively used by ear, nose, and throat doctors as a local anesthetic for mucous membranes of the oral and nasal cavities.

Of course, our nation has no quarrel with the cultivation of the coca crop for the aforementioned lawful purposes. It's the use of the coca leaf for cocaine purposes, by far the main use of the leaf today, which we want to eliminate. Apart from the difficulty inherent in monitoring coca cultivation for lawful as opposed to unlawful purposes—an attempt to measure the immeasurable—the possibility of eradicating even a substantial percentage of coca cultivation is virtually nonexistent.* For instance (per the March, 1990, U.S. Department of State International Narcotics Control Strategy Report), in 1988, 6,896 hectares of cocaine were manually eradicated in Peru, Bolivia, and Colombia—up to that point by far the highest ever—yet

---

*In the United States, the only major drug which is eradicated by the federal government is marijuana. Since its inception in 1982, the Domestic Cannabis Eradication/Suppression Program (DCE/SP), the sole nationwide law enforcement program that exclusively addresses marijuana, has eradicated (in many states by herbicide, in others, manually) several million outdoor marijuana plants a year, with a high of 7.5 million in 1992. DCE/SP is a DEA-coordinated program in which the DEA works with local and state law enforcement as well as the National Guard, the Civil Air Patrol, and federal agencies like the U.S. Forest Service, National Park Service, and Bureau of Land Management. The states with the largest annual marijuana cultivation are usually California, Hawaii, Illinois, Indiana, Kentucky, Tennessee, Arkansas, and Alabama. By all accounts, today's marijuana is significantly more potent than it was during the Woodstock era.

it only amounted to less than 4 percent of the 193,136 hectares unlawfully cultivated in those countries that year.

In 1989, President Bush, amidst much fanfare, launched his so-called "Andean strategy," a five-year, $2.2 billion plan to attack and halt the supply of cocaine at its source. The plan was to substantially increase economic aid to wean the economies of these nations away from drug production, and provide military assistance (to combat the traffickers) to the main source countries of Peru, Bolivia, and Colombia.*

But that year, 1989, not only did the number of hectares of cocaine being cultivated increase to 217,075, but the number that were eradicated decreased to 4,490, a minuscule 2 percent eradication rate. The year 1990 was hardly any better: 9,030 hectares out of 220,850 cultivated were eradicated (4 percent). In 1991, the numbers were 212,658 and 6,458 (3 percent). In 1992, 217,808 hectares of cocaine were cultivated and 6,108 eradicated (3 percent). By the end of 1992, it was clear to everyone except the undaunted Bush Administration, which managed to remain sanguine even while standing on quicksand, that the increased infusion of economic and military aid to the Andean nations to halt cocaine trafficking at its source was a failure. The number of hectares cultivated remained essentially the same, as did the number eradicated, and just as much cocaine as ever was reaching the United States. In 1992, Senator Joseph R. Biden, Jr. (D–Del.), the Senate Judiciary Committee chairman, said: "The simple fact is that more cocaine enters this country now than before we began our Andean strategy."

In recognition of this reality, when the Bush Administration requested $387 million in counter-narcotic funds to the Andean nations for fiscal year 1993, Congress slashed the amount to $174 million, a 35 percent cut from that of the prior fiscal year. Just as more aid had no positive effect, cutting the aid had no demonstrable negative effect. Per the 1994 U.S. State Department Report, in 1993, 197,893 hectares of cocaine were cultivated in the Andean nations of Peru, Bolivia, and Colombia, and only 3,193 were eradicated (2 percent). In 1994, 207,410 hectares of cocaine were cultivated and

*In the Cartagena (Colombia) "summit" in February, 1990, President Bush and the presidents of Peru, Bolivia, and Colombia, set forth in their eleven-page Declaration of Cartagena no specific new steps, other than increased economic and military aid, to combat trafficking. The four political leaders did manage to add to the cosmetic slogans of the drug "war": They formed, they told reporters covering the conference, "the first anti-drug cartel."

6,010 eradicated (3 percent). Unbelievably, in Peru, the major source country, *not one hectare of cocaine was eradicated by the Peruvian government in 1994* (page 106 of the 1995 State Department Report). What this reveals is that irrespective of our efforts, the Andean nations produce just as much illicit cocaine as is called for in this country.

The only law the narco-traffickers do not violate is the law of supply and demand. It is well known that the Andean nations only plant the coca crop in a small percentage of the lush, fertile area available to them. If the demand for cocaine were to increase, more hectares would be cultivated. Even now, the drug czar's office admits that "current [1995] coca cultivation is three times what is necessary to supply the needs of the U.S. drug market."

One of the principal reasons why this nation's attempt to get the Peruvian and Bolivian governments to eradicate illicit coca cultivation has been, and will probably always be, stillborn, is that cooperation from these governments, despite periodic public pronouncements of resolve and commitment, has consistently been at modest levels.

There are several reasons for this. Although Peruvian President Alberto Fujimori's administration has successfully reversed Peru's economic decline, Peru, and particularly Bolivia, are poor nations, and coca production for cocaine purposes has infused their economies with hundreds of millions of much-needed dollars. The incentive for stricter control of coca cultivation, therefore, is minimal. Moreover, both governments are politically unstable and wield little actual influence over several regions of their countries where coca is grown.

Then, too, there are the great inherent problems of the eradication process, mostly carried out manually with blade cutters. There are approximately 10,000 coca bushes per hectare. In a country like Peru alone, where approximately 108,600 hectares were unlawfully cultivated in 1994, that's 1,080,600,000 (over 1 billion) bushes to be manually eradicated, a prohibitive number. Also, even where the bushes are cut to ground level, they fully regenerate in eighteen months.

The alternative of uprooting the bush is not an easy one. The coca plant is very hardy, with an extensive root system, and it usually takes two people to pull it out by its roots. This is why the DEA and U.S. State Department have concluded that manual eradication is not practical, and the answer, if any, is in the aerial spraying of the herbicide Tebuthiuron ("spike"). Although spike is selective—killing only the coca plant and not contiguous crops—there are prohibitions to its use. The Peruvian government, though considering it, has thus far not agreed to the spraying of coca crops, and in Bolivia, a law specifically prohibits it. Moreover, at least as to the herbicide spike, Eli Lilly, its U.S. manufacturer, announced a few years ago that it will no longer sell the herbicide for use against the coca crop.

Additionally, if herbicide spraying of any kind is initiated, most Bolivian and Peruvian officials predict a social uprising by the *campesinos* (peasant farmers). More and more, voices in Peru and Bolivia are saying that we have no business attempting to eradicate coca crops in their countries; that the problem lies not with them, but with "the demand for cocaine by the gringos"; that without America's cocaine hunger, there obviously would be no massive coca cultivation, i.e., we should clean up our own act before inserting ourselves into the internal affairs of another country.

Widespread corruption among the military and police in Peru and Bolivia also continues to constitute a major impediment to the eradication efforts of both countries. Reporting in March, 1992, from Yurimagues, a town in Peru's upper Huallaga Valley, the world's largest single coca-producing region, *New York Times* reporter James Brooks observed: "Few police or army officers are willing to seize planes [Colombian drug planes picking up coca base for transportation back to Colombia to be refined into cocaine]. Indeed, officers often bribe their superiors for transfers to the Huallaga Valley. Landing fees [paid by traffickers to Peruvian police and military] for drug planes at airports in the region can go up to $5,000." In 1993, one trafficker told Francisco Reyes, a reporter for the Lima-based newspaper *La Republica*, that the traffickers sometimes even use Peruvian army helicopters to transport the coca base out of the jungle. "We pay $50,000 per helicopter flight, $30,000 for the commanding officer, and $20,000 for the crew," the trafficker told Reyes. "There is no war on drugs here," Reyes writes from Lima, Peru's capital.

The alliance that exists between the traffickers and the Peruvian army and law enforcement (particularly the army) is such that the DEA estimates less than one-half of one percent of Peruvian coca base production en route to Colombia is intercepted. Because of the endemic corruption, in 1992 Hernando de Soto, Peru's top drug official, resigned and told President Fujimori in his resignation letter: "As all the media have reported, drugs are regularly dispatched from places controlled by the state." Robert G. Torricelli (D–N.Y.), chairman of the House Subcommittee on Western Hemispheric Affairs, states: "Our nation's strategy of using the Peruvian police and army against the traffickers is flawed because they are totally and completely corrupted."

The corruption in Peru has actually extended to the point at which Peruvian army units shoot at special Peruvian narcotics police in U.S. helicopters on interdiction missions.* These police are trained by DEA agents and anti-drug officers under U.S. State Department contract at Santa Lucia, a heavily fortified U.S.-built military base deep in the upper Huallaga Valley.

Because corruption in the military and police is so commonplace in Peru, it is not even looked upon as serious when it occurs in the lower echelons. When Peruvian authorities, from time to time, crack down on the corruption, the punishment is mild—not incarceration, but usually simply dismissal from the service or force. For instance, in December of 1994, the Peruvian Army Information Office said that approximately 200 cases of corruption had been discovered, resulting only in dismissal from the service. So the deterrence is negligible.

Peruvian corruption continues to the present time. As recently as January 9, 1995, the date book of an arrested drug trafficker documented meetings and phone calls with the Peruvian vice minister of the interior and army officials. Four army generals are presently being charged with aiding and protecting drug traffickers.

---

*The American military also has a presence in the Andean nations. Per Captain Chris Yates, public affairs officer for the United States Armed Forces Southern Command headquartered in Panama City, Panama, as of 1995 the total number of U.S. military personnel in the Southern Command theater assigned to specific counter-narcotic missions in Central and South America—mostly in Peru, Bolivia, Colombia, and Ecuador, and excluding the Caribbean and Mexico—is 603 (155 Army troops, 359 Air Force, 5 Marine Corps, and 84 Navy). Their sole mission is training and technical assistance to the host countries. They have no law enforcement function, such as the arrest of traffickers or the actual interdiction of cocaine shipments. Yates says that the number of troops assigned to each country is classified. The main pieces of military equipment, used exclusively in the anti-drug effort, are one E-3 Sentry radar plane and two F-16 fighters interceptor planes, each of which is stationed in Panama. The Southern Command also uses UH-60A Blackhawk helicopters and Navy Riverines (small watercraft) in the host Andean countries, but only in a training capacity. The number of helicopters and riverines is also classified. Yates points out that U.S. Customs agents, as opposed to the military, do operate helicopters on actual interdiction missions in the Andean countries.

The first U.S. military anti-narcotic intervention in the Andean nations is believed to have been in July, 1986, when 160 American army troops with Blackhawk helicopters were sent to Bolivia to train local forces in a four-month series of raids on cocaine-producing plants. In October, 1989, twenty U.S. Army Green Beret troops began

The situation is little different in Bolivia. Although President Gonzalo Sanchez de Lozada's administration is committed to combating corruption, according to the 1995 State Department report, "Corruption pervades the Bolivian government and judicial system, with direct involvement in narcotics trafficking within some elements of the Bolivian armed forces. Although the government has taken a strong public stand against corruption, it remains endemic." Coca crop *campesinos* in Bolivia report that Bolivian police have now taken to stealing the cocaleros' coca only to sell it to drug traffickers themselves. One of Bolivia's main drug traffickers, Jose Faustino Rico Toro, was arrested by Peruvian authorities in December, 1994. His previous job? Commander of the nation's counternarcotics police.

In addition to corruption, one of the biggest and most immediate obstacles to eradication is resistance by the coca growers. In the late 1980s, the *campesinos* and traffickers in Peru's upper Huallaga Valley formed an alliance with the Maoist-oriented paramilitary group *Sendero Luminoso* (Shining Path, officially the Communist Party of Peru) to protect them from government eradication teams. The *Sendero Luminoso* guerrillas were so effective in their violent response to the manual eradication teams (resulting in many deaths; even helicopters ferrying troops to the coca fields came under intense fire) that in September, 1989, their attacks forced a temporary suspension of the eradication effort.

There was a contemporaneous, related reason for the suspension in 1989. While America's first priority in Peru is to combat drug trafficking, for years the gravest danger to Peru's central government was not drugs but its struggle for survival against the *Sendero Luminoso*. The fanatical *Senderos*, at their peak a force of around 7,000 armed fighters, waged a bloody fifteen-year war (20,000 were killed) to overthrow Peru's democratic form of government and install an authoritarian Maoist regime. Its founder, a former philosophy professor named Abimael Guzman Reynoso, referred to himself as the "fourth sword of Marxism," after Marx, Lenin, and Mao Tse-tung. The Peruvian government saw that its crackdown on the *campesinos* only served to drive them into the hands of the Marxist rebels. Former Brig. Gen. Alberto Arciniega, who was the Peruvian army's field

instructing Peruvian police officers in jungle drug interdiction. They were recalled to the States in April, 1992.

commander in the upper Huallaga Valley region in 1990, said, "My order is: Nobody must touch the *campesino* coca grower. This doesn't mean I support drug trafficking." Arciniega added that if the coca eradication program were to be resumed, "each campesino whose crops were eradicated would become, the next day, one more *Senderista.*"

The *Sendero Luminoso* were so disruptive of Peruvian life and such a direct threat to the nation's security that in early April, 1992, President Fujimori declared martial law and temporarily shut down Peru's congress and regular court system, asserting he needed untrammeled authority to fight the terrorists. His decree allowed his police to arrest terrorists on less evidence and permitted summary trials by anonymous judges. Not surprisingly, Fujimori's suspension of civil liberties to achieve peace in the land had the support of the Peruvian people. "Shining Path's ferocity was so traumatic that people were willing to tolerate anything," explained Diego Garcia-Sayan, the executive director of the Andean Commission of Jurists, a human rights group. Fujimori's bold initiative paid off. In September, Guzman was captured by Peruvian national police. In a ten-day trial following immediately thereafter, the judge, wearing a hood to protect his identity from Guzman's followers, held Guzman responsible for over 20,000 deaths and $20 billion in damages since the Maoists' revolt erupted in 1980. On October 14, 1992, Guzman was sentenced to life imprisonment.

The capture of the charismatic and forceful Guzman caused the *Sendero Luminoso,* who promised retaliation for the capture of their leader and a fight to the bitter end, to plunge into precipitous decline. Guzman himself recorded statements to his diehard followers to lay down their arms, and although small factionalized remnants of the group remain (the largest of which is commanded by Oscar Ramirez Durand, the son of a retired Peruvian general), it no longer is a destructive force in Peruvian society. Fujimori succeeded in neutralizing the most violent and powerful rebel force in South American history.

With the demise of the *Sendero Luminoso,* the Bush Administration expressed hope that the tide in the losing war against illicit coca production in Peru would be turned around, but as we have seen from the cold statistics, it did not happen. Although the *Senderos* are no longer there to protect the coca crops from government eradication and interdiction efforts, in those instances where the Peruvian military and law enforcement have not been bought off, the *campesinos* themselves oftentimes forcibly repel eradication efforts. This is also true in Bolivia. For instance, during the Bolivian government's manual eradication in 1992 of illicit coca crops in Chapare Valley (the nation's principal coca area, producing more unrefined coca paste than any area except Peru's upper Huallaga Valley), angry farmers resisted, damaging nine of the eradicators' vehicles and wounding five of the drivers. Additionally, *campesinos* in Peru and Bolivia have organized into unions to strongly oppose eradication.

The governments of Peru and Bolivia both agree that a highly funded and aggressive crop substitution program is the only way to get their *campesinos* to stop growing coca, and with limited U.S. funds and technical assistance, a modest effort has been made to accomplish this. But by all accounts it has been unsuccessful, although slightly less so in Bolivia than in Peru. To develop alternative crops and markets in regions ideally suited, unfortunately, for the coca crop is a monumental task. Even where attempts have been made, the alternative crops, such as coffee, corn, cacao, and fruit, still aren't nearly as profitable to the *campesinos* as illicit cocaine. Since the cocaine explosion of the late 1970s, *campesinos* have enjoyed a standard of living heretofore never dreamed of. It is difficult to persuade the close to 350,000 Peruvian and Bolivian *campesinos* to discontinue coca cultivation when the coca crop provides them with up to five times more profit than any food crop. This is so for several reasons. Most alternative food crops take a few years of hard labor before they yield a good harvest, which even then is usually only once a year. Coca requires minimal care and is harvested three times a year. In addition, food crops have to be transported through a mostly roadless jungle to market, and once there, sales are not assured. With coca, not only are sales assured, but the traffickers pick up the coca leaves from the *campesinos* at their source. No transportation is required. A field agent for DIRECO, the Bolivian government agency that oversees coca eradication, told *Los Angeles Times* reporter William Long that *cocaleros* who have given up their coca cultivation "can't make a living" with other products. "The alternative development program isn't working."

And the *campesinos* (called *cocaleros* in Bolivia) themselves have shown that the drug traffickers have no monopoly on corruption. A U.S. State Department investigation in 1992 revealed that many Bolivian farmers, who were being paid $2,000 per hectare to eradicate their coca crop, were destroying only their worst plants, collecting the money, and replanting farther in the jungle.*

Despite the demonstrated futility of the eradication effort in Peru and Bolivia, our nation's leaders, at least publicly, remain undaunted. Melvin Levitsky, former assistant secretary of state for international narcotics, says, "We have to have the patience and stamina to persevere." And the 1995 National Drug Control Strategy report points to "a new focus" on the source countries, emphasizing economic development programs, eradication, and interdiction of drug planes at the source countries themselves (isn't this what we've already been doing for years?). But the 1996 fiscal year budget for the source countries of Peru, Bolivia, and Colombia—only $137 million—betrays our recognition of the futility of eradication as a solution to the problem, and hence only the most perfunctory efforts are being conducted. How perfunctory and superficial? Examples are always illustrative. The Pentagon, whose signature throughout the years has been financial profligacy and waste, *never even requested* from Congress in its 1996 budget that any additional C-130H cargo planes be built, but unbelievably, the House National Security Committee, on its own, ordered up eight more of the behemoths, at a cost of $290.4 million; i.e., we're spending over two times as much for planes the Pentagon *doesn't even want* than we are to eliminate or reduce the source of nearly 100 percent of the highly destructive cocaine entering this country.

In April of 1993, coca leaf growers from Peru, Bolivia, and Colombia met in Cuzco, Peru, and issued a declaration that "the West, represented by the United States, is trying to carry out a definitive genocide and ethnocide against Andean people by eliminating and eradicating our coca leaf. They cannot do so. The eradication of the coca leaf would mean death for Andean people. Coca is everything for us, our material survival, our myths, our cosmic vision of the world, the joy we find in life, the voice of our ancestors, our reason for existing and being in the world." The position of the growers was that they should not suffer because the American consumer and Colombian seller want to make illicit cocaine out of their "sacred" plant, which, they said, "will outlive all of the destructive forces, surviving forever."

---

*The eradication of the coca plant and the opium poppy in Colombia has been more successful. Since 1994, Operation Splendor in Colombia has used U.S.-supplied planes and fuel and U.S.-trained pilots to spray Colombian fields with the herbicide glyphosate, eradicating 4,910 hectares of coca and 4,676 hectares of opium poppy that same year, with little resistance from the *campesinos* or the Cali cartel.

When one reads these words, one sees the silliness of the suggestion by some that a real war, with force and arrests, be waged against the *campesino*. As President Fujimori said in a February 3, 1991, interview with *La Republica*, "The social cost" of such a war on drugs where there was "strict application of the law," would be "terrible, because it would involve jailing 260,000 families, condemning 1.3 million people to misery, and would create a nationwide commotion." Fujimori told the *Miami Herald* (while attending the thirty-three-nation Summit of Americas in Miami in December of 1994) that U.S. efforts to promote crop substitution, eradicate drug plants, and subsidize Peruvian law enforcement agencies have failed and were "a disaster."

Returning from a trip to La Paz, where he met with Bolivian President Sanchez de Lozada, American drug czar Lee P. Brown told reporters on August 29, 1995, that the Bolivian government was not "seriously enforcing its narcotic laws,"* but that the Bolivian president would face "substantial political difficulties" if he ordered significant eradication of the coca crop.

But none of these situations and obstacles is the reason why the possibility of extinguishing coca crops is for all intents and purposes nonexistent. The reason lies, again, in the nature of the beast: the fact that, as with interdiction, if you eradicate hectares of coca crops in one place, they will emerge somewhere else. Although the coca plant is indigenous to Peru and Bolivia, it can grow easily in subtropical climates at elevations from 1,000 to 6,000 feet, and can be harvested as much as four times a year. In other words, it can grow in many regions of the world. The DEA reports that Venezuela, a major transshipment point for Colombian cocaine, and the immense country of Brazil are starting to grow coca. Coca has also been successfully grown in Java, India, Ceylon, Formosa, and certain areas of Africa. Common sense tells us that the moment there was any serious interruption in the cultivation of coca in the present principal source

---

*A 1988 Bolivian law prohibits the growing of new coca plants, but there is little enforcement of the law. Although President Lozada, fearful of a threat by the United States to decertify Bolivia as a country receiving U.S. aid ($87 million in 1995), has recently been threatening the *cocaleros* with forcible eradication of their coca crops, he also sends contradictory signals. "When we bear down on these people [*cocaleros*]," he explains, "we are perceived [by the majority of Bolivian people, per polls] as giving some very poor people a very hard time on behalf and for the benefit of a very wealthy country [the United States]. I think these people, if they see that their livelihood and their family's livelihood are endangered, will quickly accept being armed by the narcos, and we will end up with a very serious situation. We don't know if our economy, our society, could support the social and the human and economic cost of an insurgency."

countries of Peru and Bolivia, the coca crop would sprout up like wildflowers in a hundred different places.

Because of this reality, even one with the most myopic vision can see that coca crop eradication is an impossibility. And even if a method were ever devised to entirely or substantially eliminate coca production, the drug lords would simply shift to synthetic cocaine, which has already been manufactured.* Synthetic drugs like phencyclidine (PCP) and methamphetamine (speed) are already being produced in substantial quantities in domestic clandestine laboratories, and pose an increasingly ominous threat. Then there are the so-called designer drugs, a relatively new phenomenon. These drugs result when unethical chemists manufacture altered versions of prohibited drugs. Since their exact chemical structures are not covered by the Controlled Substances Act of 1970 (21 U.S.C. §812, which sets forth five "schedules" of prohibited drugs), until they are eventually brought under the act, they are not illegal. An example is the synthetic opiate fentanyl, a drug more powerful than heroin.**

A concomitant alternative to eradicating the coca crops is destroying the laboratories ("kitchens") that produce the cocaine. Although most of the labs are in Colombia, they have now surfaced all over South America, particularly in Bolivia. The DEA and State Department launched a very aggressive effort to knock out the labs, first with Operation Stop Prop/Blast Furnace in Bolivia in 1986, and then Operation Snowcap throughout South America in 1987. Though the labs are frequently isolated and hidden by extremely dense jungle and mountainous terrain, because of excellent intelligence information it is estimated that as many as 10 percent of them were located and destroyed in a two-year period. American Huey helicopters (the

---

*Rubber provides a parallel. With the blockade of Germany by the British during World War I, Germany succeeded in producing a synthetic rubber. Likewise, here in the United States at the onset of World War II, due to the possibility that America's source of natural rubber would be cut off, fifty-one plants were constructed to produce synthetic rubber on a mass scale. In fact, since the 1950s, automobile tires are made primarily of synthetic rubber.

**It must be mentioned that although the military search-and-find proposal for the drug crisis set forth subsequently in this book (see Chapter 3) would obviously not be applicable to domestically manufactured synthetic and designer drugs, the second solution, which deals with the interdiction of drug-profit monies (see Chapter 4), would be viable, as the high-level dealer in synthetic and designer drugs, like his counterpart in cocaine, heroin, and marijuana, has to launder his drug earnings. It should also be noted that for obvious reasons, it would be infinitely easier for this nation to substantially reduce and cripple domestic production of illicit drugs than it is for us to do so in far-off countries like Colombia and Burma.

workhorse of the Vietnam War), carrying troops or police from the various South American countries and accompanied by DEA special agents, swooped down on the labs, and physically dismantled and destroyed them. An indication of Operation Snowcap's effectiveness is that from April 10 to December 31, 1987, 1,375 cocaine laboratories (this number includes coca paste and coca base labs) in Colombia, Bolivia, Peru, Costa Rica, Guatemala, Panama, Brazil, and Chile were neutralized. The effect (not effectiveness) of all this? Nothing at all. More cocaine is being produced by cocaine laboratories than ever before. Operation Snowcap was discontinued in 1994.

A further illustration of the utter futility of attempting to solve the drug problem by destroying all the cocaine laboratories: In January, 1989, Colombia's National Police Anti-Narcotics Unit destroyed a complex of twenty-six labs on a ranch outside Puerto Triunfo. The labs had a capacity (though they were not actually reaching it) of producing 6.6 tons of pure cocaine a week. At 341 tons a year, *this one complex alone* could supply more than the yearly consumption of cocaine in this nation.

What this all means is that the task of eradicating illicit coca crops and cocaine laboratories, like that of drug interdiction, is a "Mission Impossible." As with interdiction, the Band-Aid approach is flawed from its inception. Even if it were possible to eliminate virtually all these crops and labs, for the effort to continue to work, a very substantial American military force would have to permanently occupy almost every country in South America. We already know from years of experience that Latin American countries, by themselves, would be unsuccessful at—much less even be inclined towards—effectively suppressing the inevitable reemergence of illicit coca production. Without our permanent occupation, the coca crops and cocaine labs would start reappearing the moment the engines of the jets carrying our troops back to America were turned on. And a very large and permanent American military presence throughout South America not only would be prohibitively costly but also would be unlawful and create immense geopolitical problems for us in the Western Hemisphere.

This nation's effort—what there is of it—to solve the drug problem could be likened to that of exasperated parents flitting aimlessly (within a set and circumscribed range of options) from one plan to another to control an incorrigible child, often helplessly returning to previous methods they've forgotten have failed. For years, the greatly predominant means to combat the drug problem was through law enforcement and interdiction. With the enactment of the Drug Abuse Office and Treatment Act of 1972, however, federal policy changed to emphasizing drug treatment and prevention initiatives over law enforcement and interdiction. The 1972 act established the National Institute for Drug Abuse to handle research, prevention efforts through education and treatment, and rehabilitation programs. From fiscal year 1973 through 1977, in fact, demand reduction programs (education, treatment, etc.) received more of the drug-fighting federal dollars than supply reduction (law enforcement, interdiction, eradication, etc.). In 1978, however, the thrust of federal funding shifted back to emphasizing law enforcement and other supply reduction programs over demand reduction efforts. But in 1994, though supply reduction continued to get the lion's share of the drug-fighting dollar, our nation once again started going in the direction of placing increased emphasis on education and treatment. This pendulum effect will, of course, continue indefinitely unless we can come up with something completely new and potent. The old nostrums, by themselves, won't do.

With respect to *law enforcement*, it has become clear that once the coca leaf is grown, processed into cocaine, and smuggled into the United States, American law enforcement cannot, by the process of arrest and prosecution, make any significant dent in the drug epidemic. As *Washington Post* columnist Richard Cohen has observed: "For every drug pusher who's put in jail, another will take his place. Nothing really changes. There's an inexhaustible supply of amoral people looking to make a quick buck." Law enforcement officers on the local, state, and federal levels are fighting hard and courageously (many have lost their lives) in the trenches against the drug cancer, but this task has proven to be as impossible as stopping rain from falling.

Although former drug czar William Bennett, and his successors Bob Martinez and Dr. Lee P. Brown, have placed primary reliance on law enforcement as the solution to the drug problem, the consensus among law enforcement authorities markedly differs. Thomas C. Kelly, who retired in 1988 as the DEA's deputy administrator, echoes what one hears from law enforcement veterans around the country: "I've been in law enforcement for twenty-five years," he says, "but I'm not ashamed to tell you that law enforcement is not the answer to the drug problem." Former FBI Director William Sessions adds: "The solution isn't in the hands of law enforcement." The nation's former chief law enforcement officer, Attorney General Richard Thornburgh, goes further: "If we want to lose the war on drugs, we should just leave it to law enforcement." Isaac Fulwood, the recent chief of police in Washington, D.C., perhaps said it best: "We can't arrest our way out of this problem." If we haven't learned this reality from decades of futile law enforcement, we never will.

The following are excerpts from the June 9, 1989, editions of the *Los Angeles Times* and *Los Angeles Herald Examiner*. They illustrate what has been repeated, with variations on the main theme, thousands of times in cities throughout the nation to this very day:

> More than 100 officers using a tank-like battering ram stormed 10 suspected rock houses in South-Central Los Angeles as part of a major cocaine raid, Los Angeles police announced yesterday. Several neighborhood residents complained about the violence of the raid . . . but police defended their actions as necessary in the continuing battle to quell the city's burgeoning drug problem. At least two shots were fired at officers preparing to enter one of the heavily fortified houses with the aid of the six-ton battering ram. . . . Undercover officers had made cocaine purchases at each of the houses during a month-long investigation. "The dope moved from house to house," one of the officers said. "It was like a shell game—which house is it in today?" Shortly after police left and the battering ram rumbled away, drug sales in the neighborhood resumed, residents said. "Drug dealers were running up to cars and asking the occupants what they needed no more than 30 minutes after the police left," said a neighborhood resident. A narcotics officer acknowledged yesterday that cocaine remained readily available on East 47th Street.

On those occasions when law enforcement is successful in ridding a neighborhood of drug trafficking, the dealers and pushers simply move to an adjacent neighborhood. And so on, around the country.

And while *education* of the dangers of drug abuse should continue to be vigorously pursued and increased and should theoretically help lower the demand, we must take cognizance of the fact that nearly every adult in America who uses and abuses drugs *already* knows of these very dangers and still elects to use drugs. With respect to educating our nation's youth, close to 50 percent of them are already receiving state-mandated drug education and prevention classes between the fifth and eighth grades (believed to be the critical years), yet drug use among our young is on the rise again, and remains dangerously high. One would almost automatically assume that D.A.R.E. (Drug Abuse Resistance Education), a seventeen-week school program designed to discourage youths from using drugs, would have a measurably positive effect. However, it apparently has not been successful among the targeted fifth and sixth graders. Initiated in 1983 by the Los Angeles Police Department and city officials, the celebrated anti-drug program is taught by local police to over 25 million students in fifty states and several foreign countries. Although D.A.R.E. officials report that their surveys show that "kids who take the D.A.R.E. course are much less likely to use drugs later in life," independent studies, in which researchers look at children who took D.A.R.E. and those who didn't and see which groups used more drugs in the following years, reflect that D.A.R.E. has not been effective.

Gilbert Botvin of the Institute for Prevention at Cornell University says that it's "well established that D.A.R.E. doesn't work." A 1991 National Institute of Drug Abuse study of D.A.R.E. found, like virtually every other survey, "no statistically significant difference between experimental groups and control groups in the percentage of new users of cigarettes, alcohol, and marijuana." A 1990 Canadian government-funded survey also concluded that "D.A.R.E. had no significant effect on the students' use of any of the substances (marijuana, heroin, crack, cocaine, LSD) measured." In 1994, the U.S. Department of Justice commissioned the Research Triangle Institute of Durham, North Carolina, to conduct a statistical analysis of all the research nationwide on the issue of D.A.R.E.'s effectiveness. Their verdict after analyzing eight studies involving 9,500 children? D.A.R.E. has "a limited to essentially nonexistent effect" on drug use. A comprehensive 1995 study of 5,000 students from 240 schools commissioned by the California Department of Education came to the same conclusion. And according to the 1995 National Drug Control Strategy Report, "The evaluations suggest that D.A.R.E. is not, by itself, a sufficient community response to the drug problem. . . . Some studies question the value of increasing knowledge of drug consequences and creating anti-drug attitudes among students who do not (and will not soon) face choices about drug use. One implication is that programs such as D.A.R.E. might be more appropriate for older children."

Our goal, of course, should be to educate 100 percent of America's youth. But even if we achieve this exposure, and even if the drug education were 100 percent effective—which it cannot, and never will, even approach—this would only solve the drug problem for the future. The horrendous drug problem as we know it today would continue for many years, a totally unacceptable situation.

The situation is similar with *treatment*. Although few disagree that treatment should be available to all addicts (only an estimated 20 percent of America's addicts presently receive treatment), and can only help, there are divergent statistics on the efficacy of treatment. Some show that the recidivism rate after treatment is very high. For example, a 1991 U.S. Department of Justice study showed that 62 percent of state inmates and 55 percent of federal inmates who used drugs in the month before their latest offense had previously been in a drug-treatment program. However, a $2 million survey conducted over a one-and-a-half-year period between 1992 and 1994 of cocaine, heroin, and alcohol addicts in California showed much more positive results, *at least in the short term*. The California Drug and Alcohol Treatment Assessment (CALDATA) study of 3,000 addicts recently discharged from treatment centers or presently undergoing treatment reflected a significant decrease in addiction of about two-fifths, and in drug-related crimes of close to two-thirds. Moreover, a cost-benefit analysis showed a $7 return for every dollar invested, mostly due to a reduction in crime and health care.

Quite apart from a certain amount of recidivism that naturally takes place even with the best treatment, a 1993 GAO survey for the House of Representatives found that "a number of treatment facilities were not effectively treating the addiction." Also, treatment is inherently limited. Irrespective of the wide range of physical and psychological problems it addresses itself to, the treatment facility has no capability of ameliorating the often profound social and economic problems which have contributed to the addiction, which, in the long term (in excess of two years), usually results in the individual returning to his or her addiction. In any event, treatment is after the fact. It only addresses itself to the result of America's drug problem. It cannot be a solution to the existing problem itself.

Nor can all the other stopgap, modest measures which our nation's leaders come up with year in and year out to solve the drug problem. The fact that those elected and appointed officials who represent us think that these measures will is a very disturbing commentary. An example of what those in charge of the farm have come up with is set forth in former Customs Commissioner William von Raab's personal letter to then–Attorney General Edwin Meese on May 26, 1988. Von Raab was an energetic and resourceful public servant who shepherded the transformation of U.S. Customs in recent years from a cargo-and-luggage checker into a sophisticated and combative enemy of the drug smuggler. And his agency has done an excellent but futile job as the lead federal agency in drug interdiction. Von Raab prefaced his suggestions by stating that the letter was "in response to the President's request for new ideas to fight the drug war." He continued by stating that he met with his executive staff to formulate the ideas, which he said he hoped would have merit in attempting to "achieve our goal of a drug-free America." These were some of the new ideas set forth in the commissioner's letter: (1) Anyone who is a drug offender should be required to report to Customs when entering or leaving the United States. (2) The arrest of all persons caught crossing the border with drugs should be announced to their local newspapers. (3) Urge states to suspend or revoke driver's licenses of persons caught at the border with drugs in their cars. (4) There should be car window or bumper stickers to identify convicted drug offenders. (5) Drug offenders should be required to register with local police when they move into a locality. (6) Artificial drugs (benign, look-alike, pseudo-narcotics) could be placed into circulation to flood the distribution system, confuse users, and disrupt the market.

In all deference to the commissioner (who also, in fairness, had at other times recommended much stronger measures, such as shooting down smuggler planes) and his staff, other than inducing a chuckle and a smile on the faces of the drug lords, how can our nation's leaders expect these types of Band-Aid measures (or those like the 14-mile steel fence along the first part of the 1,933 mile U.S.-Mexico border, starting at the Pacific Ocean and extending eastward) to cause more than the tiniest occlusion against the sea of drugs entering our nation?

Throughout the years and right up to the present, there has been a spirited division of opinion among those fighting the drug war as to what is the real "source" of the drug problem. Many experts speak of the user as the true source, and hence, they want the emphasis to be on deterrence (law enforcement), education, and treatment. Others feel that most of our efforts should be directed to eliminating the coca crops and/or cocaine laboratories, which they consider to be the true source. But when we hear talk of "going to the source" to solve the drug problem, it has to be a source whose attack by us has a reasonable probability of success. There are many "sources" of the drug problem, but as we have seen, the ones against which we have directed our resources simply don't lend themselves to extinction.

True, in one sense the source of the drug problem is the user. If we could stop the user from using drugs, we'd obviously no longer have the drug problem we have today. But we cannot do so. True, in another sense the coca fields are the source of the drug problem, because if we could stop the cultivation of the coca crop, we'd no longer have our current drug problem. But we can't. And true, in yet another sense, the cocaine laboratories are the source of the problem, because if we could stop the laboratories from producing the cocaine, again, we wouldn't have our current crisis. But we can't. I view these aforementioned sources as being secondary or derivative sources, and hence, though our assaults on them should continue, our efforts to solve the drug crisis will be misdirected until we fix our primary gaze elsewhere.

Facts are stubborn little devils, and since we have all the facts and evidence that even an inveterate skeptic would ever need, and then some, that we cannot stop the nation's voracious demand for drugs, nor keep the supply of drugs from entering our porous borders, there appear to be only two conceptual ways to solve the drug crisis, and they both are directed toward the true source of the drug problem, and the only source that can be successfully defeated: the drug lords who start the whole process and make it all happen. The whole process by which the coca plant is grown for illicit purposes, processed into cocaine powder, and smuggled into the United States obviously just doesn't "happen" (i.e., coca crops do not have feet of their own, nor cocaine laboratories hands of their own). There are several people at the top of the pyramid who make all of these things occur. *And if these people decide they don't want to do it anymore, it's not going to happen. It's as simple as that.* How do we make them not want to do it anymore? That's what this book is all about.

"Going to the source" of the problem, then, a phrase one often hears in the war against cocaine, does not involve going to the laboratories that produce the drug, or even the Andean fields that produce the crop from which the cocaine is made. The seminal source, almost by definition, is the minds of the people on top who make it all happen. The war against cocaine, not a conventional war, will be won, if at all, not by the expenditure of billions of dollars, or by the sweat and blood of great numbers of men and women on the drug battlefield (we've already done all of that), but by new and piercing measures employed in such a manner that the minds of the adversary (drug lords) will gladly give up the fight.

This book discusses two proposals to achieve this objective. Unlike the 1988 Anti-Drug Abuse Act, which, even though it contained nothing new of any significance, had as its utopian objective a "drug-free America," these proposals will not bring about an America free of drugs. We will always have some drug use and abuse in America. The proposals, instead, are calculated to substantially and quickly reduce the drug problem down to manageable proportions; i.e., they give promise of eliminating the drug *crisis* presently confronting this nation.

The efficacy of these two proposals is based on an elemental reality. It is always said that the demand for drugs creates the supply. But if the supply were cut off because the supplier no longer desired to continue his trade, of necessity the demand would eventually wither away.

Just like no one, not even a Houdini, can pull a rabbit out of the hat when there is no rabbit in the hat, there cannot be widespread use of drugs if little is available. As the 1989 Bennett Drug Strategy report pointed out, "when drug availability declines, few people are likely to seek out drugs and consume them." Before the enormous infusion of cocaine into this country in the late 1970s, millions of Americans weren't using cocaine and its derivative crack, nor did we have the disastrous social crisis we have today, *did* we? Moreover, if a cocaine addict no longer has cocaine, he is *forced* off the drug.

There is an important caveat to all of this. To be successful, the reduction of the cocaine supply has to be very substantial. If it is slight or perhaps even moderate, the reduction, at least in terms of drug-related crime and violence, will cause more harm than good, triggering more warring by rival gangs over the shrinking availability of the drug. Also, the increased street price for cocaine brought about by the reduced supply will necessitate the commission of more crimes by addicts to support their habit.

The two proposals that follow are:

1. Make the drug lords realize the high probability (not possibility) that if they continue their trade, they will pay with their lives (Military Search-and-Find Mission), and/or
2. Make it so unprofitable for them (Interdiction of Drug-Profit Monies) that they will automatically go elsewhere or into some other line of business, perhaps basket-weaving.

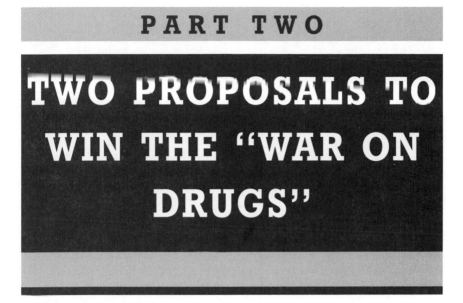

PART TWO

TWO PROPOSALS TO WIN THE "WAR ON DRUGS"

PROPOSAL 1
Military Search-and-Find Mission

T his proposal calls for the deployment of a U.S. Army Special Forces unit (or U.S. Marine Expeditionary Force) on Colombian soil for the specific and limited purpose of apprehending and bringing to the United States for criminal prosecution the drug kingpins who are responsible for the cocaine blitz of America.

When I first recommended this course of action in 1991, I set forth two additional measures to help ensure that no successors will want to take the place of the arrested kingpins. If they are implemented, the probability is very high that the whole process set in motion by the kingpins by which coca plants are converted into cocaine and the cocaine is smuggled into the United States will, for the most part, cease. One of these measures, the death penalty for drug lords, is now federal law (see page 161 et seq.). The other measure is the creation of a special federal court to expedite the trials and appeals of the drug lords (see page 164 et seq.).

The precise stratagem of a military search-and-find mission (not an invasion) has not previously been publicly urged. On those very infrequent occasions when military intervention by way of combat troops *is* discussed as a solution to the problem, the principal options bandied about are: invasion; sending our troops to Colombia to assist the Colombian military in fighting the drug cartels; utilizing U.S. Special Forces as assassination squads in Colombia (prohibited by

§2.11 of President Reagan's December 14, 1981, Executive Order 12333); and sending military troops to Peru and Bolivia to eradicate the coca crops. By and large, the American government has almost reflexively rejected all suggestions of military intervention of *any* kind whatsoever on foreign soil (over and above money, material resources, and military advisers) to solve our drug crisis, recoiling from the notion the way the devil does from holy water. One reason is that for well over a century, this nation has been operating under the incorrect assumption that it is prohibited by law from using the military in a law enforcement capacity in foreign countries (see Posse Comitatus discussion beginning on page 125).

In addition, the government has given these reasons, among others, for the inadvisability of U.S. military intervention: "We are acutely aware of the sensitivity of Latin American nations to U.S. intervention"; "It would inflame nationalist sensibilities in Central America," and so forth. Translation: The mere sensitive *feelings* of some of the leaders and citizens of a few foreign countries are apparently far more important than our own country's horrendous drug crisis and the desire of our nation's citizens to end it. (But, as we shall see, when, *for infinitely far less valid reasons*, this nation's leadership wants to massively invade a Latin American country, such as Grenada or Panama, these considerations no longer apply.) If it ultimately comes down to a choice between offending the sensibilities of those in Latin America who would object to our violating their national sovereignty by apprehending drug lords within, and witnessing the continuing destruction of millions of American lives because the supply of cocaine into this country by these drug lords isn't stanched, can there really be any question what our choice has to be?

This chapter will point out not only the advisability and lawfulness of a military search-and-find mission, but also the *explicit constitutional duty* of this nation's chief executive to pursue this course of action.

A military *invasion*, which conjures up the notion of large numbers of men, ships, tanks, and airplanes invading the boundaries of another nation, would obviously not be required, since we would not be "at war" with the government or people of Colombia, nor do we have any reason to be. In fact, polls consistently show that although corruption is rampant and cocaine has become the leading product of the Colombian economy, the Colombian government and most of the country's 36 million citizens are opposed to the very people a military raid would seek to bring to justice. Former Colombian presidents Virgilio Barco Vargas and Cesar Gaviria Trujillo waged a bitter but unsuccessful war against the drug lords in the late eighties and early nineties. And Colombia's current president, Ernesto Samper, although plagued first by whispers and now accusations to the contrary, has given all indications (by his near decimation of the Cali cartel) that he is anti-cartel. As opposed, then, to a typical military invasion, this would be *a very limited search-and-find mission by that type and number of American military personnel deemed necessary by the Joint Chiefs of Staff to accomplish the job.*

Lest there be any confusion, it must be stated off the top that the December 20, 1989, invasion of Panama *was not* an example of the search-and-find proposal discussed in this chapter. In the first place, it was a full-fledged military invasion. Second, as we shall see, its principal purpose was not really to help win the war on drugs. Obviously at pains to justify the invasion, the Bush Administration asserted that in addition to protecting both the lives of Americans in Panama and the integrity of the Panama Canal treaties, a further reason was the war on drugs: to apprehend Panamanian dictator Manuel Antonio Noriega so he could be brought to the United States to face federal drug charges in Miami.* Though this was excellent PR for the American people, if even one of the strategic reasons for the invasion truly was to aid the drug war by seizing Noriega, then we would have obviously gone into Colombia at the time and gotten the *real* drug lords.

Noriega, to be sure, was guilty of drug trafficking, but he was never a drug trafficker in the genuine sense of the word. The Panamanian leader was involved neither in the production nor the sale of drugs; he was simply one of many "facilitators" who sold his services to the traffickers, permitting them, among other things, to use his nation, as several other small nations are used, as a money-laundering haven. As the *Los Angeles Times* noted, Noriega only "aided and abetted the drug traffickers."

No one disputes anymore that the Carter and Reagan administrations knew of Noriega's association with the narco-traffickers and

---

*On April 9, 1992, Noriega was convicted in Miami of eight out of ten charges of drug trafficking, racketeering, and money laundering brought against him by the U.S. Attorney's Office. The federal jury found, among other things, that Noriega had helped the Medellin cartel set up operations in Panama, hid some of its leaders after the assassination of Colombia's Justice Minister in 1984, took a $4 million bribe to authorize creation of a

simply looked the other way. In testimony before a 1988 Congressional Subcommittee on Terrorism, Narcotics, and International Operations, Francis J. McNeil, a career State Department official, said the United States was "coddling Noriega beyond any time when one would reasonably doubt Noriega's involvement in drug trafficking." Then–DEA Administrator John C. Lawn told the subcommittee that Noriega's name appeared in more than eighty separate DEA investigative case files between 1970 and 1987.

At the time, Noriega was furnishing U.S. intelligence agents with valuable information about leftist movements throughout Central America and assisting in the Contra effort. But when the Panamanian bad boy's venality got the best of him and he also began funneling arms and supplies to the Sandinistas, Cubans, Palestinians, and Libyans, as well as making not-so-sly hints that he possessed some sort of dirt on President Bush ("I've got Bush by the balls"), and giving vent to his ingenerate anti-American instincts, he became, as *Newsweek* said, "Bush's biggest foreign policy embarrassment." Washington rumbled with rumors that Bush was personally irritated with Noriega.

There is rather compelling proof that bringing Noriega to justice on the drug charges was never a main objective of the Bush Administration. On December 20, 1989, the U.S. State Department confirmed that at a meeting in October between U.S. officials and Noriega representatives, the U.S. representatives promised that it would not make any effort to extradite Noriega on the drug charges if he gave up his power and left Panama. Noriega declined. Senate Armed Services Committee Chairman Sam Nunn (D–Ga.) and Senator John W. Warner (R–Va.), the ranking Republican on the panel, as well as then–White House Press Secretary Marlin Fitzwater, also confirmed the offer to Noriega. Earlier, the Reagan Administration had even hatched the idea of dropping the drug charges altogether in exchange for Noriega's removal from power. And that, it appears, was what the invasion was all about. For once, there was near unanimity among observers of the political scene that the overriding goal of the invasion was to oust Noriega from power and install a stable and friendly democratic government.

---

cocaine laboratory in Panama, laundered drug profits, and generally assisted the Medellin cartel in efforts to import cocaine into the United States. The fifty-eight-year-old Noriega, who did not take the stand in his own defense, is presently serving a forty-year sentence at a federal prison near Miami.

THE DRUG LORDS AND THEIR CARTELS

Colombia

Up until 1991, the heart of the Colombian cocaine industry was the Medellin cartel, a criminal empire formed in the early 1980s that employed thousands of people and whose vast illicit fortune enabled it to wield political power not just in Colombia, but in other Latin American countries as well. The cartel had powerful associates, but only three men—Pablo Escobar, Jorge Ochoa, and Rodriguez Gacha—ruled the roost, and with an iron hand.

The cartel leader was Pablo ("El Padrino," the Godfather) Escobar Gaviria. He was also, by far, the most visible member of the cartel. Escobar began his career in crime as a petty thief stealing headstones from cemeteries, then removing the inscriptions and selling the stones to others. Together with Rodriguez Gacha (before the latter was slain), he had been responsible for nearly all of the violence perpetrated by the cartel. In the early years of the cartel, before murder and terrorism became its signature, indications were that Escobar was second among equals to Jorge Ochoa; at least when cartel leaders summoned Colombian drug traffickers for "summit" meetings, Ochoa invariably presided. [In the mid-1980s, two American drug traffickers penetrated the inner circle of the cartel, Barry Seal (since murdered) and Max Mermelstein. Seal referred to the Medellin cartel as "the Jorge Ochoa cocaine cartel," and Mermelstein said that in each other's presence, Escobar deferred to Ochoa.] Escobar, who was described by friend and foe alike as highly intelligent, demonstrated that an individual on the wrong side of the law can nevertheless possess some traits that many on the right side should have. His largess in providing aid to the poor gave him a legendary Robin Hood aura among some in Colombia. Among other things, he built and donated a housing project in Medellin called Barrio Pablo Escobar for 550 impoverished families. Escobar even built soccer fields and a zoo for the disadvantaged.

Up until January 15, 1991, when he turned himself in to Colombian authorities in exchange for a promise of no extradition to the United States, the second most powerful member of the cartel was Jorge Luis Ochoa Vasquez ("El Gordo," the Fat One), the middle son of Don Fabio and Dona Margoth Vasquez, an old-line Colombian family whose original source of modest wealth was cattle-raising and a family-run restaurant. The most discreet and least violent member of the cartel, El Gordo was quietly efficient and did not even use drugs himself, nor permit them to be used in his presence. With his father, he shared a passion for horse breeding, including the Paso Fino show horse. Ochoa has two brothers, Juan David, and Fabio Jr. Fabio Jr. surrendered to the authorities on December 18, 1990; Juan David on February 16, 1991. The Ochoas were known in Colombia as the "first family of cocaine."

The third member of the cartel, Gonzalo Rodriguez Gacha, was slain on December 15, 1989, by Colombian troops near the Caribbean town of Coveñas. The rough-hewn Gacha, known as "El Mejicano," because of his fondness for Mexican food and music, had risen to power as Escobar's underling, and allegedly personally killed a political leader who interfered with his coca *campesinos*. Though Escobar's power seemed to have stabilized, and Ochoa's, if anything, had waned, the stature of Rodriguez Gacha, who operated out of his small hometown of Pacho, about seventy-five miles southeast of Medellin, continued to increase, and some predicted he would one day be El Padrino. Like Escobar, he had been generous with his money in helping the poor.

Although never quite a member of the ruling cartel troika, a prominent narcotic chieftain in his own right was the flamboyant and indiscreet Carlos Lehder, since convicted in 1988 by a Jacksonville, Florida, federal jury on multiple drug-trafficking charges. In the late seventies and early eighties, Lehder, from the small Bahamian island of Norman's Cay (a transshipment point to the United States for Colombian cocaine located 200 miles southeast of Miami), became the first big cocaine smuggler for the Medellin cartel. In 1989, American financier Robert Vesco, now in exile in Cuba, was indicted by a U.S. grand jury in absentia for having facilitated Lehder's narcotic-trafficking activities. Vesco lived in the Bahamas during Lehder's drug-trafficking days and is believed to have bribed Bahamian officials to overlook Lehder's illicit activities.

In the short span of a few years, Ochoa, Escobar, and Gacha, referred to by *Newsweek* in 1990 as perhaps "the most successful criminals in history," had become among the world's richest men. The July 24, 1989, edition of *Forbes* magazine listed the three cartel leaders as among the world's only ninety-two billionaires. The authors of *The Cocaine Wars* (Paul Eddy, with Hugo Sabogal and Sara Walden), a 1988 book on the cartel, referred to the cartel as "without doubt, the largest and most profitable criminal conspiracy in the world. What was once a group of disparate and rival gangs has been molded into a sophisticated, determined, and ruthless multinational conglomerate that has effectively brought Colombia to its knees through fear and intimidation."

And murder. Organized crime in the States, as opposed to Sicily, has consistently and religiously stayed away from murdering public officials. Realizing that there is enough heat on them already without going after public officials, Mafiosi killings are usually internecine in nature. The Medellin cartel, being much stronger in Colombia than the Mob ever was in this country (in Colombia, the cartels are called the mafia), exercised no such reticence with public officials. In fact, officials were their primary targets, and the higher the position they occupied, the more attractive they became to the cartel; that is, if the official could not be bribed and was vigorously opposing them. The cartel's victims included not only scores of soldiers, police, and public officials, but (per the Colombian National Association of Judicial Officials and Employers), unbelievably, 43 Colombian judges, 179 lower-level judicial employees, and 12 Supreme Court justices. Other victims have included three presidential candidates; Colonel Jaime Ramirez Gomez, the incorruptible and highly regarded head of the Colombian National Police's Anti-Narcotics Unit; Carlos Mauro Hoyos Jiminez, the nation's attorney general; Rodrigo Lara Bonilla, Colombia's justice minister and a leading architect of a 1979 extradition treaty with the United States; and the Bogota judge who investigated Bonilla's murder and allegedly uncovered evidence implicating the cartel (in Colombia, "judges of instructions" are responsible for compiling evidence to determine whether charges should be brought).

The emergence of the cartel gave rise to the Colombian expression "plata o plomo" (silver or lead), meaning "take the bribe money or the bullet." The fact that a considerable number of high Colombian officials paid with their lives is incontrovertible proof that they forcefully opposed the cartel and did not take the silver. The following lament from then–government minister Carlos Lemos Simmonds before he resigned in March, 1990, was representative of the pervasive fear among Colombian officials because of the unprecedented death toll among Colombian leaders: "I go from an armored car to a guarded office. My feet have not touched the streets for weeks. My family lives in terror." In 1989, Justice Minister Monica de Grieff resigned out of fear and fled the country with her family.

Even journalists were not exempt. From January, 1984, to early 1991, thirty-one editors and reporters were murdered by the cartel for publishing strong anti-cartel pieces, including Guillermo Cano Isaza, editor of the anti-drug crusading Bogota daily *El Espectador*, and Raul Echeverria Barrientos, managing editor of the Cali daily *El Occidente*.

Anyone influential who was a foe of the cartel lived in fear. Rafael Santos, news editor of *El Tiempo*, described the change his life had taken: "Armored cars, bodyguards, and guns have become part of my life. I am warned by security officials to change routes to and from my office, to leave and arrive home at different times. Two other newspaper buildings have been blown to bits by narcos wishing to silence the press. My office building looks like a fortress. Reporters, reluctant to cover stories about drugs, refuse to put bylines on the articles. Editorial columnists . . . will never mention extradition publicly. That would be signing our own death warrant."

Most of the assassinations ordered by the cartel were carried out by bands of teenage *sicarios* (paid killers) from northeast Medellin, the meanest and most squalid quadrant of the city. The *sicarios* zipped through the clogged traffic on motorcycles and, pulling alongside their target's car, emptied their submachine guns on the victim and his bodyguards. As often as not, the *sicarios* themselves were killed in the return gunfire from the victim's bodyguards, but life was so wretched for the destitute assassins that its loss wasn't so important. "I am going to die," said one fifteen-year-old *sicario* in an interview, "but my mother will remember me because I gave her a beautiful new refrigerator."

"The institutions of this country are crumbling so rapidly that we don't even know what is happening," Colombian sociologist Eduardo Velez said at the time. "They're killing judges, and no one does anything." Many judges went into hiding or left the country, including the one (Consuelo Sanchez-Duran) who charged Escobar and Gacha with ordering the December, 1986, killing of Guillermo Cano, the Bogota editor. Referring to the Medellin cartel, *El Tiempo*, Colombia's largest newspaper, noted: "The country's legal structure is not enough to counter such a powerful empire, which can buy off anyone."

In 1990, the Colombian government initiated a nationwide manhunt and offered a $1 million reward for information leading to Pablo Escobar's arrest. The Colombian government's war against the Medellin cartel was really a war against violence, not cocaine trafficking per se, as the reward flyer for Escobar's capture, which was distributed throughout Colombia and which made no reference to drug trafficking, illustrates. To the side of Escobar's picture were these words in Spanish: "Author of terrorist acts against citizens and the national police." At the bottom of the flyer were these words: "Help . . . don't be the next victim." Juan Carlos Pastrana, editor of the Bogota newspaper *La Prensa*, said at the time: "It is a war against Escobar and Rodriguez Gacha [the other violent Medellin cartel leader]. I haven't seen any war against the other drug traffickers." Escobar went into hiding, and for months on end, pursuing government forces were unable to find him.

In fact, from the mid-1980s through the early 1990s, the Colombian government actively sought to find and arrest Escobar, Ochoa, and Gacha, yet never succeeded in finding Ochoa (as indicated, he turned himself in), and it wasn't until the deaths of Gacha in 1989 and Escobar in 1993 (after a shootout with Colombian police) that they met with success. It was widely believed by American drug experts that the Colombian government's failure for several years to find the drug lords was attributable to pandemic corruption in military and law enforcement ranks, enabling the cartel leaders to know well in advance every move their pursuers made. Per a ranking U.S. drug expert in Bogota, the intentional dereliction of duty also extended as far as misdirecting and even failing to carry out assigned raids. As Agusto Nunez, managing editor of the Brazilian newspaper *O Estado de São Paulo*, put it at the time, the drug lords' ability to evade arrest "can only be explained by the fact that their circle of friends includes men in strategic positions of power." Former Colombian Interior Minister Fernando Vasquez Velasquez acknowledged in testimony before the Colombian senate in September, 1989, "that there is massive infiltration by narco-traffickers in the government, the armed forces, the police, and congress." As reported in the December 24, 1990, edition of the *New York Times*, "The cartel's infiltration of the police and army is believed to be so great that helicopter anti-drug units are often given precise destinations only after they are airborne."

This problem, of course, would not have been present if the pursuers had been American military forces.

Making the Colombian government's failure all the more inexplicable (that is, without the explanation of corruption in the military and among the police), is the fact that up until 1989 the Colombian government, as well as our DEA, which maintains offices in Colombia (Bogota and Baranquilla), even knew where the drug lords lived. Years before Escobar went into hiding due to the government's

nationwide dragnet and offer of reward money for information leading to his capture, Escobar normally walked freely around his principal abode, a 50,000-acre ranch, *Hacienda Napoles*, in the river town
of Puerto Triunfo, fifty miles east of Medellin. Ochoa used to divide
his time between *Hacienda Veracruz*—his vast cattle ranch between
Baranquilla and Cartagena on Colombia's picturesque northern
coast, which had a multi-thousand-acre wildlife preserve and a mile-
long paved landing strip that could accommodate a 747—and his
parents' estate, *Las Lomas*, on a hillside south of Medellin.

With a promise of leniency from the Colombian government, Escobar surrendered in June of 1991. Pending his trial on charges of terrorism, he was "incarcerated" in a special prison in the Medellin
suburb of Envigado, his hometown. His quarters were the equivalent
of a luxurious and spacious residence, with a soccer field, personal
gym, 60-inch TV, waterfall, and trout pond. Worse, it was widely
believed that he continued to run his drug-trafficking empire from
Envigado through a handful of associates who could enter and leave
the prison at will. When criticism in Colombia mounted over Escobar's continued drug activity and five-star hotel accommodations,
President Gaviria ordered that Escobar be moved to a military jail.
On July 22, 1992, the day of the move, Escobar and several of his
lieutenants, who were incarcerated with him, overpowered the
guards and escaped. The reward for information leading to his arrest
was immediately increased to $3.4 million, $2 million of which was
posted by the U.S. State Department. In early August, Colombia's
national police and army formed a 2,000-member task force to pursue Escobar full-time, and the search for him became so intense that
survival, not running his drug-trafficking empire, occupied all his
time. A vigilante group comprised of relatives of those murdered by
Escobar ("Pepes," for "People Persecuted by Pablo Escobar") also
joined in the manhunt. Escobar successfully eluded capture until December 2, 1993, when he was gunned down after a shootout with
Colombian police while running barefoot across the roof of his Medellin hideout. He had two nine-millimeter pistols in his hands.

"Colombia's worst nightmare has been slain," President Gaviria
triumphantly proclaimed. In life, Pablo Escobar was the man who
built cocaine trafficking into a global market and terrorized a nation
(Colombia) in the process. In death, he was mourned by some as a
folk hero. To chants of *"Viva Pablo!"* by thousands from the barrio
shantytowns of Medellin, he was laid to rest atop a hillside cemetery.

"In the future, people will go to his tomb to pray, the way they would to a saint," one of the mourners said.

When Escobar was slain, many believed that perhaps a light at the end of the tunnel could be seen in the war against drugs. But it was only the light of an oncoming train. As the *Chicago Tribune* editorialized, "If only killing Escobar were enough." With the demand for cocaine still extant, and billions of dollars to be made by the traffickers in meeting that demand, the flow of cocaine into America following Escobar's death never skipped a beat.

The cartel that replaced the Medellin cartel, which for the most part died with Escobar, was the Cali cartel, a fierce competitor with the Medellin cartel for the cocaine market since the late 1980s. In fact, before the government war against the Medellin cartel diverted its leaders, the two cartels were engaged in a blood feud over U.S. cocaine markets, and the Cali cartel seemed to be getting the worst of it. Forty-seven drugstores and six radio stations owned by Gilberto and Miguel Rodriguez—the Cali cartel's leaders—were dynamited and bombed, and in February, 1989, Gilberto Rodriguez's chief bodyguard was murdered in downtown Cali. But as early as April, 1991, two months before Escobar surrendered to authorities, Charles Gutensohn, the DEA's chief of cocaine investigations, told me that the Cali cartel, headquartered in Colombia's third largest city, was responsible for "most of the cocaine reaching America. The Rodriguez brothers are currently the biggest cocaine traffickers in the world." This was due to the Colombian government's crackdown on the violent Medellin cartel, as opposed to the Cali cartel. "The Medellin cartel can't function like they used to," said Gutensohn. "They used to operate openly in offices and warehouses. Now they're on the run. Pablo Escobar changes his location every night. There's no question their operations have been disrupted." However, because the Medellin cartel was still the most famous, and certainly most feared cartel in Colombia, it was at least a full year before the preeminent power of the Cali cartel became known to the general public.

Far less notorious than the Medellin cartel, the Cali cartel, like the former Medellin cartel, is not a cartel in the strict business sense of the word; rather it is an informal association of drug traffickers, the Rodriguez brothers being the most powerful. Even before the dismantling of the Medellin cartel, the Cali cartel was getting larger and pumping a considerable amount of cocaine poison into America, particularly New York City, Washington, D.C., and Southern California. Although small, scattered, and independent remnants of the

Medellin cartel still continued to operate, the Cali cartel largely swallowed up the Medellin cartel, offering limited franchises there to former Escobar lieutenants.

During the heyday of the Medellin cartel, the consensus was that it was responsible for 80 percent of the cocaine reaching America, with the Cali cartel supplying most of the remaining 20 percent. Two smaller Colombian drug cartels at the time were the Bogota cartel and the loosely knit North Atlantic Coast cartel, based mainly in the coastal cities of Cartagena, Baranquiela, Santa Maria, and Rio Hacha. With the demise of Escobar and the Medellin cartel in late 1993, most drug experts estimate that the Cali cartel soon exceeded the scope of their former rivals, and by 1994 and through most of 1995, it controlled 80–85 percent of the U.S. and foreign cocaine market. In 1994, the DEA said, "The Cali cartel is the most powerful international drug trafficking organization in history." Thomas Constantine, head of the DEA, added that "for their impact, profit, and control, they are bigger than the Mafia in the United States ever was." Due to the recent arrests by Colombian authorities of most of its leaders, the Cali cartel is weakened and in a state of flux, though at this writing it still controls the cocaine market.

For years, the Cali cartel has been dominated by the brothers Gilberto and Miguel Rodriguez Orejuela. Gilberto, a former banker known as the "chess player" because of his shrewdness, has been the strategic planner of the cartel, while his younger brother, Miguel, a lawyer, has run the organization's daily operations. Near the top with the Rodriguez brothers has been Jose Santacruz-Londono, who actually founded, with Gilberto, a small Cali-based criminal gang named *Los Chemas* in the early 1970s, from which the Cali cartel ultimately evolved.

In more recent years, other cartel leaders have emerged: Helmer "Pacho" Herrera-Buitrago; the violent Urdinola brothers, Jairo Ivan and Julio Fabio; Raul and Luis Grajales, first cousins who are related to the Urdinolas by marriage and are particularly active in Europe; Juan Carlos Ortiz; and Juan Carlos Ramirez.

The members of the Cali cartel are known as Colombia's "gentlemen" cocaine traffickers (the "gentle dons") because, unlike their former Medellin counterparts, they have a reputation for trying to avoid violence if at all possible, currying influence with bribes more than bullets. Up until the Colombian government's crackdown on the cartel starting in June of 1995, its leaders mixed easily with the wealthy elite of the city.

But this reputation for non-violence is only *
tive to the Medellin cartel, even Genghis Khan
but the myth of benign Cali drug lords cannot /
and more in the nineties the cartel has mov
their former bitter rivals. Colombian officials
1995, two members of law enforcement were
gunmen: a police officer in charge of intellig
near Cali, and in Bogota, the third highest-ranking o....
bia's equivalent of the FBI. Cali itself, a city of close to 2 million
people, has become like Medellin was when that city was the drug
capital. In 1990, Medellin had the highest homicide rate in the
world—4,637 for a city of 2.4 million. In 1984, Cali had 200 murders. In 1994, murders had jumped tenfold to nearly 2,000, mostly
drug-related. (Colombia itself has a per capita murder rate that is
eight times higher than the United States' and three times higher
than that of any other nation in the world.) "The majority of the
violence in the Cauca Valley [which surrounds Cali] is committed by
drug traffickers protecting their interests," says Carlos Alberto Mejia,
the regional attorney general for Valle del Cauca state.

As far back as 1991, *Los Angeles Times* reporter Stan Yarbro wrote
on assignment from Colombia that "the picturesque town of Mar-
sella, on the Cauca River, is an impromptu mortuary for victims of
Colombia's drug war." Yarbro reported that since January of 1988,
219 such victims had been washed ashore downstream on the Cauca
River from Cali. Some of the victims included perceived enemies,
informants, and peasants hired by the traffickers to work in the cocaine laboratories for short periods at relatively high pay and then
killed to protect the secrecy of the operation. In fact, in September of
1991, while the dreaded Medellin cartel, though somewhat debili-
tated by Escobar's incarceration, was still a powerful and violent
force, the Colombian attorney general's office reported that the
Cauca Valley had the highest rate of disappearances of any state in
Colombia.

Perhaps incongruously, the most powerful of the Cali traffickers,
the Rodriguez brothers, have been the least violent. They reportedly
liken themselves to America's Kennedy family, arguing that the latter made their fortune during Prohibition before becoming pillars of
American society. While the Rodriguez brothers continued their trafficking operations, they sought respectability by making charitable
contributions, purchasing a network of legitimate businesses (including hotels, office buildings, and car dealerships), and owning

ıca," a professional soccer team. Most of the eleven children
e two brothers have been educated at colleges and universities
Europe and the United States, including Boston College and Stanford.

But the new breed of Cali traffickers, perhaps best exemplified by
Ivan Urdinola, have become increasingly violent. Colombian
human-rights officials say Urdinola, who has almost completed serving a light sentence in a plea bargain, is often seen with up to twenty
bodyguards, and is believed to be responsible for many of the murders
in the Cauca Valley. The big distinction, by far, between Cali-cartel
vis-à-vis Medellin-cartel violence is that up to recently* the Cali traffickers sought out specific victims and eliminated only them—i.e.,
their violence was very focused, whereas the signature of Medellin
cartel violence, which ultimately led to its downfall, was terrorism
against Colombian society as a whole. To kill a victim they wanted,
buses, buildings, even airplanes, were blown up, resulting in the
death of hundreds of innocent Colombian people. Thus, the term
narco-terrorism.

At its peak in 1993, 1994, and much of 1995, the Cali cartel was
believed to have generated between $25 billion and $30 billion annually in worldwide sales of cocaine and heroin, with profits believed
to be $6 billion–$7 billion per year. The cartel is famous for its sophisticated drug-smuggling techniques, including the use of semi-
submersible boats, almost like submarines, to carry drug cargo, and
for having the best intelligence network in Colombia. "The C.I.A.
tells me that the sophistication of the Cali cartel is about at the level
of the KGB when the Soviet Union fell apart," Defense Minister Botero said in June of 1995. For example, as reported in *Time* magazine,
lieutenants of the cartel leaders "moved about Cali with laptop computers linked, via radio, to a mainframe that contains such information as records of every long distance call into and out of the city."

Cali leaders had woven themselves into the political, cultural, and
law enforcement fabric of Cali to such an extent that prior to a series
of arrests in the summer of 1995, every operation against them had
been compromised.

Reporting from Cali in June of 1995, *Los Angeles Times* reporter

---

*On June 10, 1995, a bomb exploded at an outdoor music festival in Medellin, killing
29 people and injuring 205. According to then–Colombian Defense Minister Fernando
Botero, intelligence reports indicated that the bombing had been carried out by the Colombian guerrilla force The Revolutionary Armed Forces of Colombia on behalf of the Cali
cartel.

Kenneth Freed wrote that "corruption, which used to be quiet here, has spread and become more obvious. . . . City and provincial officials are on narcotic payrolls, and hundreds of police officers and government security agents have been suspended or are under investigation for corruption." A local businessman confirmed to Freed what was already common knowledge, per U.S. drug officials: "The narco-traffickers have taken over. They control business, politics, everything. Cali is a sewer of corruption."

In August of 1994, newly elected President Ernesto Samper Pisano, in testimony before the Colombian senate, said: "We have to dismantle all of the corruption of police and judges" protecting the Cali cartel. But the corruption's tentacles may have extended all the way up to Samper himself. Samper's commitment to earnestly fighting the traffickers has been questioned by U.S. officials in light of a verified tape-recording that surfaced shortly after he was elected, in which Cali cartel traffickers are heard offering a $3.75 million donation to his 1994 campaign (the April, 1995, edition of *Semana*, Colombia's leading weekly, quotes a witness, described as credible by U.S. authorities, as asserting that the Cali cartel also contributed $1 million to Samper's earlier bid for the presidency in 1989).

Responding to the negative, front-page publicity over the revelation, Samper immediately acknowledged the $3.75 million offer from the cartel to his campaign but denied accepting the money from the narco-traffickers. He also had some compelling circumstantial evidence to prove he was not in bed with them. As he pointed out in a letter to Senator Jesse A. Helms (R–N.C.) on July 15, 1994: "The four bullets still lodged in my body are a constant reminder of the 1989 cartel attempt to assassinate me at Bogota International Airport."

But the question was, would Samper go after more than just the corrupt police and judges protecting the Cali cartel—would he go after the cartel leaders themselves?

After the dissolution of the Medellin cartel by the killing of Escobar, and with narco-terrorism thereby no longer a threat, the Colombian government had become demonstrably weaker in its anti-narcotic posture. Both U.S. and Colombian officials concede that the tracking of Escobar and his ultimate death at the hands of the Colombian police was carried out with significant help from the Cali cartel leaders, who were rewarded with a more lenient, *laissez-faire* attitude toward them by the Colombian government. Left for the most part unfettered in their drug activities, the Cali cartel not only effected a stranglehold on the international cocaine market, but got into heroin trafficking to such an extent that Colombia is now the number-two seller of heroin in the world, behind the Southeast Asian countries. The cartel's marijuana production also increased appreciably. Washington let its dissatisfaction with the Colombian government known by ratcheting up its pressure on Colombia to be much more aggressive in its law-enforcement efforts against the Cali cartel. In March of 1994, the United States also suspended evidence-sharing by the DEA with the Colombian government on narcotic investigations because on more than one occasion it was confirmed that the evidence was being turned over to the traffickers.

Finally, the United States informed Colombia that unless Colombia got more serious about its anti-narcotic efforts, it would not certify Colombia as a nation fully complying with the provisions of the 1988 United Nations Convention against Illicit Traffic and Narcotic Drugs and Psychotropic Substances. Decertification would have precluded Colombia from receiving any economic assistance from the United States, and also would require that we veto loans to Colombia from the World Bank and other international lending institutions. * Under this threat, and because of the incriminating tape that caused the United States to question his counter-narcotic bonafides, Samper sought to allay U.S. concerns over Colombia's commitment to combat the narco-traffickers by launching a joint police and military effort against the Cali cartel. Beginning in late 1994, 6,000 men, including an elite military and police "search brigade," conducted searches and raids on Cali cartel strongholds. The Rodriguez brothers, who heretofore moved freely in the social life of Cali, went into hiding. A $1.25 million reward for the capture of each of them ($825,000 for that of five underlings) was also offered. The manhunt, though once again, as with Escobar, inhibited by corruption, enabling the Rodriguez brothers and their associates to stay one step ahead of their pursuers, finally paid off on June 9, 1995, when Gilberto Rodri-

---

* On February 28, 1995, President Clinton, in a memorandum to the secretary of state, declined to decertify Colombia. The president waived economic penalties and invoked a clause in the Foreign Assistance Act that, despite noncompliance with the United Nations act, allows for certification when it is in the "vital national interest" of the United States to do so. The State Department, in its 1995 International Narcotics Control Strategy report, said it would be counterproductive to decertify Colombia. "Colombia is the primary source of cocaine to the United States, [and] continued cooperation with the government of Colombia is very important to this country. . . . The net result of decertification would be an increase in the flow of narcotics from Colombia to the United States."

guez was arrested by Colombian police in his luxury apartment in the posh Santa Monica neighborhood of suburban Cali. Rodriguez was found cowering in a hidden compartment built into a bedroom. After his arrest, Rodriguez, age fifty-six, told authorities: "I'm not a criminal like Pablo Escobar. I don't murder or plant bombs." He added, however, that he could not be the leader of the Cali cartel, since no such organization existed.*

"This is the beginning of the end for the Cali cartel," President Samper exulted from Bogota. Keeping the pressure on, on July 4, 1995, the cartel's number three man, Jose Santacruz-Londono, was arrested in a Bogota restaurant as he drank lemonade with three associates. (However, on January 11, 1996, Santacruz escaped from Bogota's La Picota prison, and at the time this book went to press, he has thus far eluded a nationwide manhunt.) A week and a half later, Henry "the Scorpion" Loaiza, believed to be the cartel's chief assassin, surrendered to the authorities. Other lesser traffickers also surrendered. With the Urdinola brothers already behind bars (Jairo Ivan was arrested in April of 1992 and Julio Fabio surrendered in March of 1994), much of the cartel's leadership was presently in custody. But U.S. officials, though heartened by the arrests of several of the cartel leaders, were guarded in their optimism. Gilberto Rodriguez was behind bars, but his brother, Miguel (as well as Helmer "Pacho" Herrera-Buitrago), was still at large, and DEA officials pointed out that it was Miguel (not Gilberto, "the chairman of the board") who had actually been running the day-to-day activities of the cartel. "Miguel is the hands-on operator," said DEA head Thomas A. Constantine. "He deals in the most intimate details of the cartel whether the operations are in Queens [New York], Spain, or anywhere else in the world." But on August 6, 1995, Miguel Rodriguez and four of his associates were captured in an early-morning raid by 500 Colombian police on Rodriguez's tenth-floor apartment in an exclusive residential area of Cali. Rodriguez, in his underwear, was trying to hide in a secret compartment in his master bedroom. He did not resist arrest and, in fact, congratulated the officers, saying the intelligence service that led them to him was excellent. Colombia's foreign minister, Rodrigo Pardo, immediately declared, "The Cali Cartel is dead." With most of the main leaders of the cartel now behind bars (only

* Speaking for nonattribution, more than one U.S. intelligence official has said that the CIA, which by all accounts has been expanding its anti-narcotic activities in foreign countries, provided intelligence support and loaned technicians to Colombian authorities leading up to Rodriguez's arrest.

Helmer "Pacho" Herrera-Buitrago was still at large at the time), similar declarations were voiced by drug officials in Colombia and the United States. The obituaries were premature.

Even before the arrest of Miguel Rodriguez, Joseph B. Treaster, in the June 12, 1995, edition of the *New York Times*, quoted U.S. officials and experts as saying that even if and when Miguel Rodriguez was apprehended, "there are half a dozen other senior executives of the $25-billion-a-year enterprise and perhaps 500 mid-to-upper-level managers ready to keep the world's drug users supplied."

The reason, of course, is not only the vast wealth that awaits a whole new generation of traffickers but also, due to Colombia's notoriously lenient punishment for drug trafficking under Colombia's Judicial Code, the lack of any real deterrent to engage in this activity. Under a 1993 law, approved after intense pressure from Cali cartel-corrupted legislators, twelve years is the maximum sentence for the crime of drug trafficking. And under Colombia's plea-bargaining and sentence-reduction system as set forth in its Code of Criminal Procedure, traffickers who surrender, confess to just one crime, and furnish information (consistently useless, observers say), are entitled to have their sentences significantly reduced even further—by up to two-thirds, at the discretion of the prosecutor or judge. This is so regardless of how high up in the drug-trafficking enterprise their position is. Moreover, even where the drug trafficker is captured—and hence, there is no surrender—by confessing to the one crime, all other pending charges against the trafficker have to be permanently dismissed. A January, 1995, report by Colombia's justice minister revealed that in 38 percent of the cases, those convicted of a drug crime never served even one day in prison. Colombia's Chief Prosecutor, Alfonso Valdivieso Sarmiento, characterized the situation this way: "The plea-bargaining system results in virtual impunity" for the traffickers. The system is so lenient that the average sentence for defendants with long histories of major drug trafficking has been just three years. Jorge Ochoa, one of the three leaders of the Medellin cartel, only received a sentence of eight years in 1991, and is expected to serve just six. Contrast that with the United States, where a conviction for a onetime sale of only fifty grams of crack by a street pusher in the ghetto results in a mandatory minimum sentence of ten years.

Currently, the Cali cartel leaders in custody are negotiating with the Colombian government over their sentences, and the DEA estimates that these negotiations could stretch out for over a year. No one, including the Rodriguez brothers, is expected to be sentenced in excess of twelve years. In fact, the *New York Times* reported in its June 27, 1995, edition that under Colombia's existing plea-bargaining and sentence-reduction system, even the main cartel leader, Gilberto Rodriguez, "could spend as little as eight years in jail." "The ace up their sleeve," a mid-level cartel employee told *New York Times* reporter James Brooks, "is what they have on the politicians." Bernardo Hoyas, a Catholic priest who is the former mayor of Baranquilla, says that in mid-June of 1995, Miguel Rodriguez showed him copies of canceled checks reflecting cartel payments in excess of $17 million to presidential and congressional campaigns in 1994. American columnist Steven Gutkin adds: "Many politicians can only pray the traffickers stay quiet. With an intelligence network far superior to the government's, they have amassed tons of dirt on Colombia's politicians." In an earlier, unsuccessful July, 1995, raid to capture Miguel Rodriguez, police reportedly found a suitcase containing documents reflecting $25 million in payoffs to nearly 2,000 politicians, police officers, journalists, and officers of the Colombian military.

On July 26, 1995, Chief Prosecutor Valdivieso's office arrested the treasurer of Ernesto Samper's 1994 presidential campaign, Santiago Medina, on charges that he accepted a $50,000 check from a Cali cartel front company. Small potatoes, Medina said, telling investigators that during the same campaign, Defense Minister Botero, Samper's then–campaign manager, instructed Medina to solicit over $6 million from the Cali cartel, which he claims they gave him after demanding and receiving a receipt signed, he says, by Botero. Miguel Rodriguez, Medina told authorities, quipped: "This [the receipt] is the smallest but most expensive Botero I own," an obvious allusion to Botero's father, Colombia's most famous painter (Guillerme Pallomari, the cartel's top accountant who fled Colombia in September, 1995, and turned himself in to U.S. authorities, has confirmed the $6 million contribution to Samper's campaign). Botero resigned as defense minister on August 2, 1995, and was arrested on August 15.

Before he approached the cartel pursuant to Botero's instructions, Medina said he told Samper of Botero's instructions and alleges Samper replied: "Do what has to be done, but don't let me know about it." Samper once again vehemently denied having any knowledge of the Cali cartel's contributions to his campaign, and Miguel Rodriguez, upon his arrest, denied contributing to Samper's campaign. Labeling Medina a liar, Rodriguez declared: "The president is an honest man."

Valdivieso is presently looking into charges that the cartel made payoffs to Colombia's attorney general, comptroller general, president of the lower house of Congress, and eleven other members of Congress. Valdivieso, the cousin of Luis Carlos Galan, the anti-cartel presidential candidate slain by the Medellin cartel on August 18, 1989, says his mission is to carry out Galan's dream of ridding Colombia of narco-trafficking. Appointed by the Colombian Supreme Court in 1994 to complete the term of the retiring prosecutor general, Gustavo de Greiff, the diminutive Valdivieso immediately launched a campaign to root out the corruption by the traffickers of Colombia's governmental and judicial system. Polls show him to be Colombia's most popular public figure, someone of impeccable rectitude who is held in equally high esteem by Washington. Valdivieso's mandate is limited to going after drug traffickers, so he cannot prosecute President Samper. Accordingly, he has been forwarding any evidence on Samper revealed in his other investigations to the Committee of Accusations of the Colombian Congress, which was considering investigating Samper for possible impeachment.

In September, 1995, amidst references to Watergate and the downfall of the Nixon presidency by the Colombian media, Samper gave formal testimony before the committee denying the Medina allegations. Earlier, on August 16, 1995, Samper imposed a ninety-day state of emergency (which allowed him to issue decrees without legislative approval) to combat organized crime and violence in Colombia. Interior Minister Horacio Serpa concurrently announced that as of August 16, 19,662 people had been slain in the country, many by leftist rebel and guerrilla groups who have been fighting the government for over thirty years. Samper's action was widely perceived as an attempt to divert the public's attention from the burgeoning drug-corruption scandal. On October 18, 1995, the country's Constitutional Court struck down Samper's state of emergency, holding that the conditions did not exist for the government to adopt such an extreme measure. On December 14, 1995, the threat of impeachment for Samper was eased when a Colombian congressional committee voted, 14 to 1, against opening a formal investigation into charges that Samper personally approved the acceptance of campaign contributions from the Cali cartel. "If definitive proof arises, there will be a formal investigation," a member of the committee said.*

---

* In a January 21, 1996, television interview (just a few days before this book went to press), former Defense Minister Botero, who is awaiting trial on charges of illicit enrichment over the Cali cartel campaign contributions, said that Samper had knowledge of the contributions. Samper immediately denied the accusation and accused Botero, his long-

Joe Taft, who recently retired as the chief of the DEA's Bogota office, estimated that "50 percent to 75 percent of the Colombian Congress" has at one time or another been influenced by cartel money. Most other observers don't put the figure quite that high.

Since the arrests of most of the Cali cartel's leaders, U.S. authorities have noticed no significant diminution in the flow of cocaine from Colombia into this country, and only an incurable Pollyanna would have expected otherwise. The recent arrests have had a demonstrable effect on the price of cocaine "only in certain locales in the United States, mainly in the New York City and Detroit areas," per Jim McGivney, chief spokesperson for the DEA. In New York City, for instance, the wholesale price of cocaine has increased nearly 50 percent and the retail, street price 30 percent. The crackdown on the Medellin cartel by the Colombian government produced a similar increase in cocaine prices for around four months in late 1989 and early 1990. McGivney said that at this point, no one knows for sure whether this is price-gouging by the traffickers (lying to their buyers that supplies have been diminished because of the recent crackdown of the cartel leaders), or there actually is a short-term supply problem brought about by the arrests. Most feel it's the former, noting that the Cali cartel has always been known to have large stockpiles of cocaine warehoused in Mexico, and they doubt this supply would be depleted this soon.

Moreover, nothing has illustrated the continuing ability of the Cali cartel to organize and transport large shipments of cocaine more than the landing of a Caravelle jet near the Baja California village of Todos Santos near Ensenada on November 5, 1995. Witnesses saw twenty men wearing the black windbreakers of the Mexican federal police unload what was believed to be a $100 million cargo of cocaine, which has since disappeared. The federal police were observed to have then tried to destroy the identity of the plane and bury it in the sand. But Mexican and U.S. officials retrieved serial numbers from the jet's turbines and traced its ownership back to the Cali cartel. The federal police commander in Baja and all twenty-nine of his officers were transferred within days after the plane landed to Mexico City headquarters, but no arrests have yet been announced.

U.S. Ambassador to Colombia Myles R. R. Frechette says: "Even

---

time friend and adviser, of being a liar. Amid growing pressure to resign, on January 24, 1996, a day before the final draft of this book was submitted for publication, Samper met with his cabinet to consider a referendum asking Colombians whether he should resign.

if you get all these guys" at the top of the Cali cartel [only Jose Santa-cruz-Londono and Helmer "Pacho" Herrera-Buitrago are not presently in custody], "there are ambitious lieutenants just waiting to fill their spots." Clifford Krause, in the August 13, 1995, edition of the *New York Times*, wrote: "Most experts agree that putting the Rodriguez brothers and their cronies behind bars will most likely have no lasting impact on the supply, price, and purity of the cocaine and heroin that tens of thousands of Americans, whether in inner city parks or suburban patios, still smoke, snort, and shoot into their arms."

McGivney said the DEA has confirmed that a "second-tier of traffickers in Colombia have already stepped up to fill the power vacuum created by the recent arrests." For the most part, they are ambitious lieutenants of the Cali cartel leaders, the latter still retaining, McGivney said, a "semblance of control over them, but nothing like before." Gilberto Rodriguez, perhaps disingenuously, says: "Nobody controls these kids. They have more power and money than they can handle." Greg Passic, a senior special agent of the Financial Crimes Enforcement Network (FinCEN), who is in regular contact with U.S. drug agents in Colombia, says that about twenty "baby cartels" have started to emerge from among the pack seeking to become the next Cali cartel, and "we already know the identity of about one-half of their leaders." DEA Administrator Thomas Constantine, in testimony before the U.S. Senate in mid-August, 1995, said that "these newly emerging groups could rise to an equal or superior footing with the Cali mafia."

The Rodriguez brothers and Jose Santacruz-Londono are each believed to be multibillionaires. When there's an opportunity to become unimaginably wealthy, and the only risk, if at all, is a few years of incarceration, Colombian drug traffickers eager to export cocaine to America will remain as common as pebbles on a beach.

Even if, as virtually no one predicts, Colombia ceases to be the major source of refined cocaine for the world's markets, other nations will soon take over. Even before the recent crackdown on the Cali cartel, not all of the Peruvian and Bolivian coca base and paste were shipped to Colombia for refinement into powdered cocaine. Bolivia, in particular, has been responsible in recent years for over 5 percent of the world's refined cocaine. And Peru's Demetrio Chavez-Pena Herrera, known as "El Vaticano," has been trafficking not only in coca base and paste, but in shipments of kilos of refined cocaine to the United States.

The nation U.S. drug agents fear the most, however, is Mexico. With the crumbling of the Cali cartel, the DEA fears that Mexican traffickers, who for years have been mules for the Colombian cartels, may seek to get in at the front end of the cocaine trade. By employing the Andean coca growers themselves and running their own laboratories in Peru and Bolivia, they can bypass Colombia and control production as well as delivery. Constantine says the Mexican drug organizations certainly have the potential to do this. "These guys could turn Mexico into the next Colombia," he says. James Jones, U.S. ambassador to Mexico, concurs. "If we don't stop [the Mexican traffickers] soon," he says, "I'm afraid Mexico will eventually become the hemisphere's next drug headquarters."

We don't know yet who will actually end up replacing, if at all, the Cali cartel specifically or Colombian cartels in general. What we do know is that if the Colombian cartels cease to be the main traffickers in cocaine, it will be just a matter of time before we read that somewhere, some other person or group has gained control over "X" percent of the cocaine market. That you can bet on.

Mexico

Since the release of my book *Drugs in America* in 1991, some feel that Mexico has become, in the words of Eduardo Valles Espinoza, the former special adviser to the attorney general of Mexico, a "narco-democracy." Dan Burton, the Republican congressman from Indiana who is chairman of the House Foreign Affairs Western Hemisphere Subcommittee, only disagrees slightly. Mexico is "almost, although not quite, a narco-democracy," he says. Mexican President Ernesto Zedillo, who is trying to move Mexico, after sixty-six years of one-party rule by a corrupt and entrenched oligarchy, into a democracy based on the rule of law, said in his State of the Union message on September 1, 1995, that drug trafficking "has become the most serious threat to national security, our societies' health, and civic peace."

One may ask why the military approach herein recommended against Colombia is not therefore likewise being recommended, at least at this time, against Mexico. The reason is that while Mexico is, indeed, a major source country for 60–80 percent of the foreign-grown marijuana available in the United States, and 20 percent of the heroin, as stated earlier these two drugs don't even come close to being responsible for this nation's present drug crisis. As to the drug that does, cocaine, virtually no coca plants are produced in Mexico. Although Mexico has become the main transshipment point for Colombian cocaine imported into the United States, Mexican drug lords are for the most part only the "delivery agent," or middlemen, for the Colombian cartels, responsible for the transportation of the cocaine across the Mexico-U.S. border. Picking the cocaine up from Colombian pilots landing in Mexico or from containerized cargo from ships in Mexico's seaports, they deliver the cocaine to distributors in the United States. Unlike their employers in Colombia, the Mexican narco-traffickers are in no way involved in the growth of the coca leaf in the main source countries of Peru and Bolivia, nor for its conversion into illicit cocaine. Therefore, a military search-and-find mission against the drug lords of Mexico would not be attacking the "source" of the cocaine problem.

The Mexican traffickers themselves—who, more and more, are being paid by the Colombian cartels not in cash, but in part of the cocaine load, and who for years smuggled marijuana and heroin across the border and distributed the drugs here in the United States—are now also in many instances the distributors of cocaine, particularly in the western states. But even in this latter situation, they obviously are not the "source" of the problem.

Mexico is a nation which, by President Zedillo's candid admission, has "never had a culture of the rule of law. It is a problem very deep in our cultural and historical roots." Luis Astorga, a prominent Mexican sociologist, says: "You're talking about institutions that have been corrupted from the beginning. The normal thing is to be corrupted." The corruption doesn't just exist among higher and mid-level public officials. "All Mexicans," writes *Miami Herald* reporter Peter Slevin from Mexico City, "know about *la mordida*, the bite that street cops, meter-readers, and petty clerks of every description claim as their sacred right." And as the country has become a leading player in the drug world, as surely as night follows day, official corruption and violence, as in Colombia, have become even worse.

According to Phillip Jordan, director of the El Paso Intelligence Center (EPIC), the eyes and ears of the DEA, for years Guadalajara has been and continues to be the central base of operation for most of Mexico's narco-traffickers. They live there, feel comfortable there, have meetings there, and are involved in drug activity there, although their primary drug-trafficking activities are in other areas of Mexico. Guadalajara was the base of operations of Miguel Angel Felix Gallardo, the one-time "godfather of Mexican cocaine" and principal supplier of cocaine to the United States for the Medellin cartel in the 1980s. Gallardo was arrested in 1989 and is presently serving a forty-year sentence in Mexico for several drug-related crimes, including his participation in the 1985 killing of DEA Special Agent Enrique Camarena.

The latest EPIC intelligence indicates that there are presently four major drug "organizations" in Mexico (the DEA refers to "corridors" of influence, or "organizations," in Mexico, not "cartels," as the DEA does with the Colombian narco-traffickers). Most of these organizations have loose ties with each other, and work together from time to time. Moreover, several of the organizations are actively involved in drug-trafficking activities within corridors in Mexico other than the one in which they have major influence.

The *Gulf of Mexico* organization has for several years been the principal conduit into this country of Colombian cocaine. Based in the southeastern border city of Matamoros, which is across the border from Brownsville, Texas, its leader, Juan Garcia Abrego (now in custody), is known as the "Mexican Escobar." Garcia Abrego, who has been indicted on drug-trafficking charges in the United States, was the first international drug lord to be placed on the FBI's "Ten Most Wanted Fugitives" list. The U.S. government also posted a $2 million reward for his capture. Garcia Abrego's drug empire is believed to be worth $10 billion–$15 billion. U.S. and Mexican authorities estimate it is responsible for the murder of at least thirty-five people and protection payments of millions of dollars to Mexican police commanders and regional prosecutors.

On the evening of January 14, 1996, fifteen Mexican federal drug agents arrested Garcia Abrego at a private ranch of his in the village of Villa de Juarez, near Monterrey, Mexico. He was deported the very next day to Houston, Texas, where he faces a September 24, 1993, federal indictment charging him with heading a criminal enterprise responsible for transporting and distributing millions of dollars of cocaine and marijuana into the United States.

The violent *Ciudad Juarez*, or *Chihuahua* organization, controlling the middle area of the Southwest border, is headed by Amado Carillo Fuentes, who, per a May 29, 1995, report in *Time* magazine, has "littered the streets of Juarez with the bodies of informants each time one of his drug shipments is seized by U.S. agents." Two years ago, Carillo himself survived an assassination attempt on his life at the hands of hit men for Garcia Abrego. Three of Carillo's bodyguards were killed in the spray of machine-gun fire at a chic seafood restaurant. Because of the intense pressure on, and ultimate arrest of Garcia Abrego, the strength and activity of his organization is in decline, and the thirty-nine-year-old Carrillo is believed to be Mexico's most powerful drug trafficker at the moment, making inroads into the territory of at least three other organizations.

Carillo is highly meticulous and elusive and has managed to avoid having any current criminal charges brought against him in Mexico. He is under two federal indictments in the States, however, for drug smuggling: one in Miami (1988) and one in Dallas (1993). Carillo took over his organization when Rafael Aguilar Guajardo was killed in 1994 in the southern resort city of Cancun by several hit men hired by other still-unidentified traffickers. A young American girl was killed in the spray of bullets. It was Guajardo who was responsible for smuggling into the United States in 1989 the 21.4 tons of cocaine seized from the Sylmar, California, warehouse. Today, Carillo is a hero to the residents of Guamuchilito, Mexico, the dusty village where he grew up, building a church for the people, giving tractors to the farmers, and through his mother, who still lives there, money to the poor.

The *Tijuana* or *Pacific* (coast) organization is headed by the Arellano Felix brothers—Benjamin, Javier, and Ramón—nephews of imprisoned kingpin Miguel Angel Felix Gallardo. Juaquin (Chapo) Guzman was also very competitive in this corridor prior to his arrest in June of 1993, as was another recently arrested trafficker, Hector Luis Palma-Salazar.

The *Sinaloa* organization, Mexico's fourth largest, is headed by Juan Esparragosa-Moreno. Guzman and Palma-Salazar were also the leading traffickers in this corridor before their respective arrests.

Like their former Medellin cartel counterparts, the Mexican drug lords live in regal splendor with many bodyguards and vast entourages, and either bribe or kill whoever stands in their way. No one disputes that many of the country's federal police commissioners and assistant attorneys general, as well as local officials, are on the payroll of the drug lords. The most shocking example is that of Mario Ruiz Massieu, the self-styled crusader against government corruption, who was the number-two man in the Mexican attorney general's office and the nation's top anti-narcotics official.

Massieu was appointed by President Zedillo to head the drug effort, but later also led the investigation into the September 28, 1994, assassination of his brother, Jose Francisco Ruiz Massieu, the secretary-general of Mexico's ruling Institutional Revolutionary Party.

Massieu resigned his office in November, 1994, claiming the Mexican government "continues to condone corrupt and criminal activity." In early March, 1995, after being questioned by Mexican authorities about his alleged cover-up of information that Jose Francisco's murder was ordered by Raul Salinas de Gotari,* the brother of Mexico's former president, Massieu fled Mexico, but was arrested by U.S. Customs agents at the Newark airport en route to Spain. Shortly thereafter, U.S. officials discovered $9.3 million in Texas bank accounts bearing his name.**

Mexican officials allege that during Massieu's brief nine-month tenure as Mexico's top narcotics fighter, he ran a "franchising operation" for narco-traffickers in key states across the nation, appointing federal attorneys handpicked by the traffickers to head narcotics enforcement in the subject states. The top federal enforcement job in the northern border state of Tamaulipas was reportedly sold by Massieu for $1 million. Testimony was taken in Mexico that Massieu regularly received suitcases of money from corrupt federal police and prosecutors while serving as the chief narcotics official of the Mexican government. In extradition hearings in a Newark federal courtroom over a period of months, the Mexican government vigorously sought the return of Massieu to face charges of embezzlement and of obstructing justice in the cover-up of his brother's murder. But on June 22, 1995, the federal judge rejected the Mexican government's request that Massieu be returned to Mexico, concluding that the evidence Mexico had gathered against Massieu had been obtained by torture and was there-

---

*Raul Salinas de Gotari is presently in custody in Mexico on charges he masterminded the murder of Ruiz Massieu. In late November, 1995, Mexican and Swiss prosecutors confirmed that de Gotari's wife and brother had been arrested by Swiss authorities while trying to withdraw a staggering $84 million in cash from a Swiss bank. (U.S. and Mexican investigators told Los Angeles Times reporter Mark Fineman that Raul Salinas's accounts in Switzerland and elsewhere in Europe, as well as in the United States, "may well exceed $250 million.") Mexico's national comptroller has reported that Salinas—on a government salary that peaked at $70,000 a year from his government position as a top planner at an agency that distributes corn and other subsidized foods—owned twelve homes, at least one ranch, fifteen apartments, and seventeen plots of land, with forty-five different bank accounts in Mexico alone. Mexican and American officials have said there is a "certain presumption" but no evidence thus far that Salinas's fortune represented drug money.

Although there has been a flood of speculation in Mexico that Raul Salinas's brother, former President Carlos Salinas de Gotari, is somehow connected to whatever corruption is undoubtedly involved here, a spokesperson for the DEA in Washington said emphatically that his office has no evidence of any kind that the former president was involved in drug activity.

**Massieu's former chief deputy, Jorge Stergios, who deposited the drug payoff money for Massieu in the Texas bank accounts, is presently a fugitive.

fore unreliable. On December 22, 1995, the judge again rejected the extradition request, this time ruling that the American prosecutors handling the case for Mexico had failed to show that the charges against Massieu were true.

Among the more prominent recent murders attributable to the Mexican narco-traffickers are the murder of Tijuana Police Chief Jose Federico Benitez, on April 28, 1994 (just ten days after, his secretary said, he was offered and turned down $100,000 to call off his aggressive anti-drug operations), and the May 10, 1995, murder in Guadalajara of Leobardo Larios Guzman, the former Jalisco state attorncy general, who led the investigation into the May 24, 1993, murder of Juan Jesus Posadas Ocampo, Guadalajara's Roman Catholic cardinal. The Arellano Felix brothers, who head the Tijuana organization, are believed to be behind the murder of Guzman. On August 30, 1995, the Mexican government announced that a two-year investigation into the cardinal's murder led them to the tentative conclusion that the cardinal was killed when the assassins—believed to have been sent by the Arellano Felix brothers—mistook him for Joaquin Guzman, the Sinaloa trafficker with whom the Arellano Felix brothers had been fighting for years.

U.S. officials believe that President Zedillo (as did his predecessor, de Gotari) would genuinely like to stem the growing tide of narcotics activity in his country. He has appointed a new and respected attorney general, Antonio Lozano, to clean up the Mexican justice system, and has continued his country's cooperative drug-interdiction effort with the United States in the Northern Border Response Force (referred to earlier). And over a ten-day period in late November and early December of 1995, Mexico and all seven Central American countries carried out what has been described as "the biggest multinational counter-narcotics blitz" in history. In Mexico alone, where most of the arrests and seizures were made, the Mexican army, navy, and police forces seized more than five tons of cocaine, nearly forty tons of marijuana, two aircraft, six ships, and more than 650 suspected drug traffickers.

Lozano, however, has acknowledged that corruption is so deep and entrenched that it may take as long as twelve years to rid just his own organization (federal police and prosecutors) of it. He is currently in the process of establishing an elite counter-narcotics squad to break the nexus between the drug syndicates and the regional *federales* (federal judicial police officers). A blatant example of how open is that umbilical cord was the June, 1995, arrest of Hector Luis (El

Guero) Palma-Salazar, one of the leaders of the Sinaloa drug organization. Palma was protected by thirty-three armed *federales,* including the deputy regional commander, and was only taken into custody on a federal warrant when 200 army troops broke through that protection.

Another such blatant example occurred in November of 1991 at a remote airstrip in the eastern state of Veracruz, only this time the bad guys were the army. Mexican soldiers protecting a cocaine shipment killed seven federal police officers who chased the planeload of drugs to the airstrip. A videotape of the murders was taken by U.S. Customs pilots who had followed the officers to the scene. The tape shows that some of the police officers were shot dead at point-blank range.

Then there was the almost laughable incident on August 4, 1994, in the central state of Zacatecas. A cargo plane laden with ten tons of Colombian cocaine landed near the desert town of Sombrerete. The load was seized by federal transportation police, but as they were driving it to the Zacatecas state capitol, about sixty *federales,* a separate force, hijacked eight tons of the shipment from them. The eight tons turned up shortly thereafter in Southern California.

Like the situation in Colombia, Peru, and Bolivia, as well as in the United States, the drug forces in Mexico have proven to be powerful and resilient. Large seizures, even arrests, are simply part of the cost of doing business. Despite small setbacks here and there, the Mexican drug lords are successfully smuggling more cocaine into this country than ever before, and as well intentioned as Zedillo and his current administration might be, they seem powerless to do anything about it. Corruption is so systemic and blatant that cargo jets laden with cocaine from Columbia continue to land routinely at small airports throughout central and southern Mexico under the protective eyes of cooperating local police officials.

Fighting the Mexican narco-traffickers could be expected to be ineffective under any circumstances in Mexico. But recent events have exacerbated the problem. The armed insurrection by peasants in Chiapas in 1994, coupled with the assassination of two-high ranking members of the ruling party—presidential candidate Luis Donaldo Colosio in March, 1994, and the party's number-two official, Jose Francisco Ruiz Massieu in September, 1994—have stunned the nation to its core and necessarily diverted some government attention and resources away from anti-drug programs. Per the U.S. Department of State's 1995 International Narcotics Control Strategy Report, the seizure of cocaine by Mexican authorities dropped dramatically from 46.2 metric tons in 1993 to 22 metric tons in 1994. The 1995 statistics were not yet published at the time of this writing.

And there is a more pernicious influence on the affairs of state in Mexico, which at least explains to some why, notwithstanding Zedillo's public stance and ostensible efforts, the drug situation in Mexico continues to deteriorate. Mexico's current economic crisis, brought about by the devaluation of the peso, would be substantially worsened by the elimination of the billions of narco-dollars that infuse the country and help to sustain its economy at tolerable levels. U.S. prosectors estimate the annual earnings of the Gulf of Mexico organization, Mexico's largest, at between $10 billion and $15 billion. As columnist Andrew A. Reding observes: "Even taking the lower end of the range, than halving it, would leave the income of the Gulf cartel alone in rough parity with the value of Mexico's single most important legal export to the United States—oil."

Suffice it to say that our neighbor to the south will continue indefinitely to be a hospitable temporary repository and transshipment point for Colombian cocaine destructively entering this nation's bloodstream. But currently, no search-and-find mission to Mexico is herein recommended.

INTERNATIONAL LAW CONSIDERATIONS

One seeming problem with a search-and-find mission to Colombia is really (though it sounds serious) illusory: that of international law. It's a basic principle of international law that absent a treaty between the two subject nations providing for extradition of those charged with felonious crime, a sovereign state (in this case, Colombia) has the right to grant asylum to any person (normally, a citizen of the sovereign state) seeking refuge, and no other country has the right to forcibly abduct said person for criminal prosecution purposes. International *law*, however, is a misnomer, since—apart from treaties or agreements between specific nations—we are not referring to actual laws, but rather to international *custom* and general *principles* of law recognized by civilized nations. Despite the existence of an International Court of Justice—the judicial organ of the United Nations at The Hague in the Netherlands to which disputes between nations are sometimes submitted—the United Nations Charter (which, in Art. 2, par. 4, obligates "all members" to "refrain . . . from the threat

or use of force against the territorial integrity or political indepen-
dence of any state") does not give the court any coercive sanctions to
carry out its judgments.* Because of this, many scholars feel that
international law has more the character of morality than law; particularly when it comes to extradition, where some writers on the law
of nations assert that countries, irrespective of treaty, have a moral
duty to extradite criminals because the interests of society demand
that serious crimes be punished. They assert that an extradition
treaty adds nothing new to the substance and character of the moral
obligation, giving it only a contractual measure of certainty.**

Even in the theoretical likelihood that our action would be deemed
to be "unlawful under international law" (as was the case when
members of the Israeli Intelligence Service [Mossad] entered Argentina and located and arrested Nazi war criminal Adolf Eichmann in
a Buenos Aires suburb on the evening of May 11, 1960; Eichmann
was returned to Israel, tried, and subsequently executed), the U.S.
Supreme Court has explicitly held (as recently as 1992, in *United
States v. Alvarez-Machain*) that the forcible abduction of an individual in violation of international law is no bar to an American court's
exercising jurisdiction over the case once the individual is brought
before the court.***

We *had* a valid extradition treaty with Colombia (1979); but in
November, 1985, something happened in Bogota, Colombia's
capital, that wouldn't even happen on the Hollywood set of a Mob
film. Certainly neither Al Capone nor Lucky Luciano, in the Mob's

---

*In the unlikely event that Colombia, claiming its sovereignty had been violated by
a search-and-find mission, submitted the matter to the International Court of Justice,
theoretically the U.N. Security Council could deem the proposed military raid an "act of
aggression" against Colombia, and under Articles 41 and 42 of the charter, call upon the
members of the United Nations to apply such measures against the United States as sever-
ance of diplomatic relations, a blockade, and a "complete or partial interruption of economic relations and of rail, sea, air, postal, telegraphic, radio and other means of
communication. . . ." Anyone who would believe that any of these things would happen
or even be considered would believe someone who said he had seen an alligator doing the
polka.

**In *United States v. Alvarez-Machain*, 112 S Ct 2188 (1992), the U.S. Supreme Court
dealt dismissively with Mexico's assertion that in addition to the abduction of Dr. Alvarez-
Machain (by kidnappers in Mexico acting at the behest of our DEA) violating the U.S.-
Mexico extradition treaty, it was also prohibited by international law. The Court referred
to the rule that one government "may not exercise its police power in the territory of
another state" as only a "principle," and went on further to say that there are "many
actions . . . including waging war" which can properly be taken by a nation that violates
this principle.

***The first case enunciating this doctrine was *Ker v. Illinois*, 119 U.S. 436 (1886). See
also *Frisbie v. Collins*, 342 U.S. 519, 522 (1951), and *United States v. Insull*, 8 F.Supp.
311 (1934).

heyday, would have even fantasized in these terms. Aware of the increasing U.S. pressure on Colombia to extradite the drug kingpins, the drug forces mounted a constitutional challenge and a campaign of fear against the legislation implementing the extradition treaty. The twenty-four justices of the Colombian Supreme Court, the majority of whom were believed to be in favor of upholding the treaty, were scheduled to vote in the near future. Among the many threatening acts the drug forces employed was sending miniature coffins to the justices. On November 6, 1985, they went beyond threats. A busload of thirty-nine heavily armed leftist guerrillas (called M-19) entered the Palace of Justice and cold-bloodedly murdered eleven of the justices, including Chief Justice Alfonso Reyes Echandia, each of whom—as confirmed by Roger Yochelson, at the time an assistant U.S. attorney in the Justice Department's Office of International Affairs, which handles all extradition for the federal government—was known to be a solid supporter of the treaty.* A twelfth justice, Hernando Baquero Borda, who had negotiated the treaty with the United States and was its strongest advocate, was not present at the Palace of Justice on November 6, 1985. But on July 30, 1986, Borda and his bodyguard were murdered. More would have been killed on November 6 if the security forces of then–President Betancur had not quelled the slaughter, killing all of the guerrillas.

With this type of mortal lesson, the new members of the reconstituted Colombian Supreme Court could hardly be expected to ratify the treaty, but it is a testament to the bravery of several of the new justices (a bravery displayed by many of the public officials in Colombia who have paid for their courage with their lives) that when the Court voted on June 25, 1987, the Colombian law implementing the treaty was held to be unconstitutional by only one vote. On July 22, 1987, Colombian judges voided three U.S. requests for the arrest and extradition of Medellin cartel leaders Ochoa, Escobar, and Gacha.

For a while the state of extradition was up in the air. The ambiguity owed its origin to three assassinations in Colombia ordered by the drug traffickers within a forty-eight-hour period. On August 16, 1989, a few hours after he upheld an arrest warrant for Pablo Escobar

---

*Of course, the statistical probability of it being a coincidence that only pro-treaty justices were murdered (a few survived) is extremely low. Although initial government inquiries concluded that the Medellin cartel was not involved (Justice Minister Enrique Parejo said they probably were, the only high-level government official willing to say so publicly), as stated in the 1989 book *Kings of Cocaine* (by Guy Gugliotta and Jeff Leen), a year after the mass murder "every Colombian in a responsible public position would accept *without question* that the traffickers ordered and paid for the Palace of Justice assault."

on a double-murder charge, Magistrate Carlos Valencia Garcia was gunned down as he left a Bogota courthouse. On August 18, in Medellin, the cartel murdered Col. Waldemar Franklin Quintero, the chief of police of Antioquia province (of which Medellin is the largest city). Quintero had led several major raids against the cartel, resulting in the seizure of several tons of cocaine. But it was the bullets that killed Sen. Luis Carlos Galan four hours after the Quintero murder that brought to life Colombia's biggest crackdown (up to that point) against the drug cartels.

Galan, a very popular presidential candidate and avowed pro-extradition cartel foe, who was considered to be the frontrunner to replace President Barco (who could not succeed himself) in 1990, was assassinated as he was about to deliver a speech before 10,000 people in Soache, twenty miles south of Bogota. Within hours of the Galan assassination, Barco, using his state-of-siege powers, reinstated the extradition treaty previously struck down by the Colombian Supreme Court and launched the aforementioned crackdown against the drug traffickers that included a nationwide dragnet to apprehend the cartel leaders and the confiscation of their real and personal property. Under Barco's decree, twenty-two lower-level Colombian drug traffickers were eventually arrested and extradited to the United States.

In retaliation, the drug cartels immediately declared "total and absolute war" on the opposition. Their purpose was clear: to intimidate Colombian society into bringing pressure on the government to make peace with them and, most importantly, end the extradition of accused traffickers to the United States for trial, which they feared above all else ("We prefer a tomb in Colombia to jail in the United States," declared one cartel communique). Colombia's major cities were rocked by hundreds of explosions set off by the traffickers at banks, newspapers, radio stations, schools, and supermarkets, causing hundreds of deaths and injuries. Two other presidential candidates for Barco's seat, Carlos Pizarro and Bernardo Jaramillo, were assassinated—on the orders, the government claimed, of Pablo Escobar. Pablo Escobar was also believed to be behind the explosion of an Avianca airliner on November 27, 1989, over Bogota, which killed 107 passengers, including two Americans.*

---

* Escobar and an associate, Dandeny Munoz-Mosquera, were indicted on August 13, 1992, in Brooklyn, New York, under a 1986 terrorism statute making it a crime to kill U.S. citizens abroad. Munoz-Mosquera, known as the number-one paid assassin and enforcer for the Medellin cartel, was arrested in the United States in 1991 when it was learned that he had traveled here just as President Bush and other world leaders were

Additionally, the cartel offered a special bounty of $4,300 for every police officer killed. Upward of 250 officers in Medellin and other Colombian cities were indiscriminately murdered on the streets. The fear and terror, which caused millions of Colombians to stay at home and business to slow dramatically, took its toll, as evidenced by increasing voices within the Colombian government and among its people urging "negotiation" with the traffickers so Colombia could return to normalcy. With this type of internal pressure, plus the history of twelve of their predecessors being murdered by the cartel just four years earlier in a successful effort to influence the Court's vote on extradition, most believed that the Colombian Supreme Court would hold Barco's decrees on extradition and confiscation to be unconstitutional. But on October 3, 1989, in a singular display of courage and judicial responsibility, the court upheld Barco's state-of-siege decree on extradition, though it overturned the confiscation decree. The war immediately escalated.

The first side that blinked in the war was the government. On July 26, 1990, President Barco lifted emergency military control over three suburbs of Medellin that were strongholds of the cartel. It was a sign that Colombia had had enough and, though not capitulating, was taking a pragmatic approach that the nation could not continue to be convulsed by violence, particularly when the root cause of the war was the insatiable demand for cocaine in the United States. Apart from the ultimate wisdom of its decision, few fair-minded persons could denounce Colombia for its new stance. *El Tiempo*, Colombia's largest daily newspaper, editorialized that "it's worth asking whether the war on drug trafficking should be fought in this country." The weekly publication *Semana* wrote that "in the war against drugs, the United States is ready to fight to the last Colombian."

The very day after Barco's emergency-lifting gesture, the Medellin cartel—itself weakened and reeling from the war, which had forced it into going underground and resulted in the slayings of Gacha and such other prominent members as Gustavo Gaviria, Escobar's cousin, and Juan Jairo Arias, a leader of the cartel's network of hired killers—declared an end to the violence. The cartel communique

arriving in New York to address the United Nations. In December of 1994, a federal jury in New York convicted Munoz-Mosquera of the Avianca bombing and thirteen other counts of drug-related crimes. Witnesses at the trial from Colombia testified that Munoz-Mosquera carried out the bombing because Escobar wanted to intimidate the Colombian government into ceasing its war against the Medellin cartel. Other witnesses revealed how Munoz-Mosquera himself had killed over 100 Colombian police officers. He was sentenced to life imprisonment without the possibility of parole.

said: "We decree a unilateral, indefinite ceasefire, and we suspend attacks against police, bombings in all Colombian cities, and the execution of politicians, journalists, judges, and other functionaries."

Although there was a welcomed cessation of violence, no one took the traffickers at their word. On August 7, 1990, Colombia's new president, Cesar Gaviria, who had run on a strong anti-cartel platform, vowed in his inaugural address to bring peace to his battle-scarred nation. "No nation in the history of humanity," Gaviria said, "has paid as high a price as Colombia for confronting the most powerful criminal organization in memory." He went on to imply the possible end to extradition, but only if the "terror first disappears." In a series of September, 1990, decrees, Gaviria officially took the next step, promising all accused traffickers who surrendered and confessed to at least one crime that they would not be extradited to the United States. They would be tried in Colombia, he said, and if convicted, receive prison sentences reduced by a quarter to a half.

On November 17, 1990, the government announced a new decree guaranteeing that no trafficker, no matter how many crimes he committed, would serve more than thirty years. Justice Minister Jaime Giraldo then made the most dramatic concession thus far, stating that if Pablo Escobar, accused by the Colombian government of murdering hundreds of people, "confesses all of his crimes he would enjoy a reduction by half of Colombia's maximum sentence, and would serve fifteen years."

Public opinion polls showed that Colombians supported Gaviria's concessions, as enormous as they were. "It's time to stop pursuing a war that only interests the United States," said Humberto Samorano, a twenty-three-year-old university student. "It's their problem if they can't educate their people to stop taking drugs," he told a correspondent for the *New York Times*. Vicente Jimenez, a twenty-seven-year-old engineer, said, "I agree with Gaviria's policy of stretching out his hand to the drug traffickers, because we need peace." Marie Isabel Ruedos, a Colombian columnist, added: "We are tired. We have lost. We have to do something different. We have to find a formula for peace."

President Gaviria's offer not to extradite the narco-traffickers if they surrendered was a definite signal that Gaviria was going in the direction of officially nullifying Barco's state-of-siege extradition decree, thereby leaving in place the June 25, 1987, ruling of the Colombian Supreme Court invalidating the extradition treaty. But the traffickers weren't waiting for Gaviria. Besides, being a politician, he could not be completely relied upon to continue in the direction they wanted. On December 9, 1990, special delegates to the Colombian National Assembly, whose express purpose was to "rewrite the Constitution," were elected by the Colombian people. A very low turnout of voters (only 3½ million, as opposed to 8 million in a March, 1990, congressional election) enabled several well-financed candidates believed to be sympathetic to even further accommodation with the cartel to be elected. Though many members were not in league with the drug lords, the assembly was referred to by some as the "Narco-Assembly." And on July 4, 1991, the assembly, after heavy lobbying, bribes, and intimidation by the narco-traffickers, passed a new Colombian constitution (replacing the original one of 1886), in which extradition was expressly prohibited. It was now safely out of the whimsical hands of the courts and politicians. No Colombian drug trafficker, no matter how much illicit cocaine he exported to the United States or elsewhere, and regardless of how much misery, harm, and destruction he caused to this nation's citizens, would ever be extradited to America to face justice.

Without the proposed search-and-find mission set forth in the following pages, the Colombian drug lords will be able to continue to violate this nation's laws and cause prodigious harm to this country with total impunity.

For reasons of sovereignty, it is highly unlikely that the Colombian government would give its official consent to our military raid. The amount of flame and passion with which their objection would be made, however, is not clear at all. In February of 1994, Colombia's Counsel of State, the highest authority on government administration, complained to then-President Gaviria about the presence of 250 U.S. soldiers in Colombia (130 combat engineers on a humanitarian mission to build a school, build a medical clinic, and improve a road; the others to maintain a U.S.-built radar station to monitor drug-trafficking flights). Colombia's sovereignty was being violated, they said. The normally placid Gaviria, his voice trembling, ignored the complaint. "Sovereignty is in greater danger when a nation is handed over to drug traffickers, and the state does not have the capacity to respond," he said.

Gaviria's predecessor, President Barco, told President Bush only that his government "would not request" American combat troops to help the Colombian military and police during its civil war with the narco-traffickers—not a strong anti-interventionist statement.

Bogota *did* object to our deployment in January, 1990, of a naval task force off the coast of Colombia to monitor and intercept air and seaborne drug traffic, and the deployment was discontinued a few months later.* On the other hand, in late 1989, Bogota approved of our flying American military planes over Colombian airspace to monitor suspicious air traffic, and the secret operation was only curtailed when an American EC-130 spy plane nearly collided with two Colombian airlines over southern Colombia on March 29, 1990.

While Colombian officials would object to our military raid, it is not so obvious that the majority of Colombian people would do so. Although the Colombian economy is being shored up by the cocaine commerce, most Colombians are painfully aware of the pernicious effect the drug industry has had on the nation's culture and everyday life, and would love nothing better than to be rid of it. A May, 1995, nationwide poll of Colombians showed 76 percent in favor of the recent anti-cartel campaign by the government.** Many Colombians, proud of their heritage as Latin America's oldest democracy, fear the narcotics traffickers will eventually transmute their system of government. "Our way of life is being threatened," Bogota prosecutor Francisco Bernal Castillo says. In other words, apart from the anticipated formal denunciation by the Colombian government of any search-and-find mission, a very limited U.S. military intervention might be privately welcomed by a great many in Colombia. And although no public officials in Colombia have been murdered by the cartels in the last few years, fear ebbs slowly, and they can never feel serene that intimidation of them by violence won't resume again. It therefore strains credulity to believe that these officials would not be privately in favor of any measure that would end the fear and danger.

Even those Colombians of less noble instincts have long ago become alarmed at the deep and widespread harm narco-trafficking has

---

*One reason for the objection, however, was that such an operation would undoubtedly interfere with legitimate Colombian commerce. For instance, on March 9, 1990, two U.S. Coast Guard cutters stopped and searched two Colombian ships 125 miles north of Colombia. The freighters were suspected of transporting cocaine, but no drugs were found aboard.

**A few Colombian intellectuals, however, have tried to make a case on behalf of the cartels. Though denouncing the aspect of violence, in his *Impacto del Narcotrafic en Antioquia*, Mario Arango argues that the cartels have stanched the social deterioration of Colombia. In a January 8, 1989, *Washington Post* interview, Arango said that narcotrafficking has spawned an egalitarian "social revolution. With narcotics, the mestizos, mulattoes, and blacks have had the opportunities to enter consumer society and gain substantial wealth. The best vehicles that are driven in the city of Medellin are in the hands of people who have black or dark skin."

brought to their country. At the beginning, the drug cartels were of mild concern. "They were getting rich off the gringos, an entirely respectable way for a Latin to assimilate wealth. Our children weren't taking cocaine, so everything was fine," one middle-class mother offered. But today, thousands of young knife-wielding addicts high on a very low-grade cocaine called *basuco* (South America's toxic equivalent of crack) roam the streets, willing to kill for the price of a fix.

CONSTITUTIONAL CONSIDERATIONS

If, for whatever reason, the Colombian government would not authorize our military intervention, then we should intervene without their blessing. There is ample legal and constitutional justification for such an action.

Before discussing the particular facts of this case and applicable law, some general background will be helpful. Article I, §8 [11] of the U.S. Constitution gives Congress the power to declare war. The basis for this power is Art. I, §8 [1], which states that Congress shall "provide for the common defense and general welfare of the United States." Although the military intervention contemplated in this chapter would not even be close to the type that would necessitate a congressional declaration of war, nevertheless, the language of Art. I, §8 [1], though pertaining to Congress, provides the very kind of rationale that has been used throughout this nation's history by presidents employing American forces on foreign lands in the absence of a declaration of war by Congress.

For instance, upon the intervention of the Chinese Communists in Korea, on December 16, 1950, President Truman employed our armed forces in Korea by issuing Presidential Proclamation #2914, which declared that Communist aggression constituted a "grave threat" to this country, and the nation and its people had to respond by making whatever sacrifices were necessary "for the welfare of the nation."

By a military search-and-find mission in Colombia, would we not be defending our nation by neutralizing the very source of that which is almost mortally wounding the "general welfare" of this country? No semantic stretching is required to reach that conclusion.

However, inasmuch as any presidential employment of military force in Colombia would undoubtedly be *without* a formal congressional declaration of war, and inasmuch as one of the primary challenges to such a course of action would undoubtedly be based on the contention that it was unlawful, an analysis of the legality of such an action is necessary.

Although Art. II, §2 [1] does provide that "the President shall be Commander-in-Chief of the Army and Navy of the United States," technically this only places the president at the head of this nation's armed forces. It clearly envisions, as a predicate to his conducting war as the head of the nation's armed forces, that war has been declared. And Art. I, §8 [11] ("The Congress shall have power . . . to declare war") exclusively and unambiguously gives that power to Congress, not the President. To assume that §8 [11] only gives Congress the power to utter the words, in fact in writing, "We declare war," not actually to initiate war, is to assume that the framers intended to confer upon Congress a totally idle and meaningless power. And while no one disputes the inherent power of the presidency to engage the nation in war, without first securing congressional approval, to repel an invasion, the Constitution does not authorize the president to *initiate* war. As the United States Supreme Court as far back as *The Prize Cases*, 67 U.S. (2 Black) 635, 646–647, 649, 660 (1863), said: "This is a Government created, defined, and limited by a written Constitution, every article, clause and expression in which was pondered and criticized, as probably no document in the affairs of men was ever before tested, refined and ascertained. . . . In this . . . Constitution, it was explicitly and exclusively declared, in words as plain as language affords, where this tremendous power should reside. To Congress is entrusted the power to declare war. . . . War is reserved to the judgment of Congress itself." The Court went on to say that the war power means that only Congress can "initiate war, put the country in a state of war."

Although the subject Articles of the Constitution need no interpretation to determine the framer's intent, Alexander Hamilton, writing in *The Federalist*, No. 69, at 465 (Cooke ed. 1961) in 1788, a year before the Constitution went into effect, said: "[T]he President is to be Commander in Chief of the army and navy of the United States. In this respect his authority would be nominally the same with that of the King of Great Britain, but in substance much inferior to it. It would amount to nothing more than the supreme command and direction of the land and naval forces, while that of the British King extends to the *declaring* of war . . . which by the Constitution would appertain of the Legislature."

It has been suggested by proponents of the position that the president has power to initiate war that if the framers at the 1787

Constitutional Convention in Philadelphia had intended that power to reside in Congress, they would not have changed the word *make* war to *declare* war in Art. I, §8 [11]. In *The Records of the Federal Convention of 1787*, p. 313 (edited by Max Ferrand), the "journal" entry for Friday, August 17, reads: "The question being again taken to strike out the word 'make' and to insert the word 'declare' . . . it passed in the affirmative." But in James Madison's notes of the debate on that date at the Convention as set forth on pages 318 and 319 of the *Records*, the change appears to have been made *only* to confirm the Executive's right to repel sudden attacks, not to give him the right to initiate war: "Mr. M [Madison] and Mr. Gerry moved to insert 'declare', striking out 'make' war; leaving to the Executive the power to repel sudden attacks." The Madison notes reflect that only Pierce Butler of South Carolina supported giving the president the right to make or initiate war, and that the other colonial representatives were against it. In addition to his opposition, Madison writes that "Mr. Gerry never expected to hear in a republic a motion to empower the Executive alone to declare war," and that Mr. Sharman thought "the Executive should be able to repel and not to commence war." Also, "Mr. Mason was agst [against] giving the power of war to the Executive, because not (safely) to be trusted with it."

So much for the interpretation of words and phrases, and the apparent intent of the framers of the Constitution. The reality is that throughout this nation's history, presidents, *without* the approval of Congress, have time and again committed American military forces abroad. Although all presidents, during their inauguration ceremonies, swear to uphold the Constitution, when it comes to arguably the most serious and important (in terms of consequences) part of the Constitution—who has the right to commit the military forces of this nation to an armed conflict with another nation—most presidents, even self-proclaimed "strict constructionists" of the Constitution like Ronald Reagan and George Bush, have cavalierly ignored the explicit constitutional language and their presidential oath. As political commentator Russell Baker has wryly observed: "Presidents now say, sure, the Constitution gives Congress the right to declare war, but it doesn't forbid presidents to *make* war, so long as they don't *declare* it. As a result, the declared war has become obsolete. Its successor is the undeclared war."

In a 1952 U.S. Supreme Court case dealing with a different use of presidential power, the dissent noted that even as of that date, forty-four years ago, there had been "125 incidents in our history in which presidents, *without* Congressional authorization, and in the absence of a declaration of war, have ordered the Armed Forces to take action or maintain positions abroad." In fact, only five times in the nation's history has Congress declared war: the War of 1812; the Mexican War, 1846; the Spanish-American War, 1898; World War I, 1917; and World War II, 1941. In the recent Persian Gulf War, although Congress adopted resolutions authorizing the use of force (not quite the same as a declaration of war), the Bush Administration flatly asserted it had the right to commit the nation to war without a congressional declaration of any kind. A 1966 Department of State memorandum states: "Over a very long period in our history, practice and precedent have confirmed the Constitutional authority to engage United States forces in hostilities without a declaration of war."

When the president has taken this nation to war without a congressional declaration of war, Congress has ultimately always acquiesced, and the third branch of government, the judiciary—which has a history of injecting itself into virtually every conceivable area of human discord, including all the affairs of the executive and legislative branches—has surprisingly refrained from assuming jurisdiction over the matter. An example is the case of *Velvel v. Johnson,* 287 F.Supp. 846 (1968). Velvel, a professor of law at the University of Kansas, brought a class action suit against President Johnson for conducting the Vietnam War illegally, i.e., without a congressional declaration of war (some argue that the Gulf of Tonkin Resolution was tantamount to congressional approval). District Judge George Templar refused to even assume jurisdiction to hear the lawsuit. Templar said that the president has discretionary power to protect "the interests of the country. In exercising such power, the President is responsible to the country rather than to the judiciary. Since the courts lack the information as well as the competence to evaluate the data upon which the President decides military policy, *judges should refrain from subjecting presidential judgment to judicial scrutiny.*"

In a suit very similar to *Velvel v. Johnson,* during the Persian Gulf War Federal Judge Royce Lamberth ruled in favor of President Bush over a North Carolina National Guardsman who did not want to serve in an undeclared war, holding that the dispute over war powers was a "political question" outside the province of the judiciary.

So presidents, throughout our history (and even since the 1973

War Powers Resolution,* 50 U.S.C. §1541–1548, which directs that they at least "consult with Congress"), have for the most part not even bothered to seek congressional approval for the employment of military forces abroad. And they have shown no lack of affinity for Latin America. Just a few examples will suffice. President Theodore Roosevelt sent troops to Panama in 1903; President Taft to Nicaragua in 1912; President Wilson to Haiti in 1915 and to Mexico in 1916; President Johnson to the Dominican Republic in 1965; President Reagan to Grenada in 1983; President Bush to Panama in 1989; and President Clinton to Haiti in 1994. The legal justifications were anchored mostly on the following theories, behind all of which is the common thread of protecting the security and welfare of the country: the president as commander-in-chief (although we have seen that Art. II, §2 [1] does not really confer upon the president the right to declare or initiate war); the "inherent" power of the presidency (a nebulous bootstrap notion that cannot be traced to any constitutional language); the collective security theory (in the last fifty years, the United States has entered into many treaties with other coun-

---

*It would not seem that the 1973 War Powers Resolution (WPR), which requires the President, absent a congressional declaration of war, to terminate the use of U.S. armed forces abroad sixty days (an additional thirty days upon special application by the president to Congress) after their being deployed unless Congress extends the period, would apply to the search-and-find mission proposed in this work. Apart from the fact that the current administration, like its predecessors, contends the WPR is an unconstitutional usurpation of their inherent powers, the Resolution only applies if the president has introduced U.S. forces into "hostilities, or into situations where imminent involvement in hostilities is clearly indicated." The legislative history of the WPR suggests that this language refers to war or the equivalent of war (i.e., large-scale hostilities), and would not apply to a limited mission to arrest fugitives from justice under criminal indictment in the U.S. As the court said in Crockett v. Reagan, 558 F.Supp. 893, 899 (1982), the WPR, "which was enacted as the Vietnam war was coming to an end, was intended to prevent another situation in which a President could gradually build up American involvement in a foreign war, eventually presenting Congress with a full-blown undeclared war it [is] powerless to stop." Sen. Jacob Javits, an author of the WPR, said, "It is an effort to learn from the lessons of the last tragic decade of war in Vietnam. The War Powers Act would assure that any future decision to commit the U.S. to any warmaking must be shared in by the Congress to be lawful" (119 Cong. Rec. 1394 [1973]).

Since there is no likelihood that our attempt to arrest the drug lords would precipitate a war with the country of Colombia, or any paramilitary group residing therein, the WPR should not apply. But there is a greater reason why it shouldn't. As the Crockett court said, "The purpose of the WPR was to give Congress both the knowledge and the mechanism needed to reclaim its constitutional power to declare war." But here, a completely different and unrelated section of the Constitution would be involved, one that in no way is in arrogation of Congress's exclusive authority to declare war: the duty of the president under Art. II, §3 to see that the laws of this country are "faithfully executed."

Even if the WPR were deemed to apply, the search and find mission could most probably be accomplished within 60 days. If not, Congress could be expected to extend the period if apprised that the mission was proceeding well.

tries, which provide that the security of each signatory country is vital to the security of each other signatory nation); and so forth. Each of these theories, and others, while polemically tenable, are, in the last analysis, bereft of constitutional support. Yet presidential actions carried out in their name have successfully withstood all assaults on their propriety. Where a threat to the republic, however indirect, is perceived, constitutional niceties are winked at.

As opposed to prior presidential adventurism on foreign soil in our nation's history, the peculiar facts of this case give rise to the unique situation wherein the president would have clear constitutional authority to employ military forces in Colombia without congressional approval.

Apart from the fact that a search-and-find mission could not even be reasonably denominated a "war" (which constitutionally would require a congressional declaration), Art. II, §3 of the U.S. Constitution expressly provides that the president "shall take care that the laws [of this country] be faithfully executed," a duty described by President Benjamin Harrison as "the central idea of the office." The unambiguous language of Art. II, §3 needs no interpretation, but as far back as 1889, the U.S. Supreme Court, in *In Re Neagle*, 135 U.S. 1, 64, held that this section of the Constitution conferred upon the president the power and the duty to "enforce acts of Congress." The federal drug-trafficking laws violated by the Colombian cartel leaders are, of course, all "acts of Congress."

At this very moment in the U.S. District Court for the Southern District of Florida, a 9-count, 161-page Miami federal grand-jury indictment handed down on June 5, 1995 (No. 93-470 CR), charges the Rodriguez brothers, Jose Santacruz-Londono, and Helmer Herrera-Buitrago with smuggling "at least 200,000 kilograms of Cali cartel cocaine into the United States" since 1983. (There are fifty-five other defendants named in the Miami indictment on related drug-trafficking and racketeering charges, three of whom are criminal defense attorneys who were at one time assistant U.S. attorneys. One, in fact, headed the U.S. Department of Justice's international affairs office from 1981 to 1984. His job encompassed seeking to extradite Colombian drug lords, the very people he is now accused of having unlawfully attempted to shield from extradition.) Gilberto Rodriguez was already under indictment on drug-trafficking charges in New York, Los Angeles, and New Orleans, and his brother, Miguel, in New Orleans. [The Medellin cartel leaders had also been under indictment in the United States. A 39-count Miami federal grand-jury indictment handed down on August 26, 1986, charged Jorge Ochoa, Pablo Escobar, and Gonzalo Rodriguez Gacha with violating federal drug laws. Other federal indictments followed against the Medellin drug czars and their confederates, including a 12-count Jacksonville, Florida, grand-jury indictment on April 17, 1989, which, like the Miami indictment, was on drug-trafficking charges, and a 2-count Atlanta, Georgia, grand-jury indictment (Rodriguez Gacha was not named in this indictment) dated March 6, 1989, for drug trafficking and money laundering.]

The Rodriguez brothers are presently in custody in Colombia, and hence, obviously cannot be the subject of any search-and-find mission. But prior to their arrest in Colombia by Colombian authorities, this nation's president, under Art. II, §3, not only had the constitutional right to send military forces to Colombia to capture and arrest these cartel leaders, he had an express constitutional *duty* to do so. Since they were under indictment in this country, our failure to arrest them (and their predecessors—Escobar, Ochoa, and Gacha—who, as indicated, were also under indictment) and bring them back to this country to stand trial on the charges against them meant that the laws of this country were not being enforced and "faithfully executed."

It should be noted that obviously no state would ever send members of its National Guard, nor any city or county its police or sheriff's force, to Colombia to apprehend the cartel leaders. Furthermore, they wouldn't even have the authority, since the indictments are all of *federal* crimes. States, and their local entities, would be devoid of authority even if the indictments were for violations of state narcotic laws. As the U.S. Supreme Court declared in *United States v. Pink*, 315 U.S. 203, 233 (1942): "Power over external affairs is not shared by the States; it is vested in the national government exclusively."

The U.S. Circuit Court, in the *Neagle* case, 39 Fed. Rep. 833, 359–860 (1889), said that "the power and duty imposed on the President to 'take care that the laws are faithfully executed,' necessarily carries with it all power and authority necessary to accomplish the object sought to be attained." Because no other established and legal means are available, either the president dispatches forces to Colombia, or the cartel leaders can continue to commit their prodigious crimes in America with complete impunity.

Although the U.S. Supreme Court has never had the occasion to expressly rule on the constitutionality of the American military enforcing American narcotic laws on foreign soil, two relatively recent Supreme Court cases not dealing with the military give every indication that the Court would look upon such an action in a friendly way. Both arose out of the February 7, 1985, kidnapping and eventual torture-murder of DEA agent Enrique Camarena near Guadalajara, Mexico, by Mexican narcotic traffickers.* In January of 1986, DEA agents working in concert with officers from the Mexican Federal Judicial Police searched without a warrant the residences of Rene Martin Verdugo Urquidez in Mexicali and San Felipe. The purpose of the search was to secure evidence of Verdugo-Urquidez's narcotic-trafficking activities and his involvement in Camarena's murder. Rejecting Verdugo-Urquidez's contention that since it was an unjustified, warrantless search the evidence recovered should be excluded, the Supreme Court ruled, in *United States v. Verdugo-Urquidez*, 494 U.S. 259 (1990), that the Fourth Amendment prohibition against "unreasonable searches and seizures" does not apply to foreign citizens where such searches and seizures take place outside the United States. Even though the American military was not involved in *Verdugo-Urquidez*, the Court, by way of dictum, made this telling observation: "For better or for worse, we live in a world of nation-states in which our Government must be able to function effectively in the company of sovereign nations. Some who violate our laws may live outside our borders under a regime quite different from that which obtains in this country. Situations threatening to important American interests may arise halfway around the globe, situations which in the view of the political branches of our Government require an American response with armed force. If there are to be restrictions on searches and seizure which occur incident to such American action, they must be imposed by the political branches through diplomatic understanding, treaty, or legislation."

A factual situation even closer to the military intervention proposal in this book was presented in *United States v. Alvarez-Machain*, 112 S Ct 2188 (1992). In *Alvarez-Machain*, the mindset of the Court being sympathetic to such an intervention is even more apparent, if possible, than in *Verdugo-Urquidez*—to the point where the Court engaged in transparent illogic to reach its decision. Alvarez-Machain, a medical doctor, was indicted in Los Angeles for

---

*Camarena's Mexican pilot, Alfredo Zavala-Avelar, was also murdered.

his role in the Camarena murder. DEA agents believed that Machain prolonged Camarena's life so that others could further torture and interrogate him. DEA Special Agent Hector Berrellez, head of operation Leyenda (the DEA's investigation of the Camarena murder) instructed a Mexican informant to tell his associates that the DEA would pay them a $50,000 reward plus expenses if Dr. Alvarez-Machain were delivered to the DEA in the United States (prior to this, the DEA had unsuccessfully attempted to secure Machain's presence in the United States through informal negotiation with representatives of the Mexican government). Pursuant to the offer, on April 2, 1990, several armed men burst into Dr. Machain's office in Guadalajara and forcibly kidnapped him. He was then flown by private plane to El Paso, Texas, where he was arrested by DEA agents.

The fly in the ointment was the 1978 extradition treaty between the United States and Mexico. Machain moved to dismiss the indictment on the ground that his abduction violated the treaty. The Mexican government, demanding Machain's return to Mexico, also formally protested the abduction to our Department of State. The Supreme Court, in upholding the abduction, ruled that since the language of the treaty did not expressly prohibit such abductions, and was silent with respect to any reference thereto, the treaty was not violated. It is not easy to argue with the inherent logic of the dissenting opinion in *Alvarez-Machain* that such a prohibition is implicit, in that an interpretation of the treaty that condones unilateral action could not foster cooperation and mutual assistance—the stated goals of the treaty. As the dissent said: "Provisions [in the treaty] requiring sufficient evidence to grant extradition (Article 3), withholding extradition for political or military offenses (Article 5), withholding extradition when the person sought has already been tried (Article 6), withholding extradition when the statute of limitations for the crime has lapsed (Article 7), and granting the requested State discretion to refuse to extradite an individual who would face the death penalty in the requesting country (Article 8), would serve little purpose if the requesting country could simply kidnap the person. As the Court of Appeals for the 9th Circuit recognized in a related case, each of these provisions would be utterly frustrated if kidnapping were held to be permissible governmental conduct."

Nonetheless, the Court's eagerness, at the expense of logic, to uphold the DEA's conduct in *Machain*, certainly augurs well for its upholding the constitutionality of any military intervention in Colombia. This is particularly so since any such intervention would not even have to deal with the thorny impediment of an extradition treaty. As previously indicated, as of 1991 we no longer have an extradition treaty with Colombia. The U.S. Supreme Court, in effect, has held in *Alvarez-Machain* that it is not constitutionally impermissible for U.S. government agents to abduct foreign citizens on foreign soil to enforce American law. The fact that the abductors in *Machain* were Mexican nationals is a distinction without legal substance. When they acted at the behest of American agents, legally they became "agents" of our government.*

The question still to be addressed is whether abduction of foreign drug lords by the American military to enforce American law would likewise be constitutional.

The primary objection to this nation's use of the military on foreign soil to enforce narcotic laws will be the law of Posse Comitatus.

POSSE COMITATUS

Just as surely as night follows day, the proposal of U.S. military intervention on Colombian soil to enforce American civil law will evoke a strident chorus of naysayers much more interested in playing games with an obscure, quite assailable obstacle called Posse Comitatus than in solving the nation's drug problem. In fact, if the proposal is considered, almost assuredly the primary battleground will be on this issue.

Posse Comitatus (literally "power of the county") was an ancient, common-law practice in England that provided that every able-bodied male inhabitant of a county over the age of fifteen could be summoned by the sheriff to help in maintaining the public order, such as to quell a riot; that is, the sheriff could call upon the "power of the county" to assist him in his law enforcement duties. When, as an outgrowth of this tradition, federal troops enforced the civil law in the South during the Reconstruction era, Congress passed, as an amendment to the Army Appropriations Act of June 18, 1878, a law prohibiting "the Army of the United States" from being used "as a

---

*In *United States v. Juan Ramon Matta-Ballesteros* (Docket #91-50336, Dec. 1, 1995), a lower federal court, the United States Court of Appeals (9th Circuit), held that even the conduct of four United States marshals who abducted Matta from his home in Tegucigalpa, Honduras, was not unconstitutional. Though the court denounced the conduct, it held that the Supreme Court, in *Alvarez-Machain*, had ruled that this type of law enforcement action was not prohibited. Matta had been a member of a Guadalajara drug-trafficking operation and had participated in one of the meetings in which the kidnapping of DEA agent Camarena was discussed.

posse comitatus . . . for the purpose of executing the laws." The current statute (18 U.S.C. §1385) provides that unless "expressly authorized by the Constitution or Act of Congress," the "Army or the Air Force" cannot be used "as a posse comitatus . . . to execute the law."

Prior to 1981, cases interpreting §1385 held that the section was applicable to the Navy and Marines, even though they are not mentioned in the text of the section.* Any ambiguity was eliminated by the enactment of 10 U.S.C. §375 in 1981, which specifically included the U.S. Navy and Marine Corps in the Posse Comitatus prohibition.** The prohibition against executing the law, however, does not include "indirect" assistance, such as providing training, surveillance, intelligence, and loaning military equipment. By a congressional amendment to the Posse Comitatus law (10 U.S.C. §371–380), the military has been supporting law enforcement's battle against drugs in this way since 1981.***

For 117 years, the leadership of this country has inflexibly and consistently accepted the notion that any use of the American military to carry out this nation's civil laws (in this context, the "nation's civil laws" include all laws, criminal as well as civil), either here or abroad, was prohibited by the law of Posse Comitatus. The belief in this, almost as an article of faith, has been expressed throughout the years. Some illustrative examples: In testimony before the U.S. Senate and U.S. House of Representatives Committees on Armed Services on June 15, 1988, then–Secretary of Defense Frank C. Carlucci

---

* See, for instance, *United States v. Walden*, 490 F.2d, 372, 373 (1974), which based its holding on the fact that the Navy adopted the Posse Comitatus restriction by a self-imposed administrative regulation: Secretary of the Navy Instruction 5400.12, issued on January 17, 1969.

** Although 10 U.S.C. §375 doesn't use the term *Posse Comitatus*, it does expressly provide that there cannot be "direct participation by a member of the Army, Navy, Air Force, or Marine Corps in . . . a search and seizure, arrest, or similar activity . . ." However, the Office of Department of Defense Coordinator for Drug Enforcement Policy and Support has not made a determination (nor, they say, has there been any need to) on whether §375, when read in conjunction with §378 (which provides that §375 shall not be construed "to limit the authority of the executive branch in the use of the military . . . beyond that provided by law before December 1, 1981") prohibits the U.S. Navy and Marine Corps from engaging in Posse Comitatus. The question is academic, they add, because "U.S. policy is that the Posse Comitatus prohibition does apply to the Navy and Marines."

*** As a direct result of the bombing of the federal building in Oklahoma City on April 19, 1995, in which 169 people were killed, the Clinton Administration's proposed Omnibus Counterterrorism Act of 1995 would extend the "indirect" assistance exceptions to Posse Comitatus to include technical and logistical assistance by the military to domestic law enforcement "in criminal cases involving chemical, biological, and other weapons of mass destruction."

III asserted: "I remain absolutely opposed to the assignment of a law enforcement mission [in the war on drugs] to the Department of Defense. I am firmly opposed to any relaxation of the Posse Comitatus restrictions on the use of the military to search, seize, and arrest. I have discussed this matter with the President and other senior members of the Cabinet, and I can report that these views are shared throughout this Administration." Gen. Colin L. Powell, when he was chairman of the Joint Chiefs of Staff, stated: "*By law* and tradition, [the use of the military in law enforcement] is an inappropriate role for servicemen." Stephen M. Duncan, assistant secretary of defense under Dick Cheney, and DoD coordinator for Drug Enforcement Policy, said in a prepared statement on April 19, 1990, to the House Armed Services Committee, Subcommittee on Investigations: "The provisions of the Posse Comitatus statute place strict limitations on the authority of the Armed Forces to make arrests and to conduct searches and seizures. And while the Armed Forces of the United States will be actively involved in the *support* of law enforcement agencies, the DoD will *not* become a law-enforcement agency." Briefing the news media on April 27, 1995, Pentagon spokesman Dennis Boxx said: "We are very, very restricted [under the law of Posse Comitatus] to what we can do as a part of any law enforcement. . . . We still believe in that concept."*

There are two legitimate reasons to justify the continued existence of the Posse Comitatus law as a general proposition, neither of which, however, applies to the proposed military search-and-find mission.

First, the courts have pointed out that military personnel are trained to operate under circumstances where constitutional freedoms are not considerations, and if they enforce civil laws by making

* By its very language, the law of Posse Comitatus only applies to *federal* troops. The National Guard, being a *state* organization, is not subject to this law. In fact, 32 U.S.C. §112 (f)(1) specifically provides that the National Guard, "while not in federal service" can engage in "any law enforcement activities authorized by state and local laws and requested by the Governor," which, of course, would include making arrests. However, it is the policy of the National Guard not to do so. When the National Guard is "federalized" by the president (which it was, among other times, by President Eisenhower in 1957 to help ensure the admission of black students in Little Rock, Arkansas, and by President Johnson in 1967 to help quell a riot in Detroit, Michigan), it is subject to the law of Posse Comitatus. Under those circumstances, the Guard cannot make arrests. It can only detain someone it believes to be violating the law until local law enforcement arrives to make the arrest. Being federal troops, the Army's 101st Airborne Division, which was also in Little Rock, and the 82nd Airborne Division, which was in Detroit, were operating under the same constraints.

arrests, searches, and seizures, the danger of their violating the constitutional rights of American citizens in the process is great. This justification for the law's existence clearly would not apply to the arrest by the military, not of American citizens on a widespread scale, but of a few drug lords in a foreign country. The Posse Comitatus law, a law most Americans have never heard of, was enacted, after all, for the benefit of this nation's citizens, not that of our mortal enemies, in this case, foreign drug lords.

Second, the Department of Defense has consistently opposed a relaxation of this nation's historic separation of the military from civilian activities because it would interfere with the primary function of the military: to defend the nation from hostile foreign attack. In his September 15, 1986, interview with Pentagon reporters over a House bill allowing the president to order the military to seal our borders from drug smuggling, then–Secretary of Defense Caspar W. Weinberger stated: "Drug smuggling is a criminal enterprise. The time that would be diverted into stopping this is enormous. You would have to have [military] commanders and witnesses testifying in court *in thousands of cases,* and those things are never over quickly. You'd have to have all manner of informants and profiles of likely suspects. You'd have to construct a whole new law enforcement agency. Then, of course, that has a terribly adverse effect on [military] readiness."*

Again, nothing even distantly approaching such a massive scale of drug interdiction, which would be an ongoing process requiring hundreds of thousands of military personnel and eventually thousands upon thousands of arrests and court appearances, would be involved in any military search-and-find mission in Colombia.

Although the *rationale,* then, for keeping the Posse Comitatus law does not apply to the proposed military raid of Colombia, does the existence of the law itself (§1385) nevertheless pose a *legal* impediment to such a raid? There are a number of separate and independent reasons why it does not.

1. It is very doubtful that the law even has any extraterritorial application; i.e., whether it prohibits the use of the military to carry out civilian law enforcement functions *outside* this nation's borders.

---

*Per the DoD, the current worldwide military strength of the U.S. armed forces is 1,559,515. It is hard to imagine how more than one or two thousand personnel at the very most would be required in any military mission to locate and arrest the main leaders of the Colombian cartels. It is equally hard to imagine how these few troops, employed to substantially solve this nation's drug crisis, could be better utilized elsewhere.

Federal courts have held that "in the absence of statutory language indicating a contrary intent," there is a presumption that statutes apply only to conduct occurring *within* the territory of the United States (see *Chandler v. United States,* 171 F.2d 921, 936 [1948]). Here, since the Posse Comitatus statute does not expressly contain any language prohibiting the civilian use of the military outside the United States, the presumption is that such conduct is not prohibited by the statute.*

But there is more than a presumption. Since no federal court has ever dealt with the legality of using the military to enforce American civil law on foreign land** *not occupied by American forces,* the legislative history of the Posse Comitatus law is revealing and provides insight for determining its intent.

The focus of the Posse Comitatus legislative debate as reported in the *Congressional Record* (Volumes 5 and 7, 1877 and 1878) was on the *domestic* use of the military in enforcing the civil law.

During the chaotic Reconstruction period in the South following the Civil War (1865–1877), federal troops were called upon on a regular basis to enforce the law. Congressman William Kimmell argued during the debate: "The standing Army has been employed in all sorts of uses, at the request of all sorts of people, without regard even to such law as has been enacted for the direction of its employment.

---

*And in dictum, the U.S. Supreme Court has already strongly suggested in *In Re Neagle,* 135 U.S. 1, 64 (1889) that the president's constitutional duty to see that "the laws be faithfully executed" contemplated more than a domestic application. The Court said the duty extended to "treaties of the United States . . . *and international relations."* Although this is a century-old case, in constitutional matters this is largely immaterial, particularly since the high court has not ruled or indicated to the contrary since then.

**In November, 1989, at least someone in the federal government concluded what should have been obvious years ago. Although appearing only in an unreleased internal memorandum, on November 3, 1989, Assistant Attorney General William P. Barr wrote to his boss, Attorney General Richard Thornburgh, that in Barr's opinion, the Posse Comitatus law did not prohibit the use of the military in carrying out law enforcement functions outside the United States. The reason given by the Department of Justice for not releasing the memorandum was that it was a "private communication" between Barr and his "client," Thornburgh. Lt. Col. David Super of the DoD says that "the Barr memo hasn't been accepted" at the department, and official pronouncements of the DoD subsequent to the Barr memo (see pages 126 and 127) affirm this.

Although never embraced or followed, the only other vagrant murmur against the supposedly blanket prohibition of Posse Comitatus is in the January 15, 1986, DoD Directive 5525.5(c) (Encl. 4), and an oral presentation to the Office of the Secretary of Defense Posse Comitatus Conference on December 7, 1982, in which general counsel for the DoD said that under 21 U.S.C. §873(b) and in the legislative history of §375 of 10 U.S.C., there may be an exception for the U.S. Navy and Marine Corps. However, neither 21 U.S.C. §873(b) nor the legislative history of §375 contains any language that the U.S. Navy and Marine Corps may enforce the nation's civil laws.

... If the Army of the United States can be used as a posse comitatus for the execution of the laws, we are living under a military despotism unqualified and absolute, for what is military despotism but the use of troops against the people." Congressman Knott added: "This amendment is designed to put a stop to the practice . . . of military officers of every grade answering the call of every marshal and deputy marshal . . . in the enforcement of the laws."

It was particularly distasteful to the ex-Confederate states, and fraught with potential corruption of the political process, when the military oversaw and policed state elections. The South (predominantly Democratic) felt the North (mostly Republican) was wreaking vengeance on the defeated South by using the Army to police state elections and to fraudulently help "carpetbaggers" (northerners who migrated to the South after the Civil War seeking private gain through the newly established governments) and "scalawags" (southern whites who flocked to the Republican Party following the war) get elected and stay in office. Congressman J. D. C. Atkins of Tennessee, denouncing the "carpetbag system of representation and government," said: "For twelve years some of the Southern States have not known self-government or constitutional freedom. And the Army has been used as the main instrument to effect their overthrow and uphold this despotism. American soldiers policemen? Insult if true, and slander if pretended to cover up the tyrannical use of the Army keeping in power tyrants whom the people have not elected."

It is clear from a review of the congressional debate that once Reconstruction ended (1877), "the immediate objective of the legislation was to put an end to the use of federal troops to police state elections in the ex-Confederate states *where the civil power had been reestablished*" (*Chandler v. United States*).

It is difficult to see how the *domestic* legislative intent behind the Posse Comitatus law could possibly be stretched to include a prohibition against the use of the military to apprehend some *foreign* drug lords.

More specifically, if, as appears to be the case, the purpose of the Posse Comitatus law was to prevent the military from usurping the job of civilian authorities *where civil power is in effect, and capable, by itself, of enforcing the law,* inasmuch as no American civil power is, nor can be, in effect outside the United States, dispatching the military to enforce American civil law on foreign land would not be a usurpation of any civilian function, and therefore, not violative of the legislative intent of the law.

2. Section 1385 says the armed services *can* be employed to execute the law if authorized by "the Constitution." Since under the Constitution the president has the duty to ensure that this country's laws are faithfully executed, our employment of armed forces would clearly be in compliance with §1385. In any event, in any conflict between the language of a statute (§1385 prohibiting Posse Comitatus to "execute the law") and the Constitution (Art. II, §3 mandating that the president ensure that the nation's laws are "faithfully executed"), the statute has to defer to the Constitution. It is hornbook law dating back to Chief Justice Marshall's statement in *Marbury v. Madison*, 1 Cranch 137, 177–178 (1803), that "an act of the legislature, repugnant to the Constitution, is void; if both the law and the Constitution apply to a particular case . . . the Constitution . . . must govern the case to which they both apply." Any constitutional power granted the president can only be taken away, of course, by a constitutional amendment ratified by the legislatures of three-quarters of the states, not by mere congressional legislation. Therefore, it is axiomatic that insofar as the Posse Comitatus law attempts to restrict the president* (as opposed to any member of the military) in using the military to faithfully execute the law, even domestically, it is invalid because it is beyond the power of Congress.**

---

*Although a moot point due to the principle enunciated in *Marbury v. Madison*, it is not all that clear that it was even the definite intent of Congress in enacting the original Posse Comitatus statute that it apply to the president. Although there are exceptions (e.g., Senator Merrimon's remarks in 7 *Cong. Rec.* 4245), the legislative debate, in setting forth example after example of the military being utilized to enforce the law, almost invariably cited U.S. marshals and military commanders at various levels, not the president. Also, the very language of the original Posse Comitatus statute, 20 Stat. 152, Sec. 15 (1878), after providing that the Army cannot be used as a Posse Comitatus to execute the law, says that "any person" who violates the law shall be guilty of a misdemeanor. Although "any person" would, of course, include the president, when the reach of legislation is intended to include the highest office in the land, official protocol as well as simple logic would seem to demand that the president or his office (or names that are synonymous with him and his office, such as chief executive, executive branch, commander-in-chief of the armed forces, etc.) would be referred to by name. While the Posse Comitatus statute does mention the Army (and the president is its commander-in-chief), this would not seem to be adequate, since most acts ordered by lower commanders are those about which the president has no knowledge and gives no approval. Would a law intended to prohibit certain conduct by a city's chief of police and his department only mention the officers on the force, on the rationale that the chief is their leader, and prohibiting their conduct is the legal equivalent of prohibiting his? Further, the law of *respondeat superior* (the common law maxim that the master is responsible for the acts of the servant) only applies to civil, not criminal, matters, and the Posse Comitatus statute is a criminal statute.

**See also Judge Advocate General G. Norman Lieber, *The Use of the Army in Aid of the Civil Power*, pages 56 and 57 (1898): "If it be true that the Constitution directly vests the President with the duty [to take care that the laws be faithfully executed] it must follow that Congress cannot make the exercise of such power illegal."

Section 1385 expressly provides that the armed services can also be employed to execute the law by an "Act of Congress." In other words, there is nothing unyielding or sacrosanct about the Posse Comitatus law. The Coast Guard, a military service and branch of the armed forces of the United States (in time of war, or by presidential decree, the Coast Guard is under the direction of the U.S. Navy; all other times the service remains, as it is today, part of the Department of Transportation), has already been authorized by Congress to enforce federal laws and make arrests, searches, and seizures on the high seas (i.e., *outside* U.S. territorial waters) under §§2 and 89 of 14 U.S.C.* And in §379(a) of 10 U.S.C., Congress legislated that "the Secretary of Defense and the Secretary of Transportation shall provide that there be assigned on board every appropriate surface naval vessel at sea in a drug-interdiction area, members of the Coast Guard who are trained in law enforcement and have powers of the Coast Guard under title 14, including the power to make arrests and to carry out searches and seizures."

3. In the same vein, although the Posse Comitatus law is not an anachronistic relic devoid of any contemporary relevance, for the law to make any sense, Congress could (and should) enact an exception to it "in cases of national emergency," which the present drug crisis could qualify as being.

4. The president would not even have to dispatch the military to Colombia to arrest the indicted cartel leaders. He could send a large contingent of DEA and/or FBI agents, and the whole issue of Posse Comitatus would be avoided. Under §2291(c)(2) of 22 U.S.C., federal agents are not authorized in narcotics cases to "engage or participate in any direct police arrest action" in a foreign country *unless* "the Secretary of State, in consultation with the Attorney General," determines that to apply said prohibition "with respect to that foreign country would be harmful to the national interests of the U.S." With the secretary of state making the facilitating determination, DEA or FBI agents could be dispatched, then, by the president.** With 2,000

---

* See also *United States v. Chaparro-Almeida*, 679 F.2d 423, 425 (1982) and *Jackson v. State*, 572 P.2d 87, 93 (1977).

** In the event the secretary of state was recalcitrant on this issue, or the language "engage or participate" in an arrest is deemed to mean something less than "making" the arrest, Congress, which enacted §2291(c)(2), could simply amend it with new and clear language specifically authorizing foreign arrests by federal agents. A June 21, 1989, legal opinion (which does not have the force of law) by the Department of Justice titled "Authority of the FBI to Override Customary or Other International Law in the Course of Extraterritorial Law Enforcement Activities" is compatible. In that opinion, the department concluded that the FBI, without first obtaining the foreign country's consent, does have or so DEA and/or FBI agents after them in Colombia, the leaders of the Colombian cartels would be either rounded up and under arrest within weeks or on the run to the four corners of the globe. As we have seen, the U.S. Court of Appeals for the 9th Circuit has already held, in *U.S. v. Juan Ramon Matta-Ballesteros*, that such conduct by the U.S. Marshall's office, a companion federal agency to the DEA and FBI, was not unconstitutional.

Although not on all fours with the action herein suggested, related conduct by DEA agents in the *Verdugo-Urquidez* and *Alvarez-Machain* cases has, as indicated, been approved by the U.S. Supreme Court. If the Court did not invalidate the seizure of Dr. Machain when carried out by those acting at the behest of the DEA, the Court could be expected to rule that if DEA agents themselves made such a seizure, said abduction would also be upheld. Details are sketchy, but it is well known that the DEA, which has offices in Bogota and Baranquilla, already operates with a fair amount of autonomy in Colombia, and its agents not only provide intelligence, but accompany Colombian anti-narcotic agents on missions.

5. The Posse Comitatus law can also be completely circumvented by merely basing the military raid not on the president's duty to see that the laws of this country are faithfully executed, but on the same rationale that has motivated every other previous foreign military intervention absent a congressional declaration of war: to protect the general welfare and security of this nation. After all, former President Reagan, in a televised address to the nation on September 14, 1986, said, as have so many others, that the drug crisis was "killing America" and was a "threat to our national security." Congress concurs. In §4801 of the 1988 Anti-Drug Abuse Act, there is this language: "It is the sense of the Congress that, given the magnitude of the illicit drug problem and the threat it poses to the national security of the United States . . ." In September, 1989, Defense Secretary Dick Cheney termed the drug crisis a "direct threat to the sovereignty and security of our country." And President Bush, addressing the Veterans of Foreign Wars in March, 1989, said that drugs were

---

legal authority to apprehend fugitives from U.S. law in foreign countries and bring them to the United States for criminal prosecution. Upon learning about the legal opinion for the first time on October 13, 1989, Secretary of State James A. Baker III referred to it as "very narrow" and assured reporters that no FBI action in any foreign country would ever be carried out without a "full interagency discussion" of all foreign policy considerations. In 1980, the FBI wanted to enter the Bahamas to abduct fugitive financier Robert L. Vesco, but the Department of Justice advised against it, and the mission was never attempted.

"a threat [to this country] no less real than the adversaries you have battled" in the nation's declared wars.

And in President Clinton's message to Congress in 1995 at the start of his administration's National Drug Control Strategy report, he stated: "We cannot keep the American dream alive for working families if our youth are turning to illegal drug use or if the violence spawned by drug use and trafficking continues unabated. We cannot compete in the new world economy . . . while international drug trafficking is rampant. We cannot enter the new millennium as the strongest country in the world unless we . . . lead the way against illegal drugs and the terror they bring—both here at home and abroad."

In an October 22, 1995, address before the United Nations, President Clinton said: "These forces [drug traffickers] jeopardize the global trend toward peace and freedom, undermine fragile new democracies . . . and threaten our efforts to build a safer, more prosperous world." That same day he issued an executive order directing the freezing of any assets of Colombia's Cali cartel that are in the United States, and prohibiting American firms from doing any kind of business with the cartel's front organizations. The executive order was issued under the International Emergency Economic Powers Act, which empowers the president to take action such as this only where there is an "unusual and extraordinary threat to national security."

In other words, the cartels sending life-destroying cocaine to this country is no less a harm we have a right to defend ourselves against than if they were firing deadly rockets into our land, in which case no one would question our right, in self-defense, to use the military.*

One argument against Posse Comitatus that will inevitably be made by those in ivory towers is this: How would this nation like it if another nation sent its military here to capture fugitives legitimately sought by their country? Isn't this establishing a dangerous precedent? Such hypothetical and weightless obstacles, while Rome burns,

---

*The inherent right of the president to use military force in self-defense without congressional authorization was upheld in *The Prize Cases*, 67 U.S. (2 Black) 635 at p. 668 (1863), where the court said, "The President is not only authorized but bound to resist force by force. He does not initiate the war, but is bound to accept the challenge without waiting for any special legislative authority." With most of our foreign interventions without congressional sanction, such as in Grenada and Panama, the threat to our nation's security was remote, and therefore, the argument of self-defense was a weak one. Here, the massive and direct assault on this nation by Colombian cocaine has already taken place, and will continue to do so without far more forceful steps taken by us in self-defense.

are the lifeblood of those who reside in the rarefied and oxygen-lacking atmosphere of the ivory tower. In the first place, there is no comparable group of individuals in this country, nor is there ever apt to be, like the Colombian cartels, who are not only destroying another nation but are also sought by the authorities of that nation. And being the type of nation we are, if such a comparable situation did arise, we would almost assuredly extradite the American citizens to the requesting country, thereby eliminating the necessity of an incursion into this country by foreign agents to seize them.

Obviously, the military search and-find mission herein recommended should not be confused with a general policy of sending our military into another country to apprehend any fugitive from American justice, such as an American or a foreigner who robs an American bank and flees to a foreign nation. Such a policy would be not only impractical but, from a political and legal perspective, inadvisable. But here we are dealing with a situation entirely different. First, the crime committed is of unprecedented magnitude, causing the most severe internal crisis in this country since the Civil War. Second, the Colombian drug lords are not, like a fleeing bank robber, merely fugitives from justice for a single crime that has *already* been committed. They are criminals engaged in a *continuing criminal enterprise*. From their fugitive haven, they continue on a day-to-day basis to perpetrate their enormous crimes in America. Thus, in contrast to pursuing the fleeing bank robber, our action would be taken to defend ourselves. By analogy to the law of self-defense, one is authorized to use force if in reasonable fear of imminent harm. With the drug crisis, the harm is more than imminent. It's already here, and in the absence of bold action on the part of the American government, will persist indefinitely.

When we look at the propriety of a military raid in this case as opposed to previous presidential employment of military forces, the argument for a military search-and-find mission becomes even more irresistible. For instance, in North Korea and Vietnam, where we were resisting Communist expansionism, whatever the merits of our military intervention were, certain realities should be recognized: (1) The Communist aggression was thousands of miles from our shore; (2) the threat to us was indirect, speculative, and, if it were to occur at all (i.e., the spread of Communism to our shores), off in the distant future. As for the Colombian cocaine cartels, their enormous crimes are being committed not only right here in this country, but at this very moment.

We have spent literally trillions of dollars and lost thousands of lives in the past four and a half decades defending ourselves from the Communist threat. Although Mikhail Gorbachev made the Cold War obsolete with his shredding of Marx's catechism, *Das Kapital*, and the Cold War now appears to be behind us, our nation still has to be ever alert to developments in the former Soviet Union. But in almost half a century, not one single American died at the hands of a Communist *in this country;* moreover, is Communism the only threat to this country we should fight against? If we were willing to go to war at the price of thousands of American lives in far-off Korea and Vietnam to fight Communism (per the DoD—Korea: 33,746 killed, 103,284 wounded in action; Vietnam: 47,358 killed, 153,303 wounded in action), why not, for instance, conduct a simple military raid in Colombia, whose drug lords have caused incalculable harm to the lives of millions of our citizens—particularly when the mission would be swift, very inexpensive, and likely to succeed, probably without any loss of American blood?

The latter statement is viable because—unlike the large number of leftist guerrillas (*Sendero Luminoso*) who at one time protected the thousands of Peruvian *campesinos* from having their coca crops eradicated—only bodyguards protect the drug barons. And throughout the years, bodyguards have little history of armed resistance to government forces. With their small numbers, how could they accomplish anything even if they tried? Instead, the method of retaliation by the cartels, particularly that of the Medellin cartel, has been violence and acts of terrorism against members of Colombian society and institutions other than the pursuing forces. The record of those Colombian drug lords who have been arrested or eliminated provides the very best evidence imaginable for divining the consequences of our military intervention against the drug lords.

Drug chieftain Carlos Lehder was arrested by Colombian authorities at dawn on February 4, 1987, in Guarne, a small town outside Medellin. Although a startled bodyguard originally opened fire, the moment he saw the uniforms of the Colombian forces he dropped his weapon and unsuccessfully attempted to flee. Lehder and his fourteen bodyguards, none of whom fired a single shot in return, emerged from their two-story chalet and were placed under arrest. Fire *was* returned when on December 15, 1989, approximately 100 Colombian special forces troops sealed off and then advanced on a farm near the Caribbean town of Coveñas, the final refuge of drug lord Rodriguez Gacha. In the ensuing shootout, Gacha, his seventeen-year-old son Freddy (who had unwittingly led the pursuers to his father), and all five of Gacha's bodyguards were killed. No member of the special forces group was reported to have been killed or wounded.

The biggest drug lord of all, Pablo Escobar, went down shooting his pistol when he and his lone bodyguard were killed by Colombian police on December 7, 1993, in Medellin. No member of the elite police unit was harmed. When Gilberto Rodriguez, the co-leader of the Cali cartel along with his brother, Miguel, was captured in his apartment in Cali by Colombian anti-narcotic police on June 9, 1995, neither he nor his bodyguards fired a single round. "Don't kill me," Gilberto pleaded with the police, "I'm a man of peace." When his brother, Miguel, cartel leader Jose Santacruz-Londono, and several other Cali cartel leaders were arrested in the ensuing months, not one shot was fired by any of the cartel leaders or their bodyguards in resistance.

HISTORICAL PRECEDENTS

Since there is hefty precedent for presidents committing American forces on foreign soil without congressional approval, and inasmuch as there would be, in this particular case, a constitutional basis for our Colombian intervention, no historical precedent is needed for the proposed search-and-find mission. But for those who would feel more comfortable if there were, apart from the very different factual situation that induced it, there *is* a remarkably close parallel in American history. Most of the similarities will be too obvious to point out.

In 1915 and 1916, Mexican bandits from the states of Sonora, Chihuahua, Coahuila, Nuevo Leon, and Tamaulipas were crossing the Mexican-American border in Arizona, New Mexico, and Texas and plundering American border towns. The United States did not retaliate until the Mexican revolutionary, Pancho Villa, personally led several hundred men in the attack of an American garrison at Columbus, New Mexico, in the early-morning hours of March 9, 1916. Although twenty-three *Villistas* were killed, seven Americans were also killed, in addition to many injured.

On March 16, 1916, President Wilson (without congressional approval, natch) sent cavalry, infantry, and artillery, under the command of Gen. John J. Pershing, across the border to capture Villa and bring him back to the United States for trial on murder charges. This was at the height of the Mexican Civil War (1910–1921), and the Mexican government formally protested the unauthorized invasion of Mexican territory (denominated a "punitive expedition" by the American government), asking that the U.S. government "withdraw its forces from our territory." Wilson refused, responding that the expedition had "the single purpose of taking the bandit Villa, whose forces invaded the territory of the U.S., and is in no sense intended as an invasion of the republic [of Mexico], or as an infringement of its sovereignty." Wilson promised to "retire from Mexican territory as soon as our object is accomplished." (The fact that the Colombian drug lords have not themselves crossed the American border to commit their crimes, as the *Villistas* did, is legally immaterial. The U.S. indictments against them affirm this fact. Since confederates of the cartel have crossed the border at the cartel's direction and committed the state and federal crimes of trafficking in cocaine, under the law of conspiracy the cartel leaders are criminally responsible for these crimes.)

Heated diplomatic exchanges followed, during which the U.S. government stated that the underlying rationale for the expedition was to *defend* its frontier against future incursions. (Tell the U.S. Customs, Coast Guard, and U.S. Border Patrol that they haven't been trying to do this precise thing with respect to narcotics on a day-to-day basis.) As then–U.S. Secretary of State Robert Lansing articulated the self-defense theory, one that has precise applicability to our nation's current crisis: "The most effective method of preventing raids of this nature is to visit punishment on the raiders. If the Mexican government is unwilling *or unable* [shades of Colombia] to give this protection by preventing its country from being the rendezvous and refuge of murderers and plunderers, that does not relieve this government from its *duty* to take all steps necessary to safeguard American citizens on American soil."

The American forces, from their border-crossing point near Palomas, Mexico, first penetrated down to Nueva Casas Grandes, 95 miles from the international line, and eventually as deep into the interior as Hidalgo del Parral, over 450 miles south of the border. There the pursuit was halted several months after its inception by the hostility (some of which resulted in bloodshed) of Mexican civilians who aligned themselves on the side of the folk hero Villa, becoming, in effect, protectors of Villa and his band, who escaped into the vast expanse of central Mexico.

Unless one wants to argue that different rules in the enforcement of the law apply to murder as opposed to trafficking in cocaine (they do not), Wilson's "punitive expedition" in 1916 bears an uncanny resemblance to any "search-and-find mission" (or why not give it the same name as the 1916 intervention?) our nation should now employ in Colombia.

Parenthetically, Colombia clearly would not be as inhospitable as Mexico. Although Escobar, for instance, may have been a hero in the 550-unit Barrio Escobar, the Colombian mafia not only does not enjoy the passionate idolatry of the masses that Villa did, but, to the contrary, are scorned by the vast majority of Colombians.

Our full-fledged invasions of Grenada and Panama, and our instituting war in the Persian Gulf, speak even more loudly for the propriety of a military raid in Colombia.

On October 25, 1983, approximately 6,000 American military troops invaded the island of Grenada. The ostensible purpose of the invasion was to protect the lives of 1,000 Americans in Grenada, 700 of whom were medical students allegedly in danger because of a left-wing military coup that had just taken place on the island by Cuban-backed revolutionaries. The Reagan Administration's declared purpose was perceived by most to be a pretext. Not only had no American been hurt, but the new left-wing regime had assured the United States the day before the invasion that Americans on the island were in no danger and were free to leave if they wished. This only made sense. Since when has any Communist nation, not at war with us, rounded up American citizens and killed or harmed them? That a mongrel group of Marxist revolutionaries on a pebble of an island would choose to do so, for no reason other than to assure their own annihilation, is nonsensical. As the *New Republic* noted: "Medical students in the Bronx have more to fear." The obvious purpose of the Grenada invasion was to prevent further Cuban-Soviet expansionism, even on a very runty scale, in the Western Hemisphere.

But whatever the motive—be it to protect the students, the administration's need for positive public relations just two days after the slaughter of 229 Marines in Beirut (a convenient explanation but unlikely, since invasion plans preceded the Beirut tragedy), or to repel the growth of Communism—the justification of a full-fledged military invasion of Grenada, a nation that not more than one out of a thousand Americans could even point to on a map, couldn't possibly begin to even remotely approach the justification for a very limited military raid in Colombia to search, find, and arrest a handful of drug thugs whose illicit business has caused enormous and dreadful harm to our nation as a whole, and to millions of Americans individually.

To separate Grenada from Colombia by even more light-years, as opposed to the explicit constitutional authority for sending military forces to Colombia, not only was Grenada yet another example of the use of military force by an American president without congressional approval, but arguably it was even an unlawful act. The United States and Grenada are both members of the Organization of American States (OAS), the charter of which prohibits intervention by member signatory nations in one another's internal affairs.

Despite this, a *Newsweek* poll after the invasion showed that 53 percent of Americans approved of the invasion, 34 percent disapproved. Can there be any doubt that a much higher percentage of Americans would approve of a military raid in Colombia?

What about the response of the international community? With the invasion of Grenada, even the conservative government of Margaret Thatcher registered its disapproval, as did France, Italy, and West Germany. Russia and Cuba, of course, were even more high-pitched in their denunciation. And predictably, the United Nations issued a resolution deploring the U.S. action, our country casting the only negative vote. But today, all of this is long forgotten. In fact, one day after the invasion one would have been hard-pressed to detect any discernible change for the worse in our relationship with other nations, even though the Grenada invasion was very possibly not only an unlawful act but also brittle in its moral underpinnings. If this was the world community's reaction to Grenada, it seems safe to assume we have absolutely nothing to fear by militarily pursuing drug lords in Colombia or whatever other nations from which narco-traffickers are exporting their deadly poison to our shores.

With respect to the Panamanian incursion (also a violation of the OAS charter), Abraham F. Lowenthal, professor of international relations at the University of Southern California and executive director of InterAmerican Dialogue, has pointed out that the various reasons advanced by the White House to justify the U.S. military intervention "really all boil down to one—the determination to remove Noriega from office." But there is no lawful justification for this nation to invade another nation's borders for the purpose of removing a hostile regime and imposing democracy. If such were the case, and if we were so inclined, over the past several decades alone our nation would have been in a continual state of armed conflict. Just as important, although the gringo-hating, tinpot dictator of Panama had become, as previously noted, an embarrassing thorn in the side of the Bush Administration, in no way did Panama pose any type of threat to this nation, nor were any of our citizens (certainly here, and even in Panama) in any physical jeopardy from Noriega's regime.

As *Newsweek* noted, all of the official reasons for the invasion set forth by the Bush Administration "rang hollow." *Protecting the lives of Americans?* Only one American Marine had been killed, and that was in an isolated, situational context. *Protecting the integrity of the Panama Canal?* Is there any tangible evidence that it was ever in jeopardy? Or even threatened? If so, and without resorting to sophistry, how? *Noriega's "declaration of war" against the United States?* One would think the Bush Administration would have been ashamed to list this as one of the justifications for the invasion. Not that it makes any difference, but the White House language was a bit more inflammatory than what Noriega said. He declared that American provocation had created a "state of war" between the two countries. *Seize Noriega so he could stand trial on drug charges?* (See earlier discussion.)

Yet despite this, and even though twenty-three young American soldiers lost their lives (324 were wounded) in the invasion, a Gallup poll conducted for *Newsweek* on December 21, 1989, showed that an astonishing 80 percent of Americans approved of the invasion and only 13 percent opposed it.

While the United Nations General Assembly denounced the invasion, unlike Grenada, the international community hardly condemned it. Margaret Thatcher, in fact, applauded the invasion. "Someone has to uphold democracy," she said. Although virtually every Latin American country condemned the "violation of the principle of nonintervention," with the exception of Peruvian President Alan Garcia, who called the invasion a "criminal act," the denunciations were mild. Even the thirty-two-member OAS only "deeply regretted" but did not explicitly condemn it.

With this as an indicator, it would seem very clear that a search-and-find mission to seize the Colombian drug lords, where we *would* have all the moral and legal justification we would need, and where the likelihood of the loss of American blood would be vastly diminished (we faced 15,000 Panamanian soldiers in Panama, as opposed to the mere bodyguards of the drug lords), would meet with the approval of the American people.

Who, in fact, would really complain if a solar-plexus blow were delivered to the drug enemy in Colombia? Not even the old Communist refrain of American imperialism could be made, because on its very face, no effort would be made by such a raid to extend American influence and hegemony in Latin American. After we rounded up the kingpins, as President Wilson told the government of Mexico, we would immediately depart the country. Of course, some groups, who would complain if they were hung with a new rope, will inevitably protest, setting fire to the American flag in hard-to-pronounce places like Tegucigalpa, Honduras. But if our mental hide is not strong enough to withstand such protests, then perhaps we really do not want to solve the drug problem after all. As must be repeated, *either we are serious about solving the problem, or we are not.*

In determining, by way of comparative reference to Panama, the wisdom and propriety of a search-and-find mission in Colombia, one key and pivotal point has to be explored in depth.

President Bush stated that Panama was "unique" because of the risk to American lives there. But even a cursory examination of the facts reveals that no such risk existed, nor did the president seriously believe it did. The contextual background is that on the evening of December 16, 1989, in the El Chorrillo neighborhood of Panama City near Panama Defense Forces (PDF) headquarters, four off-duty U.S. officers wearing civilian clothes got lost as they were driving in a private car to a restaurant in downtown Panama City. When the car was stopped at a PDF checkpoint, an argument ensued, whereupon a PDF soldier unsuccessfully attempted to pull one of the Americans out of the car. When the car screeched away, PDF soldiers opened fire, killing Marine 1st Lt. Robert Paz. A U.S. Navy lieutenant who witnessed the shooting was beaten and his wife sexually threatened by PDF soldiers that same night.

The very day after the killing of officer Paz, President Bush made the decision to invade Panama, citing the killing of Paz and the mal-treatment of the Navy lieutenant and his wife as the triggering factor. Bush, who had previously ruled out the use of military force to assist rebel Panamanian soliders in their October 6, 1989, attempted coup against Noriega, said that the El Chorrillo incident "is what changed my mind" about the use of military force in Panama. Because of the incident, Bush said, "our people down there felt that they *didn't know* where this was going and they *weren't sure* what all of this meant and whether we could guarantee the safety of Americans there. And so I made a decision to move with enough force that we minimized the loss of life." Apart from the fact that only one American life had been lost—and *that* one in an obviously spontaneous and situational circumstance (since when does this nation, or even a dictatorial one, massively invade another nation on such a pretext? We never even retaliated militarily when 229 marines were murdered in Lebanon)—and the president had to know that many more additional American lives would be lost in the invasion, we know from the president's own lips ("read my lips") that even his advisers in Panama did *not* tell him there was *a clear and present danger* to the 35,000 Americans living in Panama. They told him they *"didn't know* where this was going, and they *weren't sure* what all of this meant. . . ." You would find more Protestants in the Vatican's College of Cardinals than you could have found observers from the Bush Administration who seriously believed that Noriega would have ordered the murder or even incarceration of Americans living in Panama. Although the bellicose Panamanian gangster was full of hubris and ended up inching too far in his flirtation with danger, there's no reason to believe he would ever have done something he categorically knew would cause swift American military retaliation.

The important point to be made is this: Even if we assume that which we know is most assuredly not true—that the lives of 35,000 Americans living in Panama were endangered—and if we accept the president's word that the well-being of these 35,000 Americans was what caused him to change his mind about the use of military force, does it not necessarily follow that he should be much more willing to use military force against the drug lords of Colombia whose cocaine blitz of America has not only endangered but also destroyed, and is continuing to this moment to destroy, the lives of *millions* of Americans? Unless the lives of Americans living *outside* the United States are somehow mysteriously worth much more than those living within our borders, what conceivable rationale can there be for protecting the lives of the former but not the latter? Even if we were to completely ignore the thousands upon thousands of drug-related robberies, burglaries, and murders that have occurred and will continue to occur in this country, as well as all the other countless horrors of the drug crisis gutting and devastating the lives of millions of *adult* Americans, was the well-being of those 35,000 Americans more important than the well-being of 225,000 innocent and helpless infants born annually with cocaine-induced physical defects such as deformed and defective limbs, hearts, and lungs? If commonsense and reason are to govern the conduct of our nation's leadership, there can be only one answer to that question.

When President Bush was asked at a December 21, 1989, news conference "if it was really worth it to send young Americans to their death" simply to overthrow Noriega, he replied, "Every human life is precious, and yet I have to answer, yes, it was worth it."

If the lives of twenty-three Americans were worth sacrificing to overthrow a vile little dictator who represented only embarrassment and irritation, but no threat to this nation's security, and who, for most of his criminally checkered career was on this nation's payroll, * why wouldn't a search-and-find mission to Colombia (where, as indicated, the loss of American life could be expected to be minimal, or nonexistent) to help eliminate this nation's drug crisis be, in President Bush's words, "worth it"?

Because the dimensions and consequences of the war against Iraq are so much greater than in either Grenada or Panama, a more thorough discussion of that war is called for.

One point has to be made as a prefatory observation. The wisdom of our decision to go to war in the Persian Gulf cannot be judged by hindsight—we succeeded in getting Iraq out of Kuwait with a small loss of American life. We have to examine our state of mind going in to the conflict. And going in, although the Department of Defense declined to issue an official estimate, word leaked out of the Pentagon to the media from several independent sources that 50,000 American casualties could be expected. And per *Time* magazine, Air Force computers projected "that as many as 150 planes would be lost the first night." CBS News learned that 40,000 body bags had been ordered by the Department of Defense. When Gen. H. Norman Schwarzkopf, commander of American troops in the Gulf, said, "We certainly didn't expect it to go this way," and chose the extreme adjective "miraculous" to describe our minimal loss of life in the Gulf War, he was merely confirming the prewar expectation that American casualties would be much, much higher. Therefore, any objective evaluation of this nation's decision to go to war logically has to deal with the 50,000-casualty figure, a horrendous price to pay for our discernible motivations in the Gulf.

By rough analogy, to judge the Bush Administration by the final

---

*In papers filed on January 18, 1991, in federal court in Miami by the U.S. Attorney's office, it was revealed that the CIA and U.S. Army paid Noriega $322,166 from 1955 through 1986. Most of the CIA money to Noriega was in monthly payments from 1971 through 1986. The payments included a period in the mid-1970s, when President Bush was the CIA director.

result rather than by its belief and intention going in to the conflict would be like exonerating one who shoots to kill if the bullet misses the victim. With that type of extravagant reasoning, if the bullet goes on and accidentally strikes down a third party who is about to kill another, perhaps the gunman should ultimately be viewed as a hero. Americans have to ask themselves how they would now feel if Iraq had been forced out of Kuwait only after great numbers of American youth returned to our shores in body bags. Since it is not even in dispute that the Bush Administration was willing to sacrifice thousands of American lives to expel Iraq from Kuwait ("No price is too heavy to pay" to force Iraq out of Kuwait, President Bush said on January 2, 1991), everything that follows is written pursuant to that high and terrible standard of risk.

The first reason cited by President Bush in August of 1990 for our presence in the Persian Gulf was economic; a "wholly defensive" action, he said, to prevent Iraq from invading and conquering Saudi Arabia. Together with Kuwait, Iraq would then control, the president pointed out, a significant portion of the world's oil reserves. Although the president also spoke of Iraq's "naked aggression," this denunciation was not made in the context of the aggression, per se, being our reason for sending troops to the Gulf, but in the context of the aggression threatening our supply of oil. Thus, on August 15, 1990, the president said, "Our way of life will suffer if control of the world's great oil reserves falls into the hands of Saddam." At an August 23 news conference, he said, "We're doing everything we can to guarantee that there will be an adequate supply of hydrocarbons [oil]." What the president was really saying was that, if necessary, he was willing to sacrifice thousands of American lives and go to war to keep oil prices low and the U.S. standard of living high. This remained his position even after the threat to Saudi Arabia ceased and only Kuwait remained an issue.

But how much of a threat to this nation's oil supply really existed? According to the *United States Department of Energy Oil and Gas Journal*, Kuwait accounts for only 5 percent of the world's production (not reserves) of oil. Even when we add Iraq (7 percent), oil experts found no cause for alarm. In a mid-November report, the Energy Department found that the loss of oil from Iraq and Kuwait "should be fully offset by surge production in other countries." (Despite the virtual shutdown of Iraqi and Kuwaiti oil production, by the end of the war in late February, 1991, OPEC was actually producing more oil than before the war commenced, and a barrel of oil was selling for

$22, virtually the same price as before the war.) Former Energy Secretary James Schlesinger noted at Senate hearings in late November that the world's oil market "has now been brought into balance without Iraqi/Kuwaiti crude." John Easton, assistant secretary of energy for international affairs and energy emergencies, said, "Do you go in to liberate Kuwait simply to free lost oil? The answer is no, it has been made up." The *Los Angeles Times* said it was a "simple truth" that "the Western world has all the oil it needs today and will have plenty for the foreseeable future, even without supplies from either Kuwait or Iraq."

The bottom line on all of this is that even completely losing Iraqi and Kuwaiti oil (a situation that never would have existed, regardless of the outcome of the crisis, since Iraq sold us oil before annexing Kuwait and would obviously want to continue to do so) would not drive the price of gasoline to the American consumer up much at all. For instance, since the Persian Gulf War, despite the absence of Iraqi oil from international markets, oil prices have remained low. At the time Iraq invaded Kuwait on August 2, 1990, according to the American Automobile Association the average cost of a gallon of gasoline in America was $1.07. During the height of the crisis in late December it rose to $1.28, an increase of only $0.21 per gallon (in Italy, a gallon of gasoline at the time was $4.58). Political commentator William Winters said in August that "our President sends up to 100,000 troops [later increased], an armada of ships and planes, at a cost of billions of much-needed dollars, to keep our gas prices from going up another 10 or 15¢ a gallon. Is that what our troops are to die for?"

When it was clear from polls, however, that Americans were opposed to waging war for such a crass economic reason as oil (e.g., a September 3, 1990, *Time* magazine poll showed only 30 percent of Americans approved of war in the Gulf to defend U.S. oil interests; "Our troops took an oath to defend our country and uphold the Constitution, but they didn't take an oath to keep gasoline at $1.29 a gallon," said Judy Davenport, whose husband was stationed in the Gulf), the president proved to be as flexible as a rubber band. Remarkably, on October 16, he now said, *"The fight isn't about oil. What we're doing is standing up against naked aggression."* Thereafter, when the subject of oil was brought up by others, the president's stock response was that Hussein could use oil in Kuwait "to finance further aggressions." In other words, keeping the price of oil down was no longer mentioned as an independent justification for our military presence in the Gulf.

But jettisoning the oil rationale and relying exclusively on resisting naked aggression didn't turn out to be too palatable, either. Polls continued to show that the majority of Americans were still opposed to war in the Gulf. Even conservative columnist Patrick J. Buchanan pointed out that if we were in the Gulf to oppose aggression, where were we at the time of "Indonesia's rape of East Timor, China's move into Tibet, Moscow's lunge into Afghanistan?" (Buchanan could have added, among others, Turkey's invasion of Cyprus.) "Why is this," Buchanan asked, "our war to fight? The 82nd Airborne ought not to have to die to restore to its throne a Sabah royal family whose own soldiers ran away rather than fight for it."[*]

Buchanan added that, unlike Israel, Kuwait wasn't a democracy and wasn't even an ally of ours. Why, said Daniel Patrick Moynihan (D–N.Y.), former ambassador to the United Nations, should we send "American men and women into battle" for the rich Kuwaitis sitting in the Sheraton Hotel in Taif, "drinking coffee and urging us to war? I remember Kuwait at the United Nations as a particularly poisonous enemy of the United States. One can be an antagonist of the United States in a way that leaves room for further discussion afterwards, but Kuwaitis were singularly nasty. And their anti-Semitism was at the level of the personally loathsome."

In a later column Buchanan perceptively wrote: "For 40 years, the United States has kept its ground forces out of the bloody conflicts of the Middle East, even though, in those 40 years, we saw allied regimes overthrown in Iraq, Libya, Ethiopia, and Iran, Israel fight six wars, and OPEC run up the price of oil from $3.00 a barrel in 1970 to $40.00 a barrel in 1979." Buchanan argued that if "none of these disasters" was sufficient cause to justify our military involvement, "how does Iraq's occupation of tiny Kuwait? Answer: It does not."

Indeed, bloody wars have been fought over land in the Middle East since biblical times. From our nation's inception over two centuries ago, we have always stayed out of them, and have never suffered for it. The Bush Administration decided to involve our nation and start

---

[*]Another conservative, Ted Galen Carpenter, director of foreign policy studies at the right-leaning Cato Institute, said that only direct threats to America's physical survival or democratic freedoms justify the use of force. "Making the U.S. the guardian of global stability is a blueprint for the indefinite prolongation of expensive and risky U.S. military commitments around the world." And the late Texas Governor John Connally said at the time that we should not shed the blood of young Americans fighting "in a distant land over a dispute of long-standing, in which we've not been involved, for a product which we could obtain elsewhere."

shedding American blood for the first time in this region of the world, a region where war and aggression have always been a staple of existence.*

Polls showed that most Americans were supportive of the president's efforts to get Iraq out of Kuwait, such as by an embargo and other economic sanctions. But not war. Certainly not after Vietnam.

A truckload of soldiers in Saudi Arabia, spotting reporters, shouted: "Why are we over here? This ain't our war. Send us home." There was an unmistakable sense in the country that we should not sacrifice American blood to rectify the never-ending litany of wrongs and aggressions committed by one nation against another throughout the world. In other words, we do not raise our children to die fighting other nation's wars when those conflicts don't threaten our national security. Although the domino theory may have been unreasonably applied as a basis for our intervention in Korea and Vietnam—and if so, our involvement in both wars was wrong—at least our motivation for those wars was to fight Communism, at the time a real threat to the United States and the entire free world. But Iraq? As the expression goes, "C'mon, give me a break."

Right in the midst of the president's declarations that we were in the Persian Gulf to resist aggression, not to protect our supply of oil, on November 13, 1990, Secretary of State James Baker in effect said that what the president was telling the American people was untrue. Why were we in the Persian Gulf? "If you want to sum it up in one word, it's jobs," Baker declared. If Hussein controlled too much of the world's oil, Baker reasoned, this would cause an economic recession that would "result in the loss of jobs for American citizens." This was a direct contradiction of the president's announced motivations from someone who was not only the nation's secretary of state but, we are told, the president's best friend, who spoke to him during this period up to twelve times a day. Can we not assume that under the circumstances he would know what the president's true motivations were? Should we really believe that the president wasn't leveling with his own secretary of state?

But the president, publicly ignoring the candid acknowledgment of his secretary of state, continued to proclaim that "naked aggression" was the reason for our presence in the Gulf. In speech after speech,

---

*When it came to the only thing that really counted in the Persian Gulf War, soldiers risking their lives, by anyone's arithmetic this was essentially an American war. Though there were twenty-eight nations in the anti-Iraq coalition, the United States alone had over five times as many troops in the Gulf as all twenty-seven other nations put together.

he made no mention, not a word, about the only reason we were there—oil. If Kuwait had not been a nation with huge oil reserves, does anyone actually believe that we would have been there?

Although the president's "naked aggression" argument met with less disapproval from the American public than keeping the price of oil down, polls continued to show that the majority of Americans were still opposed to war in the Gulf.

The president, scrambling desperately for a rationale for the war that the American public would accept, thought he finally found it in Iraq's supposed potential for launching a nuclear attack. But this fear didn't ring true. As the *New York Times* editorialized on December 2, 1990, "Four months ago, the Bush Administration insisted that Iraq's nuclear program posed no imminent danger, but in an *ex post facto* judgment, after surveys showed that Americans view a nuclear threat as the only plausible reason for war,* the White House began sounding nuclear alarms." On Thanksgiving day, the president unblushingly announced to troops in Saudi Arabia the new principal reason for war in the Gulf: "Every day that passes puts Saddam Hussein one step closer to realizing his goal of a nuclear weapons arsenal." Thus, the president said, "Our mission is marked by a real sense of urgency."

But this time it was the experts who pointed out the weightlessness of the president's assertion. "The Iraqi bomb is a red herring," said Richard Rhodes, author of the Pulitzer Prize-winning *The Making of the Atomic Bomb*. "Expert estimates put Iraqi acquisition of a limited nuclear arsenal at least ten years away." Caspar W. Weinberger, secretary of state during most of the Reagan Administration and a supporter of the president in the Gulf, said Iraq was "some years away from developing nuclear weapons." As was revealed for the first time in 1995 by the United Nations inspection team monitoring the destruction of Baghdad's weapons of mass destruction, in August of 1990, Iraq, in fact, did embark on a crash program to produce a nuclear bomb. But when President Bush, without actual knowledge of this fact, spoke of Hussein's goal of a nuclear weapon's arsenal, even his own secretary of defense at the time, Dick Cheney, felt con-

*A November 18, 1990, *Los Angeles Times* national poll showed that 34 percent of Americans believed that Iraq's potential for launching a nuclear attack would be enough to justify a major war. "That level of support," the *Times* said, "was far higher than the support offered for most of the Administration's other proposed rationales. For example, only 18 percent of those polled thought that restoring the government of Kuwait to power is worth fighting a major war."

strained to concede that if Iraq developed a nuclear device in the foreseeable future, it would be crude. "It wouldn't be anything you could deliver from an airplane. It wouldn't be anything that would be weaponized." Bush's own nuclear experts also put Iraq's acquisition of a nuclear capacity five years away.

Moreover, even assuming Hussein were a short way from possessing a nuclear capacity, if the nuclear deterrent was effective during the entire forty-five-year, postwar period against far more powerful nations than Iraq, why would Hussein, a sandbox dictator, initiate a nuclear attack when he would know that the much more lethal nuclear response from nations like the United States and Israel would immediately destroy him and his country? Last anyone heard, Hussein wanted to continue living, at least for a while.

We know now that our threat of retaliation with far less than nuclear weapons was a deterrent to Hussein. Rolf Ekens, the Swedish diplomat who is the leader of the United Nations inspection team in Iraq, told reporters on August 25, 1995, that the Iraqi officials had admitted that within days of the U.N. Security Council resolution in December, 1990, authorizing the United States to wage war against Iraq, the Iraqi government loaded the deadly chemicals anthrax and botulin (according to the U.S. Congressional Office of Technology Assessment, inhalation of even a minute trace of botulin causes death in 80 percent of people within three days) on nearly 200 bombs and warheads. But threats by President Bush and Secretary of State James Baker to hit Iraq with enormous retaliatory bombings if Iraq employed chemical, biological weapons caused Hussein, the Iraqis told the U.N. inspectors, not to use them.

Hussein Kamel, Saddam Hussein's cousin and son-in-law, who fled Iraq in August of 1995, and who had overseen Iraq's program to develop weapons of mass destruction, told *Time* magazine in September, 1995, that (as common sense would tell anyone anyway) the reason Iraq never used "unconventional" weapons during the Persian Gulf War is that to do so would have caused "the major powers to use nuclear weapons, which means Iraq would have been exterminated."

Throughout the prewar period, President Bush continued to search unsuccessfully for one clear articulation and goal he could give the American people for taking the nation to war. Virtually everyone, including Bush supporters and apologists, as well as newspaper editorial after editorial, opined that Bush hadn't yet offered a clear explanation as to why we should go to war in the Gulf. "It's not clear to my constituents why we're there, why our soldiers are over there," said Sen. Richard Lugar (R–Ind.). In a CNN interview on November 20, 1990, the president himself conceded that he hadn't "done as clear a job as I might have" in explaining to the American people why we were on the verge of war in the Gulf.

But if the president couldn't come up with a clear, transcendent goal or justification, *Time* magazine did it for him. *Time* resurrected for Bush and, it seems, reminded him, of an articulation National Security Adviser Brent Scowcroft had come up with that the president used, among others, in his September address to Congress. In his harried buckshot approach to find a justification for the war he thought the American public would buy (other than the real reason, oil), the president had apparently forgotten the notion of a "new world order."

Time magazine reported in its January 7, 1991, edition that President Bush (the man about whom critics had always said, and even supporters had acknowledged, had "no vision") had "raised a vision of a new world order. In it, the United States and the Soviet Union would cooperate to maintain peace and order" in the world. *Time* neglected to note that on November 11, 1990, the Soviet Union had already gone on record proclaiming that it would not lift one military finger to help out in the Gulf. Then–Soviet Foreign Minister Eduard Shevardnadze asserted the Soviet Union would never send Soviet troops to fight in the Persian Gulf over the Kuwait problem. "I can tell you that this option is not under consideration. This option is nonexistent," he said. And on December 4, 1990, Soviet Foreign Ministry spokesman Vitaly Churkin concurred: "The Soviet Union does not have any plans to use its forces in the Gulf."*

In any event, from *Time*'s January 7, 1991, edition on, all ambiguity about the reasons for our presence in the Gulf vanished like a breath upon a mirror. In virtually every public speech thereafter, President Bush spoke of the "new world order" as being the justification for war in the Gulf. If one read Bush's lips, the word *oil* was never used, not even once. It had become a verbal leper, and the nation quickly and obligingly forgot all the previous reasons the pres-

---

*One wonders at what point in time *Time* magazine learned that the reason for the Bush Administration's military involvement in the Persian Gulf was to implement a "new world order"? A full month after our presence in the Gulf, *Time* wrote that "The nation will not long sustain an enterprise whose *only object* is to keep Americans in the wasteful, oil-guzzling style to which they have become accustomed." In fact, as late as November 26, 1990, *Time* wrote that "the President would be well advised to clarify his goals" in the Persian Gulf.

ident had given for the war. The "new world order" of keeping peace in the world sounded good to the ears and smacked of high national purpose.

The Bush Administration tied in the whole notion of a "new world order" not just with the limited objective of reversing Iraq's forced annexation of Kuwait, but with the Neville Chamberlain-Munich appeasement analogy of "peace in our time"; i.e., if we don't stop Hussein now, he'll end up another Hitler. That is, we let Hitler get away with seizing Czechoslovakia, and look what happened. But as Michael Jochum, a research fellow in international relations at Harvard University observed, the analogy is a false one. "Did the world impose economic sanctions on Germany in 1938? Did it send 150,000 troops [as we did to Saudi Arabia] to Poland?" he asks rhetorically. Further, if Hussein posed such a serious tyrannical threat in the future, why didn't the Soviet Union, Japan, and Germany, three nations which, unlike the United States, suffered greatly from tyranny through the years, see the threat? If they did, why weren't they, not the United States, the motive force behind the coalition to stop Hussein? And why didn't any one of them even send one troop to stop this incipient Hitler?*

If Hussein posed such a threat, why didn't Bush and President Reagan see this threat when Hussein invaded Iran in 1980?** If Hussein now posed such a threat, why didn't Bush's own generals and advisers see it? Referring to the very first session of the National Security Council that Bush called on August 2, 1990, over Iraq's invasion of Kuwait, *Time* magazine reported: "At that session, once reporters had been herded out and fresh coffee had been poured, *the atmosphere was relaxed* and matter-of-fact. One by one Bush's top generals and diplomats, spy masters, and energy experts reeled off their analyses. The prevailing attitude among the group, recalled one White House official, was 'Hey, too bad about Kuwait, but it's just a gas station, and who cares whether the sign says SINCLAIR or EXXON.'

---

*Many legal scholars feel that open-to-interpretation language in Germany's and Japan's postwar constitutions would not have prevented them from sending troops if they were so inclined. Italy, for instance, with a more restricted constitution, managed to send a few troops.

**In 1980, of course, this nation was engaged in a bitter struggle of our own with Iran, and we easily embraced the Middle East tenet that "the enemy of my enemy is my friend," actually supporting Hussein by selling him critical arms to fight the Iranians. The fact that Hussein's criminal regime was on the State Department's list of sponsors of international terrorism, which thereby precluded the sale of arms to him, presented no obstacle. We simply removed Iraq from the list.

There was little sense that big U.S. interests were at stake." It was President Bush, *Time* reported, who turned the tone and attitude of the session around by deciding that our military intervention was called for. How did it happen that the man reputed to have no "vision" was the only one who saw and alerted the world that we were dealing with a potential Hitler?*

To compare the admittedly satanic Hussein with Hitler, as the president frequently did, is, of course, simply ludicrous. Hitler's Germany was a powerful, highly industrialized nation of 80 million people. Hitler dreamed of world conquest, and indeed it took several years and the combined might of the United States, Russia, and Britain to bring Germany to its knees. Iraq is a relatively backward, Third World country of only 17 million people, with a Gross National Product 1 percent that of the United States; a nation that, in eight years of fighting with Iran, a hopelessly factious and disorganized country, could barely hold its own. To compare Hussein and Iraq with Hitler and Germany shows contempt for the intelligence of the listener. As the *Los Angeles Times* editorialized on November 11, 1990, "The Saddam Hussein-as-Hitler analogy that Bush [keeps] invoking has never been convincing, only embarrassing. The Iraqi dictator is a regional menace, not a threat to civilized life on the planet." Moreover, if, in fact, Hussein ever showed unequivocal signs of becoming, like Hitler, a threat to world peace (a situation that seems quite impossible to contemplate), our overwhelming military power is such that we could have stopped him before he even came close to posing such a threat. But to have been willing to lose a great number of young American lives (let's not forget the 50,000-casualty estimate) on the speculation that Hussein intended, and had the capacity to become, a Mideast Hitler who could threaten the security of the entire world, seems inherently irrational. Dwight D. Eisenhower, who perhaps knew a little bit more about war than President Bush, said: "When people speak about a preventive war, tell *them* to go and fight it."

It has to be added that in divining Hussein's intentions for unbridled Lebensraum, here's someone who engaged in a terribly bloody war with Iran, only to inexplicably give Iran back all of the land his forces had seized. And perhaps not too much future adventurism should have been read into his annexation of Kuwait, which borders Iraq. President Bush's description of it as "naked" aggression was

---

*Although former British Prime Minister Margaret Thatcher was a hawk from the beginning in the Gulf, even she did not see or refer to Hussein in Hitlerian terms.

accurate, but it didn't tell the whole story. Although Hussein is a ruthless tyrant (as a great number of other foreign leaders whom we have supported throughout the years have been), this time the emperor may have at least been wearing socks. When Hussein proclaimed and insisted that Kuwait has always been a part of Iraq—Iraq's "19th province"—he was not speaking with a completely intoxicated mind. Prior Iraqi rulers have also considered Kuwait a province—even after Great Britain, during its colonialist period, made Kuwait a protectorate in 1914. As recently as June of 1961, the Iraqi prime minister claimed that Kuwait belonged to Iraq, and Iraq was only deterred from invasion when Britain sent military aid to Kuwait.

Although millions of Americans eventually got caught up in a seductive riptide of patriotism over their government's decision to go to war, most polls showed a slight majority actually favoring continuing sanctions over war.* Congress, though deeply divided,** authorized war on January 12, 1991. The *New York Times* said that an analysis of the road to war shows that President Bush overcame the fact that "this was a conflict *no one wanted* at the outset." Through the power of the presidency and, as we have seen, by relying on whatever would sell in Peoria, the president gradually brought a reluctant nation and many foreign nations aboard. In a modern version of *Pax Romana,* everyone went along, which is what people and nations normally do when the person they are going along with is the President of the United States, the most powerful man on the face of the earth.

After the United States bombed Baghdad on January 16, 1991, and commenced the war, the percentage of Americans favoring the war dramatically leaped 20 to 30 percent in all polls. One poll registered 88 percent. But the polls weren't asking Americans to do any thinking, which is hard work and the reason so few people voluntarily engage in it; they were only asking them to express their patriotism. Perhaps this question would have forced Americans to think and reveal the extent of their commitment *to this particular war:* Would

---

*A *New York Times*-CBS poll taken from January 5 to 7 showed 47 percent urging continuing sanctions, 46 percent urging war. A *Time*-CNN survey on January 10, just six days before the war, showed 45 percent in favor of continuing sanctions, with 41 percent favoring military action.

**And Congress had never before been so divided over authorizing war. The senate only voted 52–47, and the House 250–183 in favor of force. In the War of 1812, the Senate vote was 19–13, the House, 79–49; in the Mexican War, the votes were 40–2 and 174–14; the Spanish-American War, 67–21 and 325–19; World War I, 67–21 and 373–19; World War II, 82–0 and 388–1; Vietnam (the Gulf of Tonkin Resolution), 88–2 and 416–0.

they be willing to pay a 5 percent tax on their earnings to pay for the war? How about a 4 or 3 percent tax? What about 1 percent?

It cannot be denied that some good came out of the Persian Gulf War. If there was any fear that oil prices would have gone up appreciably absent our intervention, that fear was eliminated. Also, a vicious and ruthless despot was forced out of a nation he had invaded. The costs, however, were prodigious: Our intrusion into an inter-Arab conflict alienated many in the Arab world, with adverse economic and perhaps military consequences for decades to come; the war cost this nation approximately $9 billion; ecological damage in the Gulf is in the billions of dollars and will last for years to come; and the infrastructures of Iraq and Kuwait were for some time destroyed (a United Nations team described the effects of our bombing of Iraq as "near apocalyptic," threatening its people with "imminent catastrophe" and taking Iraq back "to a pre-industrial age"). Despite these enormous costs, the entire Persian Gulf region continues to be markedly destabilized.

The most important cost, of course, was the bloodshed and human carnage. General Schwarzkopf said that the loss of even one American life is "intolerable." Three hundred eighty-three young American men and women lost their lives in the Persian Gulf. One hates to even imagine the tears, heartbreak, and nightmares of the families and loved ones of those three hundred eighty-three American soldiers killed in the Gulf when they were told: "We regret to inform you that your son (husband, etc.) . . ." Also, many more Kuwaitis were tortured and killed by Iraqi soldiers in the closing days of the war than would have lost their lives absent the conflict. Finally, this wasn't a war in the conventional sense of the word. This was a human slaughter, an uninterrupted massacre, Rocky Marciano versus Pee-Wee Herman. As many as 100,000 virtually defenseless young Iraqi soldiers (and close to 1,000 Iraqi civilians, including women and children) were killed in the war. If, as our nation points out, all of the Kuwaitis who were killed were innocent victims, at least 95 percent of the Iraqi soldiers were also innocent victims, forced into war by a cruel and brutal dictator. And speaking of this Hitlerian dictator whom we wanted to eliminate as a threat to peace in the region and the world, at this writing he remains as firmly in power as ever, with well over half of his army and war armaments still intact to fight another day. His military is still the strongest in the Persian Gulf region. Meanwhile, tens of thousands of innocent Iraqi citizens, mostly Kurds and Shiites who tried to overthrow him after the war, as well as those whom his forces even suspected of being pro-American, have been slaughtered.*

The negative consequences, then, in the Persian Gulf War, were many, each consequence itself enormous in harm and scope. And it was all over oil. If they grew grapes or avocados in Kuwait, none of this would have ever happened.

If President Bush was very willing to send over 500,000 young Americans into combat and engage this nation in another horrible war with the potential of huge casualties for something as colossally insignificant in the scheme of things as the price of oil, how did he justify not sending a thousand or two special forces troops to Colombia to search and find the authors and architects behind the murderous flood of cocaine into this country? With full knowledge of this nation's half-hearted effort to end the drug scourge, and right in the middle of his administration's build-up for war in the Gulf, on September 4, 1990, the president vowed that the drug war would "remain the nation's number one priority" despite events in the Persian Gulf.

The "drug war" babble, of course, has become nausea-inducing. The Persian Gulf War showed the way this nation acts when it is really serious about something. It's radically different than how we've acted to end the drug curse. If our actually going to war—and mobilizing the largest invasion force since the Allies landed in Normandy during World War II—isn't enough to show the difference, consider this: In 1988, federal authorities identified eighteen (later expanded to twenty-one) countries (including Canada and Australia), islands, and colonies involved in the laundering of U.S. drug money profits. Under §4702 (the Kerry Amendment) of the Anti-Drug Abuse Act of 1988, the Department of the Treasury was required by Congress to give the "highest priority" to securing treaties with these countries providing cooperation in the effort to stop international drug-money laundering. On November 20, 1990, a classified Treasury report (obtained and revealed in the December, 1990, edition of *Money Laun-*

---

*President Bush's refusal to try to stop the massive slaughter of the Kurds and Shiites, even though he had expressly encouraged the uprising by them that caused it, is further evidence that our intervention in Kuwait had nothing to do with morality and everything to do with oil. The president's argument that it wasn't our place to get involved "in the internal affairs" of another country (Iraq) was remarkable in view of his invasion of Panama just over a year earlier to overthrow Noriega and install a new government.

dering Alert, a private Miami monthly with a large readership in the financial community) was given to select committees of Congress. Remarkably, twenty of the twenty-one countries, islands, and colonies had declined up to that point to sign a treaty with the United States.* Venezuela, the lone exception, signed one on November 6, 1990. One thing was obvious: The U.S. effort had been extremely perfunctory. In fact, the Department of the Treasury admitted that nearly one year after it was required by law to comply with the Kerry Amendment, the federal government had not even assigned one full-time staff person to the negotiations.

Commenting on the report, Sen. John F. Kerry, a leading anti-drug fighter in the Senate, said: "The Treasury Department had two years to undertake these negotiations. . . . Why an all-out effort has not yet been applied to these negotiations . . . is beyond me." Congressman Dante B. Fascell (D–Fla.), chairman of the House Foreign Affairs Committee, was even more severe in his criticism of the Bush Administration's effort. He told *Money Laundering Alert:* "I am deeply disappointed that the Bush Administration has not given this critical issue the serious attention it deserves. The report issued by the Treasury Department displays absolutely no commitment to or compliance with the law and sends a very strong signal to countries engaged in laundering practices that the United States is looking the other way."

The Bush Administration's failure to secure cooperation from the subject nations is graphic, demonstrative evidence of the low priority this country has assigned the anti-drug effort. The administration's "all-out war on drugs" was, in large part, a war of words. In the Persian Gulf crisis, President Bush and Secretary of State Baker personally and frenetically traversed the globe, twisting arms, cajoling and threatening and rewarding foreign leaders into joining the anti-Iraq coalition. In just one month, they persuaded twenty-seven nations to join. the *New York Times* referred to this "frenzied month of diplomatic activity in which the Bush Administration used arguments, rewards, and threats" to build a Security Council majority for a resolution authorizing the use of force against Iraq and forge a multination coalition. For example, Egypt, not a *sine qua non* nation in the Persian Gulf equation, had a $6.7 billion military debt to the

---

* Sen. John F. Kerry (D–Mass.) said the Bush Administration told his staff that the reason the Treasury report on the noncompliance of the twenty nations was classified was the "reluctance to embarrass those countries publicly."

United States. We forgave it in return for their joining the coalition. We had already shamefully removed virtually all of our sanctions against the murderers in Tiananmen Square (China). When we needed China's vote (or at a minimum their abstaining from voting) on the U.N. Security Council for the resolution authorizing war against Iraq, the last sanction, blocking World Bank loans to China, was quietly lifted. Yemen was threatened that if it voted against the resolution, all foreign aid to the country would cease. When Yemen nevertheless voted "no" on the resolution (along with Cuba, the only other "no" vote), the $23 million in foreign aid to Yemen appropriated by Congress for fiscal year 1990 was slashed by the State Department down to $2.9 million. To line up the support of Syrian dictator Hafez al Assad, a tyrant whose brutality, repression, and unrelieved villainy compares very favorably with Hussein, President Bush courted Assad and smiled very broadly through a hand-shaking photo session with him in Geneva. And so on.

In contrast, when the issue was the drug crisis—an issue much more important to the fabric and health of this nation—after two years, the Bush Administration had accepted without a whimper twenty out of twenty-one nations telling us to take a walk. How much pressure could this nation have possibly brought to bear on these countries if even friendly nations like Canada and Australia never cooperated? *Did the president make one trip or even one phone call from the Oval Office to even one of these nations?*

The Persian Gulf War provides proof (not just evidence), for those who don't already know, of where the true priorities are in this nation's leadership. Unfortunately, they are not to fight the war on drugs. For even if we accept, contrary to common sense and the evidence, former President Bush's assertion that the war wasn't about oil, but about Iraq's naked aggression that could not be permitted to stand in "a new world order," if the president was willing to risk the loss of thousands of American lives to get Iraq out of Kuwait, an act of aggression by Iraq that never cost America one single life (and almost assuredly would not have led to any circumstance which ever would have cost us one single life), then surely President Clinton should be willing to send a limited search-and-find military mission to Colombia to substantially eliminate a problem that continues to destroy millions of American lives.

As we have seen, a cogent argument can be made that the official reasons given by Washington for the last three wars in which this nation has engaged (Grenada, Panama, the Persian Gulf) may not have been the real reasons. But even assuming that they were, did they constitute better justification for the use of our military forces than substantially eliminating this nation's drug crisis? Particularly when Grenada, Panama, and the Persian Gulf involved massive invasions and war, and the Colombian proposal involves a mere search-and-find mission with a very small number of special forces personnel?

While our massive military intervention in Haiti in September of 1990 was unlike those in Grenada, Panama, and the Persian Gulf in that there was no invasion nor armed conflict, it shared one common denominator. Again, we were willing to go to war to achieve an objective far less compelling than ending this nation's drug crisis.

When Haiti's first democratically elected president, the populist leader Father Jean-Bertrand Aristide, was toppled from power by a military coup in 1991, the coup leaders immediately instituted a tyrannical regime in the destitute country, incarcerating or killing all known dissidents.

Although President Bush promised to "restore democracy" in Haiti, very little was done of a substantive nature under his watch to do so. Few saw any real resolve on his administration's part to remove the coup leaders (Lt. Gen. Raul Cedras; Lt. Col. Michel Francois, the police commander; and Gen. Philippe Biamby, the army chief of staff) and return Aristide to power. With uncharacteristic firmness, however, President Clinton made it clear early on that he was committed to using the U.S. military, if necessary, to oust Haiti's military dictatorship. But why? Why become perhaps irrevocably entangled in a country that never has known political stability (except by coercion) and that posed neither a military nor economic threat to the United States? And without this threat, how could we endanger the lives of young American men and women? A CBS-*New York Times* poll in September of 1993 found that 61 percent of Americans believed the United States had no responsibility to restore democracy in Haiti and 66 percent opposed an invasion.

One can probably safely conclude that President Clinton knew if he announced that the motivating force behind our military invasion was a humanitarian one—namely, ending the reign of terror in Haiti as well as preventing thousands of Haitian "boat people" from losing their lives at sea* in an effort to escape this tyranny—it would simply

---

*Because their boats were handmade and very unseaworthy—frequently constructed

not sell politically. In a September 15, 1993, speech to the nation from the Oval Office that signaled the imminent use of force in Haiti, the president candidly told the nation we had to stop "the brutal atrocities" against Haitians by the Haitian military, and we had to "promote democracy." He then added what he hoped would be two politically attractive reasons for our intervention, which, upon the slightest scrutiny, were anemic at best: "to secure our borders" (with forced repatriation, very few Haitians were continuing to set out for the United States), and to "preserve stability in our hemisphere" (Haiti is too small and impoverished a nation to cause any kind of instability in the Western Hemisphere; and for years, the barbaric and repressive rule of Papa Doc Duvalier in Haiti never prompted even a thought of military intervention on our part). "Your time is up," Clinton bluntly told Haiti's military leaders in his speech. "Leave now or we will force you from power."

But it wasn't until the early morning hours of September 18, 1993, that an American delegation—which was led by former President Jimmy Carter and included retired Gen. Colin L. Powell and Sen. Sam Nunn (D–Ga.), and which was dispatched by President Clinton to avert war—that the military troika agreed to step down, returning the nation's leadership back to Aristide. It is the consensus of virtually everyone that this agreement would never have been achieved if, during the last-minute negotiations, 20,000 well-armed American troops supported by tanks, armored vehicles, and planes, were not nearby, poised to storm ashore at Port-au-Prince in a full-fledged military invasion.

One senses that the overriding reason by far behind our Haitian intervention was a humanitarian one by a humanitarian president: stopping the atrocities against the Haitian people by the Haitian military. While this is a noble goal, if restoring democracy on a small island that is not a part of the United States is justification for mobilizing a vast military force of 20,000 American troops and, if necessary, going to war, is ending a problem *here in America* that has

---

from wood removed from the roofs of their huts—and they carried no life jackets, flares, radio, beacon, charts, or navigational equipment, hundreds of Haitians drowned at sea, many of their bodies washing up on Florida shores. President Bush, in the spring of 1992, began the process of forcibly repatriating the refugees without a hearing to determine if any qualified for political asylum. President Clinton, as a candidate for the presidency, condemned this policy as "cruel," but on January 14, 1993, a week before taking office, he announced that the Bush policy actually was saving lives and that the policy would continue.

destroyed *millions of American lives* sufficiently important to send a small search-and-find mission to Colombia?

It should be noted that the aborted and unsuccessful 1993 effort by 750 commandos of the U.S. Army's 75th Ranger Regiment to capture Somali warlord Mohammed Farah Aidid should not be viewed as an analogous situation to the proposed search-and-find mission in Colombia. First, unlike Colombia, thousands of U.S. troops were already in Somalia when the Clinton Administration sent the Rangers to Somalia to hunt for Aidid. Most importantly, while the Colombian drug lords are anathema to the Colombian people, who obviously would never physically intercede on behalf of the drug lords to protect them, as Marine Lt. Gen. Robert B. Johnston, leader of the initial U.S. intervention in Somalia, told the House Armed Services Committee: "Whether you like Aidid or not . . . in the Somalis' eyes he was a leader. To take him on, you . . . take on his entire clan. And they will fight you to the death." In fact, an October 3, 1993, firefight between Aidid's followers and U.S. troops resulted in eighteen American soldiers killed and seventy-seven wounded.

The Somali experience, however, is exceedingly instructive on the matter of U.S. priorities. Is there one sensible person in a million who will tell you that Aidid represented a greater threat to this nation's welfare and security than the Colombian drug lords who supply this nation with tons of cocaine? If not, if we were willing to send a search-and-find mission to Somalia, why not to Colombia? Particularly when, as opposed to Aidid, most of the drug lords have for years been under indictment by U.S. federal courts for having violated our nation's drug laws?

TWO ADDITIONAL MEASURES

The Death Penalty

For years, federal authorities dry-washed their hands, eagerly awaiting the day they could somehow get physical custody of Escobar, Ochoa, and Rodriguez Gacha. In fact, photos of these three prominently adorned the walls of many drug enforcement offices in this country. Those on the front lines of our war on drugs talked as if it would be the answer to their wildest dreams "if we could only get our hands on these guys." There was almost the implication that the war would be won (or the enemy severely crippled) once the cartel leaders were arrested. A Miami federal prosecutor said in 1986: "If the Colombians send us Jorge Ochoa, that will probably do more to assist the war on narcotics than anything that has happened." When drug kingpin Carlos Lehder was arrested in February, 1987, the U.S. attorney in Miami went further. "One down, three to go," he exulted, referring to Escobar, Ochoa, and Gacha. Similarly, when Cali cartel leader Gilberto Rodriguez was captured in June of 1995, a DEA official in Washington said: "This is the thing we've all been hungry for."

But as I pointed out in my 1991 book, *Drugs in America: The Case for Victory*, even with the arrest and prosecution of the then-current drug kingpins like Pablo Escobar—other than bringing them to justice under then-existing U.S. law—the drug problem would most likely continue virtually unabated as new kingpins automatically emerged to take their places. For the military search-and-find missions to have *optimum* value, there has to be more than apprehension, prosecution, conviction, and mere incarceration of the drug lords. Two other measures are necessary: the death penalty for drug lords, and a special court in which to prosecute them. As of September 13, 1994, we now have the death penalty.

In *Drugs in America* I recommended the following: "What is concurrently needed to neutralize the drug lords . . . then, is new emergency legislation providing for the death penalty . . . for anyone (not just foreign drug lords, but American traffickers) who, within a one-year period, exports or imports drugs into, or sells or distributes drugs in, this country with a street value in excess of some (not arbitrary) figure, such as $5 million. *The important point is that no killing has to be involved at all. The mere exporting, importing, selling, or distributing of drugs in excess of, for instance, $5 million, would warrant the death penalty.* We already know, for instance, the harm, including death and murder, that inevitably results from $5 million of cocaine. Inasmuch as many underlings are always involved in the drug lords' ventures, such a statute would be made to order for the granting of immunity to the lesser lights to testify against the kingpins. This, in fact, is what happened in the successful prosecutions of the preeminent Colombian drug smuggler Carlos Lehder in Jacksonville, Florida, and Honduran drug lord Juan Ramon Matta-Ballesteros in Los Angeles. Likewise, close associates of deposed dictator Manuel Noriega are currently scheduled to testify against him in Miami. As to the issue of the constitutionality of the death penalty for crimes other than murder (in this case, the exportation, importation, sale, or distribution of large amounts of drugs), other such crimes have withstood constitutional scrutiny in the past—e.g., espionage, treason, and kidnapping for purposes of robbery or extortion where there is bodily harm."

Under the federal death penalty act, a component of President Clinton's Violent Crime Control and Law Enforcement Act of 1994,* drug lords are now subject to the death penalty in the United States: 18 U.S.C. § 3591 (b) (1) provides for a sentence of death (it's not mandatory) for anyone convicted of being a principal, or one of several principal administrators, organizers, or leaders of a criminal drug enterprise that received at least $20 million in gross receipts during any twelve-month period of its existence for the manufacture, importation, or distribution of controlled substances set forth in 21 U.S.C. § 841 (b) (1) (B)—e.g., cocaine, heroine, marijuana, LSD, etc.**

By way of comparison to our death-penalty statutes, in January, 1989, Iran passed a law making the death penalty mandatory for

---

*Although it was not until 1994 that Congress got around to imposing an appropriate penalty for the drug lords, since the passage of legislation in 1987, there has been a grossly disproportionate punishment for the very smallest party in the drug enterprise. Unbelievably (and this has already happened many times), under 21 U.S.C. § 841 (b) (1) (A) (iii), a young black in the ghetto possessing—with apparent intent to sell, though no sale has to even be shown—a mere 50 grams of crack cocaine must receive a mandatory minimum sentence (the judge has no discretion) of ten years in a federal penitentiary (five grams results in a mandatory five-year sentence). To illustrate the absurdity of this law, a defendant would have to be in possession (with intent to sell) of 5,000 grams of powdered cocaine (100 times as much) to receive the same minimum mandatory ten-year sentence. In the last four years, 88 percent of those prosecuted for crack cocaine crimes were black. Whites use the more expensive powdered cocaine more than blacks do. To eliminate the gross disparity in sentencing, which resulted in far more blacks than whites going to prison for cocaine offenses, on May 1, 1995, the U.S. Sentencing Commission sent recommended draft legislation to Congress to equalize the mandatory minimum statutes for crack and powdered cocaine, but Congress rejected the recommendation, and on October 30, 1995, President Clinton signed a law retaining the harsher penalties for crack cocaine violations. However, on November 8, 1995, a Senate bill was introduced providing that the penalty for powder cocaine be raised to the same level as that of crack cocaine.

To further illustrate the absurdity of a ten-year minimum sentence for the mere possession with intent to sell just 50 grams of crack cocaine, the minimum federal penalty for attempted murder is 6.5 years; for rape, 5.8 years; armed robbery, 4.7 years; kidnapping, 4.2 years; theft of $80 million or more, 4.2 years; burglary while armed with a gun, 2 years.

**See also 21 U.S.C. §848 (e) (1), providing for the death penalty for non-drug lords convicted of being a part of a criminal drug enterprise who, in addition, kill or induce the killing of another in furtherance of said drug enterprise; and 18 U.S.C. §3591 (b) (2), providing for the death penalty for drug lords who, in order to obstruct the investigation or prosecution of their drug enterprise, attempt to kill, or direct or assist another to attempt to kill, any public officer, juror, witness, or members of the family or household of such a person.

those who sell as little as 30 grams of heroin, morphine, codeine, or methadone. In Malaysia, possession of as little as .053 ounces of heroin, 7.05 ounces of marijuana, or 1.41 ounces of cocaine constitutes "trafficking" and carries a mandatory sentence of death.

Establishment of a Special Court

The second measure that should be instituted is a special federal court apparatus exclusively for drug lords charged with violating the death penalty legislation to greatly expedite the pretrial, trial, and appeal of the drug lords, but still consistent with due process of law, and with no rights to appeal currently afforded convicted felons being sacrificed or compromised. The special court apparatus, of course, would not include the U.S. Supreme Court. The highest court in the land, however, could be urged by Congress to give priority to any of these cases they agreed to hear. Even a Third World country like Pakistan has recognized the utility of a special court that handles special cases: In early August, 1990, special "speedy trial" courts were set up to investigate and prosecute cases of corruption under Prime Minister Benazir Bhutto.

There is a precedent in the United States for the establishment of a "special" court and judicial procedure to handle an unusual situation. Under the Foreign Intelligence Surveillance Act of 1978 (§§ 1801–1811 of 50 U.S.C.), electronic surveillance (i.e., wiretapping) to acquire foreign intelligence information is not governed by the ordinary rules of federal judicial procedure, and the regular court system is completely circumvented. Application for authorization to conduct such surveillance of an American citizen (if no communication of an American citizen is involved, the U.S. attorney general, *without a court order*, can authorize the surveillance) is made by the FBI to one of seven federal district court judges designated by the chief justice of the U.S. Supreme Court. If the judge denies the application, he is directed to "immediately" provide a written statement of his reasons so that a special appellate court of three justices, again designated by the chief justice, can review the matter "as expeditiously as possible." The identities of the judges of this supersecret court are not known.

It should also be noted that to handle the explosive growth in narcotic cases across the nation now clogging the courts, there already are more than two dozen special drug courts in the nation's major cities (e.g., New York, Chicago, Philadelphia, New Orleans, Milwaukee, Miami, Oakland, etc.) that exclusively handle drug prosecutions of nonviolent offenders with substance abuse problems. Modeled after the first such court in Dade County (Miami), Florida, in 1989, the courts are funded, in part, by the federal government under Public Law 103-322. There obviously is no legitimate reason why there can't also be special courts for other particular drug defendants, namely, drug lords.

Under the special federal court apparatus contemplated, drug lords could be tried and, if the evidence was there, convicted and have their probable sentence of death carried out within a matter of one or at the most two years, as opposed to the incredibly long, drawn-out process now in place, in which sentences of death are normally imposed from between ten and fifteen years after being meted out. It is hard to believe that new drug lords would emerge knowing the fate of their predecessors, and also knowing that it would be impossible for them to conduct their business outside the reach of American armed forces, which would intervene the moment (if, under the circumstances, that moment were to occur more than once or twice) new leaders emerged.

Obviously, the proposed search-and-find mission could not be carried out against the Cali drug lords currently in custody. Other than the recently escaped Jose Santacruz-Londono, thought by the DEA to be capable of running the Cali cartel by himself, as indicated earlier, the only other Cali leader still at large is Helmer (Pacho) Herrera-Buitrago, whose personal drug empire includes a substantial part of the cocaine trade in New York and New Jersey. Up until May, 1995, he was relaxing in a penthouse atop his fourteen-story office building and residential tower in downtown Cali, and cruising around town, *New York Times* reporter James Brook says, in one out of a fleet of seventy cars, "including a bulletproofed Mazda equipped with louvers to allow his bodyguards to fire machine pistols at pursuers." Herrera's whereabouts are presently unknown, although the DEA says they are confident he is still in Colombia.

The search-and-find mission, today, would clearly be directed toward Santacruz and Herrera (against both of whom, as previously noted, there is a 1995 Miami federal indictment on drug-trafficking charges). Their capture and return to America to face a possible sentence of death would probably be enough, all by itself, to achieve the desired end. If a search-and-find mission were not directed against them, then such a mission supported by a U.S. indictment should be directed against whichever person or persons inevitably emerge to replace the Cali chieftains as the new drug lords.

With this type of deterrent in place, there is a very strong probability that the drug lords would either stop engaging in drug trafficking or, much more likely, go elsewhere—for example, Europe, where they already have been increasing their presence, though nowhere near like here in the United States.*

Colombia's cocaine cartels now supply about 65 tons of cocaine a year to Europe. Utilizing Spain and Italy as their principal countries of entry (Rotterdam, the world's busiest port, is among the many international ports that are being used), the cartels have created distribution networks that spread throughout the European Community, and cocaine seizures, addictions, and drug-related violence are on a sharp rise in virtually every European country. Most agree that the Colombian cartels have created this century's worst international crime crisis.

Even if Europe never quite developed the appetite for drugs we have here in the States, and hence would never be as lucrative a market, whatever the drug lords got there would be infinitely better than seizure by the American military and the death penalty here in the States. The analogy would be a burglar facing a home with a burglar alarm, watchdogs, and armed occupants. He is going to go next door, or wherever it will be easier and safer for him. To those who would argue that it's immoral to make this nation so resistant and unattractive to the drug lords that they will decide to concentrate on other countries (i.e., we are knowingly and selfishly doing something that can only cause greater harm to others), I suppose it's equally immoral, then, for an American homeowner to take steps to protect himself from burglars (burglar alarm, gun in the home, watchdogs, etc.), because the burglars will then commit their crimes on other people. Obviously, if other countries were to follow our lead, the drug lords would be forced to quit their trade completely.

For those who feel that a military raid and special federal court for drug lords are too radical, it must be stated again: The drug crisis has created extraordinary problems for the nation, and extraordinary

---

*The main purpose by far of the Medellin cartel's bloody war against the government of Colombia and its people was to end extradition to the United States. "Extradition was the thing the drug lords feared the most, coming to the United States and facing the sanctions that would occur here," says Thomas A. Constantine, the DEA administrator. And here, we're talking about more than jail. We're talking about the death penalty, the ultimate deterrent.

steps must be taken to solve it. If we are unwilling to take these special and necessary steps, then we are not really serious, after all, about eliminating a national crisis that, in former drug czar Bennett's words, "is destroying the lives of millions of Americans." If the search-and-find mission proposal set forth in this work is not adopted, since the narco-traffickers cannot be extradited to America (instead serving light sentences, if at all, in Colombia, which does not have the death penalty), what reason does this nation have for believing that the Colombian cocaine blitz of America will end, or that this nation's drug crisis will not continue?

If our anti-cocaine effort against the Colombian cartels has thus far been cosmetic, and anything but a "war," our effort against the heroin drug lords does not even rise to the dignity of being characterized as cosmetic. In fact, the proposed 1996 counter-narcotics budget for all of Southeast and Southwest Asia, where most of the heroin reaching this country comes from, is an incredibly paltry $6.4 million (see page 170 of the 1995 national drug control strategy budget summary). In other words, we are spending virtually nothing at all on the problem internationally.

The vast majority of the Southeast and Southwest Asian heroin imported into this country comes in through the Northeastern Seaboard, but heroin traffickers are discovering, like their cocaine counterparts, how inviting and vulnerable our Southwest border is. "Five years ago, the seizure of a kilogram [2.2 pounds] of heroin along the Mexican border was a lot of heroin," says Phil Jordan, director of the DEA's El Paso Intelligence Center. "Now it's coming across in multikilo shipments, and in greater purity." On May 27, 1995, a record-breaking (for the Southwest border) 28 pounds of heroin from Southwest Asia were seized near El Paso by the U.S. Border Patrol. However, the Southeast Asian (SEA) Heroin Task Force, a unit of the DEA, has operated with some success. On November 27, 1994, for notable instance, the Royal Thai (Thailand police force) arrested ten heroin traffickers. The arrests resulted from Operation Tiger Trap, an international investigation developed by the SEA Heroin Task Force in conjunction with the DEA offices in Bangkok and Chiang Mai, Thailand. The ten traffickers are presently in custody, awaiting extradition to the United States.

Burma (now officially called Myanmar) is by far the largest producer of opium and heroin in the world. The "Golden Triangle" of Southeast Asia, a mountainous area where Burma, Thailand, and

Laos meet, currently supplies close to 60 percent of all heroin sold in the United States, and the key country in this region is Burma. In Burma and northern Thailand, the "King of Heroin" for over two decades was the self-styled General Khun Sa (real name, Chang Chi-Fu). The sixty-one-year-old Khun Sa, who was indicted on December 12, 1989, by a federal grand jury in Brooklyn on twenty counts of drug trafficking, surrendered to Burmese authorities on January 4, 1996, ending the thirty-year reign of the world's most prominent opium baron. However, there will be no extradition of Khun Sa to the United States on the U.S. charges since a condition of his surrender was amnesty and no extradition to the United States. U.S. drug officials believe that Khun Sa's deputy, Zao Gun Jade, has taken over Khun Sa's drug empire.

For years, the major importation and distribution point in America for Khun Sa's heroin, as well as that of other Southeast and Southwest Asian drug lords, has been New York City. Since 1985, roughly half of heroin seizures nationwide have occurred in the New York City metropolitan area alone. Recently, ethnic Chinese operating out of New York City's Chinatown have replaced Italian drug traffickers (primarily the Sicilian Mafia) as the principal importers and distributors of heroin, although the Colombian cocaine cartels are now also making substantial inroads into the heroin market in America.

Khun Sa has always insisted that the heroin trade was necessary to feed his guerrilla army of ten thousand men, called the Mong Tai Army, and in 1977 actually offered to sell his opium crop to the United States for $300 million in economic aid for his subjects. In return, he said, he would use his army to destroy the heroin trade in Burma. "Why not use a bandit to catch a bandit?" he reasoned. Although former Congressman Lester Wolfe of New York actually led a congressional delegation to Khun Sa's northern Thailand headquarters to further discuss the proposal, the U.S. government ultimately rejected the offer.

According to the latest (1995) U.S. State Department International Narcotics Control Strategy Report, the Burmese government "continues to treat counter-narcotics efforts as a matter of secondary importance. . . . The government's ability to suppress Burma's opium and heroin trade is severely limited by lack of access to and control over the areas in which most opium is grown and heroin processed. This is to some extent a situation the government has created. Well-equipped ethnic armies sheltered in remote mountainous regions have been permitted [by the Burmese government] wide-ranging, local autonomy in exchange for halting their active insurgencies against Rangoon."

How is the U.S. government trying to stop the heroin drug lords? Our effort has been massive indeed, containing all the hallmarks of a real "war." I'm, of course, being facetious. For instance, in December, 1994, DEA trainers conducted a six-day course in basic drug-enforcement techniques for Burmese law enforcement personnel. And for those who feel that such a course is not quite going all-out, the previous month, a senior-level U.S. delegation, which included a representative of the State Department's Bureau of International Narcotics Matters, actually visited Burma, raising counter-narcotic issues with that country's officials, including urging them to increase the prosecution of narco-traffickers. One has to admit that that is very impressive stuff.

Per the drug czar's office, the following are among the measures currently being undertaken by the United States to stop the heroin drug lords. They are the type that one would naturally expect when a nation is "at war."

1. Continue, at appropriate levels, a "general dialogue" with Burmese authorities "regarding counter-narcotic strategy."

2. Pursuant to number 1, "exchange information with Burmese officials."

3. Continue efforts to influence Burma's neighbors—especially China and Thailand—"to exert more narcotics control pressure on the Burmese government."

4. "Continue to urge China and Thailand to conduct drug interdiction and operations along their borders with Burma."

And the endless and fruitless drug "war" goes on.

PROPOSAL 2

Interdiction of Drug-Profit Monies

I n addition to the military search-and-find solution to the drug
crisis, for the more faint of heart there is a separate, completely
independent way of ending the drug crisis: rendering the drug
business unprofitable to the drug lords who make it all happen.
This can only be done by substantially eliminating money laundering
of drug profits. The means and legal architecture for achieving this
are set forth in this chapter.

*Remarkably, this nation does not have, nor has it ever had, a cohe-
sive, step-by-step plan or strategy to stop money laundering by drug
traffickers.* * As with every area of the National Drug Control Strategy
promulgated by the White House's Office of National Drug Control
Policy (office of the drug czar), there is no specific, detailed plan to

---

* President Clinton was the only presidential candidate in the 1992 presidential campaign to even address the money-laundering issue. In a speech to law enforcement officials
in Romulus, Michigan, on October 17, 1992, the president, who has a background in
law enforcement (distinguishing himself in his brief two-year reign as attorney general of
Arkansas by creating an anti-trust division in the attorney general's office and vigorously
pursuing white-collar crime), said: "If you really want to get the big criminals, we can
focus more on the money-laundering aspects of their operations. . . . That is what the
federal government ought to focus on in the law enforcement area. Go after the money,
and we can get the big people." If the president really means those words, in view of the
fact that money laundering remains an enormous problem to overcome in the drug war,
he and his administration should give serious consideration to the two proposals set forth
on these pages.

combat money laundering, just generalities and the continuation of measures that would naturally be employed even if one were to give virtually no thought to the problem. Witness the 1991 "four point strategy" of this nation's drug czar to stop money laundering (essentially the same as set forth on pages 76–77 of the 1995 report): "Improve our intelligence capabilities on the financial activities of drug traffickers; conduct criminal investigations of money-laundering activities and arrest and prosecute those engaged in same; achieve effective regulation at both the state and federal level; and promote international cooperation."

Most cocaine drug profits end up with the drug lords in Colombia, who produce and export the cocaine. Next in line are the American distributors and suppliers (with, per the DEA, Hispanics—particularly Colombian and Mexican—dominating cocaine *wholesale* distribution in the United States, and organized groups of Mexicans, Cubans, Dominicans, and Jamaicans, as well as African-American gangs, providing most of the *retail* distribution in major American cities). But these American "high-level drug dealers," for instance, won't be a part of the drug trade if their share of the street money the cocaine earns can't be laundered. Laundering is the technique by which ill-gotten or "dirty" money from any source (in this case, the sale of drugs) is cleaned up by moving it into seemingly legitimate financial channels which disguise its unlawful origin. Saddled with millions of dollars in cash, the dealers can't live their opulent lifestyle by paying for homes and cars with boxes full of $10 and $20 bills. Apart from the impracticability, walking around with bushels of money only advertises and announces that the money may represent drug proceeds. So laundering helps the drug dealer avoid arrest and prosecution. Just as important, laundering avoids the outright seizure and forfeiture by the authorities of the money, as well as all assets purchased with the money, since the money and assets are the fruit of illicit activity. Moreover, laundering enables the drug dealer to prepare a tax return for the IRS showing an ostensibly legitimate source of income. In some cases, as we shall see, he can not only avoid paying any tax at all, but deduct fabricated interest payments on his income tax return. (Drug proceeds, in fact, are taxable income. The constitutionality of taxing illegal income was established when the U.S. Supreme Court held years ago that profits from illicit distilling of alcohol were taxable. "Congress can tax what it also forbids," Justice Holmes said. The Sixteenth Amendment to the U.S. Constitution provides that Congress shall have power "to lay and collect taxes on income, *from whatever source derived."*)

For the most part, illicit drugs enter the U.S. market on consignment. The only attempted in-depth examination ever of the division of drug-money profits between the Colombian drug lords and the American traffickers was announced by Attorney General Richard Thornburgh on April 17, 1990. Of a specific $1.2 billion in profits from U.S. drug sales, federal investigators learned that approximately $50 million never left the country, being used to pay lawyers, accountants, and other operating expenses. Almost $350 million, after initially being wire-transferred out of the country, was transferred by wire *back* to this country. Approximately one-third of the money, then, ended up in this country, with two-thirds, Thornburgh said, going to the cartel leaders in Colombia.

To achieve his purposes, the launderer seeks to convert the original street money into funds that cannot be traced. Though commencing in America, the completed laundering normally takes place in off-shore (foreign) banks in countries that provide, by statute, confidentiality and secrecy for their depositors. The prototype for most bank secrecy laws is the Swiss model, which was originally intended to shield Jewish accounts from Nazi confiscation.

There are two predominant ways that American drug money ends up in the banks of the offshore laundering haven. One is by smuggling the American currency out of this country the way the drugs were brought in—i.e., by plane, boat, car, human courier, etc.—whereupon it is deposited. The other way is by depositing the money in an American bank and then wire-transferring it to the offshore haven.*

What if these two ways were cut off in the United States, like water from a faucet? Since the drug traffickers are, in the last analysis, busi-

---

*There are other ingenious ways for drug profits to leave this country, none of which, however, would even remotely begin to meet the needs of the drug lords. One example among many: Federal authorities recently found an instance in which a legitimate Colombian businessman wished to leave Colombia with his money to live in America. However, because of its precarious economic status, Colombia seeks to keep all assets in the country. Before currency can be transferred out of the country, one has to get the approval of Colombia's Central Bank, *Banco de la Republica.* For large amounts of money not in payment of imports, this approval is nearly always declined. Even if the transfer is approved, the Central Bank collects a 40 percent tax on the money for the federal government and a 12 percent remittance tax. The businessman solved his problem by having American associates of Colombian traffickers deposit their American drug profits (profits they otherwise would have attempted to smuggle or wire-transfer out of the country) in an American account set up by the Colombian businessman. The businessman, in turn, transferred his money to an account, in Colombia, belonging to the traffickers.

nessmen who have one and only one motive for continuing their illicit operation—the profit motive—it is well within the margins of logic and common sense to assume that they would go elsewhere or find some other way to earn a living. *In other words, if the Colombian drug lords can't get their money out of this country, they're not going to send their cocaine into this country.* In reality, we can shut the faucet, or at least reduce the flow to a drip, if we are willing to make the necessary changes in our approach to the problem.

Like the military search-and-find mission, the means are revolutionary, only because revolutionary measures are needed to solve a problem that heretofore has given every indication of being insolvable. The inevitable argument of "how difficult" it would be to effectuate the plan about to be proposed should not be made. With a problem of this severity and scope, the only legitimate question is whether it is possible, not how difficult it will be. In any event, the difficulty would not be anywhere close to the incalculable time, money, and resources presently spent by this nation in its ineffectual effort to stop the flow of drugs into this country and to deal with the drug problem among our people once the drugs are ingested into the nation's bloodstream.

Whether one asks one or twenty people involved in fighting the drug war what percentage of each $100 in drug money sales is smuggled out of this country in currency form and what percentage is wire-transferred out, the answer is the same: "I don't know. Only the drug lords can tell you that."* When prodded, the authorities say that in the early 1980s, they believe over 50 percent was smuggled out, and that a shift started taking place in 1984–1985, with perhaps as much as 70 percent being wire-transferred out in the following several years. The Colombian cartel's preference for the wire-transfer option started to recede in 1989 and 1990 with the increased domestic emphasis on money-laundering controls and the cooperation, though limited, of more and more foreign countries. Everyone agrees that the pendulum has indeed swung back, and many believe the division is now roughly 50–50. Both options have their advantages and disadvantages. With the wire transfer, it is easier to send vast sums of

---

* In February, 1992, hearings before the Senate Committee on Governmental Affairs, an Arizona assistant attorney general estimated that as much as $3 billion in U.S. currency a year was being smuggled out of his state alone into Mexico. The only known official estimate on a national scale was way back in 1984, when the president's commission on organized crime estimated that of the $15 billion in illegal drug money leaving the country at that time, approximately $5 billion was thought to be transported in currency form, the remainder being wire-transferred out after deposit in the U.S. banking system.

money more quickly to their destination. Smuggling the currency out is not only slower, but there is the physical problem of sheer bulk and weight. For instance, $1 million in $20 bills weighs over 100 pounds. However, the latter method does have two advantages that appeal to the drug trafficker over wire-transferring. Since it generates no government forms, it leaves no "paper trail" back to the trafficker. Also, there is a higher margin of profit, inasmuch as there is no payment to a professional money launderer for his services.

And, if possible, smuggling money out of the country is even less likely to be detected than wire-transferring it out. The nation has thousands of miles of unguarded borders. Even where ports of entry and exit do exist, the inspection of *outbound* cargo and passengers is never given the same scrutiny as *inbound* inspection. In fact, per a March, 1994, U.S. General Accounting Office report, "only 85 of the 301 Customs ports in the nation have staff performing outbound inspections on a full-time basis. These staff total 130 of the 6,228 inspectors in Customs." With respect to planes, less than 5 percent of all outgoing flights are even targeted for inspection by customs. For instance, the General Accounting Office found that "as of September 1992, an average of 1,888 flights a month left O'Hare [Airport in Chicago] for foreign destinations. The number of flights inspected each month averaged 64." Of those flights, only one-third of the passengers were interviewed or otherwise subjected to an inspection. And U.S. Customs has no effective way to detect smuggled cash when it is hidden in ship containers. Millions of these containers are shipped out of the United States each year from ports throughout the country. But controls are weak. "The United States is probably the only country that does not have tight controls on the outbound flow of shipments," says Customs spokesman Kenneth Stroud. Unbelievably, exporters are only required to present their Shippers Export Declarations to Customs within three days *after* the cargo has already left the U.S. dock.

Chuck Davies, program manager for Outbound Enforcement for U.S. Customs in Washington, D.C., says that the amount of drug money being smuggled out in its currency form is "in the billions."*

---

*The previously referred to June 5, 1995, Miami federal indictment against the Cali cartel leaders alleges, *inter alia*, that the Cali cartel "opened front businesses in several American cities that were used to facilitate the storage of currency, and also established additional front companies to facilitate the exportation of commodities in which huge shipments of currency were hidden and subsequently shipped to Colombia."

A common practice is for the jets that transport cocaine from Colombia to Mexico to drop off the cocaine and then pick up American drug dollars for the return flight to Colom-

In my 1991 book, several examples were set forth that took place prior to 1991. One was provided by Max Mermelstein, once a leading smuggler and distributor for the Medellin cartel in America and for years the DEA's key witness against the cartel. In 1987, Mermelstein testified at a murder trial for the execution slaying of former drug smuggler Barry Seal that he had arranged for the smuggling out of the country to Colombia of "approximately $300 million" dollars in cash. Frank Retamoza, a cousin of Mexican drug lord Miguel Angel Felix Gallardo, testified at the murder trial for the killing of DEA agent Enrique Camarena that in the year 1984, he transported in his camper "a total of about $150 million" from Los Angeles to Guadalajara. And then there's Ramon Milian Rodriquez, an accountant for the Medellin cartel. During one nine-month period alone between August, 1982, and May, 1983, in forty-seven flights from South Florida to Panama in his Learjet, he transported a documented total of $151 million. When U.S. Customs agents arrested him at Fort Lauderdale International Airport on May 4, 1983, as he was about to make his forty-eighth flight, they found twenty boxes aboard containing $5,449,962 in currency. A private Saberliner jet about to take off across the border from the county airport in Kingsview, Texas (40 miles southwest of Corpus Christi), on February 6, 1985, had an even larger amount ($5,975,850) in drug money aboard. What is believed to be the largest single seizure of cash known to be destined for direct shipment to the cartel leaders took place on July 24, 1990, at a home in Sylmar, California. U.S. Customs agents seized $17,864,000 in drug proceeds already packed in thirty-eight cardboard U-Haul boxes for shipment to Colombia.

More recently, the following are among the major drug currency seizures in the country: $1,098,730 (inside checked passenger bags at airport) on November 14, 1993, in Miami; $1,117,237 (trailer crossing southwest border) on December 8, 1993, in Zukeville, Arizona; $2,813,450 and $2,433,815 (air freight at airport) on April 8, 1994, in Miami; $2,616,525 and $1,615,253 (express courier bags at courier facility near airport) on July 8, 1994, in Miami; $925,960 (cargo shipment at Miami Airport) on November 7, 1994; $2,560,381 (air freight at Miami Airport) on February 14, 1995;

---

bia. For instance, on April 17, 1995, Mexican federal agents at Benito Juarez International Airport in southern Mexico found $6.2 million in American drug proceeds on a plane (believed to have transported cocaine to Mexico) bound for Bogota, Colombia. On October 11, 1996, Mexican soldiers found $12 million in American drug money on a plane near a dam just south of Tepic in the state of Nayarit.

$1,699,150 (ship container at seaport of Miami) on March 17, 1995; $1,130,369 (on passenger at JFK Airport in New York City) on July 6, 1995; $745,303 (inside car near border in Laredo, Texas) on September 19, 1995.

U.S. Customs, aware of the magnitude of the problem, initiated a nationwide operation (Operation Buckstop) in February, 1986, to interdict the smuggling of currency out of the country. But because of limited resources and the overriding emphasis on inbound inspections, as well as the fact that outbound inspection programs are generally at the expense of Customs' inbound interdiction effort, outbound inspections continue to be the exception rather than the rule. Customs officials admit that they are very selective about when and where they decide to target a particular port to implement a Buckstop operation. In the last four years (1991 through 1994), Operation Buckstop seized $200.1 million, 95 percent of which Customs believes to be drug money. Overall, including Buckstop, Customs seized $893.3 million in bulk currency during this period (1995 statistics were not available at the time of this writing). Customs knows this sum represents only a small fraction of the drug currency being smuggled out of this country. With thousands of commercial and private air flights leaving the United States each month, 8 million ship containers leaving each year, and millions of Americans traveling abroad annually, U.S. Customs is hopelessly outmanned and overwhelmed in its effort to interdict drug money smuggled out of this country.

Everyone agrees that if one of the two principle methods that drug lords use to get their money out of this country was cut off and denied the drug kingpins, they automatically would attempt to get all of their money out the other way. Therefore, although denying the drug lords even one of the two methods would be of substantial value and importance, in order to cripple the cartel both methods would have to be denied them. In this proposed solution to the drug problem, two separate measures have to be carried out, one to automatically eliminate a substantial percentage of the problem, the other to eliminate most of the remainder. A discussion of the two measures to cut off both methods follows.

1. Two Separate U.S. Currencies

What if the stacks of American currency (like those regularly seen on the evening news sitting on a table with bindles of cocaine in front of law-enforcement officials after a "record" seizure) had no value whatsoever outside the geographical perimeters of the United States? Assigning, for the purpose of this work, a figure of 50 percent to the amount of drug money smuggled out of this country in its currency form (with 50 percent being wire-transferred out), the drug traffickers would automatically be forced to totally abandon drug money smuggling.

How could this be brought about? *Two* separate U.S. currencies would have to be utilized. The present U.S. currency (hereinafter referred to as No. 1) would be the only currency that would remain legal tender outside the United States, and would no longer have any value domestically. In due time, obviously, this currency would dry up as it was repatriated by foreign banks for credit to their U.S. dollar accounts.* Therefore, the supply of No. 1 currency would have to be periodically replenished, at least to the extent of providing U.S. tourists traveling abroad with American dollars.

The second step would be for the U.S. Treasury to print new U.S. currency (No. 2, a different color or shade of green, or a different size, a new identifying mark, etc.), which would only have value within this country's borders. Therefore, it would be useless to smuggle this currency from domestic drug sales out of the country. Several banking officials have advised that such a division of currency would be workable.

There is precedent, to a limited degree, for the dual-currency proposal. In the early 1960s, Belgium had a severe balance-of-payments

*When foreign banks repatriated (by depositing) the external American currency for credit to their U.S. dollar accounts in American banks, they could thereafter withdraw either external or internal American dollars out of that account, but they could never deposit, or get any type of credit for, internal American dollars. For instance, they could write a check on their account, or withdraw American internal dollars from it, to pay for an American purchase, but could never deposit internal dollars. To allow them to deposit such dollars would create a market for these dollars outside of the country, since the drug lords could sell these internal American dollars to the foreign banks.

Foreign banks could purchase external American dollars from American banks (with their currency, not American internal dollars) to provide a service to customers of theirs who are traveling to another country or countries and want a currency that is universally accepted in all countries, as American dollars are.

Fluctuations in the value of American currency against foreign currency would, of course, continue to take place for the external dollars, and we would have to permit a foreign citizen or bank exchanging our external dollars for internal ones not to lose money in the process.

The suggested double currency would not inhibit, because of bulky inconvenience, the purchase, for instance, of a foreign corporation or expensive commodity by an American corporation or other American buyer, inasmuch as these transactions are traditionally done by wire transfers and debits and credits to the respective accounts of the seller and buyer.

problem (imports far exceeding exports). To ameliorate the financial crisis by making the exchange rate unfavorable for imports, Belgium instituted a two-tiered foreign exhange currency system, which was in effect until 1990. Though no second currency was involved, in foreign exchange, Belgium utilized two markets, and the existing currency was dealt with in two ways. The official exchange market covered any transaction by private business as well as the government itself related to the import or export of goods or services. When the Belgian franc was used in this market it was called the "commercial" franc, and its value was controlled by the Belgian government. The second market was called the free or open market, where the value of the franc was not controlled by the government, and covered any foreign-exchange transaction other than those which resulted from foreign trade (e.g., a Belgian citizen about to visit Denmark went to a Belgian bank and exchanged his francs for kroners). When it was used in this market, the franc was called the "financial" franc.

A much closer parallel to the new currency proposal, though on an infinitely smaller scale, is what the U.S. military did in Vietnam. GIs were selling U.S. dollars to Vietnamese people for piasters (also called *dong*), the Vietnamese currency, because they could get more piasters for dollars this way than by going to an official exchange. These dollars often found their way into Communist hands, and since piasters were unacceptable to foreign manufacturers and arms merchants, the Communists would use the dollars to buy their arms and munitions. To prevent this, the U.S. military started paying GIs not in dollars but in scrip called MPCs (Military Payment Certificates). The scrip had the same value as dollars but could only be used at American facilities, such as the officers' and enlisted men's clubs. (If a GI did want to have piasters for purchase of Vietnamese goods and services, he could go to the military exchange and exchange his scrip for piasters at the current exchange rate.) Since the scrip had no value outside Vietnam, it could not be used by the Communists to buy the means of war from foreign sellers.

Utilizing U.S. currency in any way at all to solve the drug problem has been virtually ignored in this country. A lone exception is a proposal by Donald T. Regan. But it's clear the former secretary of the treasury and President Reagan's chief of staff spent little time thinking about his proposal. Regan didn't recommend, as here, *two* separate currencies, but wrote in the September 18, 1989, edition of the *New York Times*: "We should quietly print new $50 and $100 bills, either of a different color, or size, than the current ones. Then with only a ten-day warning, we should make all $50 and $100 bills obsolete—no longer acceptable as legal tender. Everyone would have to exchange their large bills for new ones." Regan says this would "trap these [drug] criminals" because they would be identified from their "huge cash holdings." Even if they didn't turn in their money, since the money would no longer have value, Regan says this "would hit the criminals where it hurts most—in the pocketbook."*

Although at first blush it sounds like a Herculean task to produce an entirely new currency, the task is not particularly daunting. According to the Bureau of Engraving and Printing in Washington, the dollar amount of American currency (not coin) presently in circulation is approximately $380 billion. The number of $1, $2, $5, $10, $20, $50, and $100 *bills* comprising the $380 billion is close to 16 billion. The cost to the government of manufacturing each bill

---

*Apart from the fact that Regan has the wrong denominations (most drug money is in $10s and $20s), and that other than when the money is commingled with that from a cash-generating business, drug traffickers and launderers do not bring their "huge cash holdings" to any one bank—instead breaking them down through the purchase of money orders and cashiers' checks at many banks, then depositing the instruments at one or a few banks—there are far more significant problems with his proposal. The drug people wouldn't have to turn *any* of their money in. They could smuggle it out of the country (which they routinely do anyway to a substantial percentage of their drug profits), deposit it in a bank-secrecy-haven country and then wire-transfer any part of it they wanted back to one or a hundred different accounts in this country.

But whatever the drug traffickers elected to do, it is difficult to decipher what Regan hoped to achieve by his proposal. For those few drug lords who, for some mysterious reason, would not smuggle their money out of the country and were crazy enough to turn it in and were identified, someone new would take their place before sunrise. And if, for whatever reason, they were able to avoid apprehension, all they would be losing anyway would be their current cash holdings, usually a week or two's profits. The next week, and every week thereafter (unless Regan wanted a new currency to be issued every other week), the drug money they received would be in the new currency. Incredibly, within days of Regan's article, some government officials (who couldn't possibly have consulted with the IRS, DEA, Customs, etc.) were reportedly giving consideration to the proposal.

The recall of $50 and $100 bills as a solution to the drug problem is so ludicrous on its face that one naturally wonders how someone with Regan's background as secretary of the treasury could come up with it. It turns out that it is precisely because Regan was, at one time, secretary of the treasury that he made the proposal. The idea wasn't even his. In 1981, IRS Commissioner Roscoe Egger forwarded a confidential internal document titled "Closing the [Tax] Gap" to Regan (a copy of which was obtained by the *National Law Journal*) in which the recall and reissue of $100 bills (and possibly $50 bills, the document said) was recommended. The document read that this would "cause those persons dealing in big bills—tax evaders, drug traffickers, illegal gamblers, loan sharks, fencers of stolen goods, and corrupt politicians, among others—to be identified for enforcement actions, civil or criminal, as appropriate."

Regan also proposed in his article that President Bush and Drug Czar Bennett "ask the chairmen and presidents of our 200 largest banks and savings institutions to take a public pledge not to accept deposits from drug dealers."

(irrespective of denomination) is slightly over 2½ cents ($.026). Hence, to replace the existing currency with new currency would cost $413 million. However, according to the Department of the Treasury (*Treasury News,* September 27, 1995), approximately two-thirds of the nation's outstanding currency is outside the United States, leaving approximately 5.4 billion bills within our borders. Since only currency that is in the United States would be replaced under the proposal suggested, the cost would be approximately $140 million, a trifling amount when compared to other federal expenditures. (Just one B-2 Stealth bomber costs $2.2 billion, over fifteen times as much.) The fourteen presses at the bureau in Washington and the twelve at its Fort Worth, Texas, plant have the collective capacity of producing 46 million bills per day. Thus, to replace the existing 5.4 billion bills with the twenty-six presses would take 117 days, too long a period. However, if the decision were made, the problem of reproduction could easily be solved simply by utilizing more presses. The reason the bureau has but twenty-six presses currently is that they are being used only to replace old and torn currency per order of the Federal Reserve System. According to Claudia Dickens, a spokesperson for the bureau in Washington, this nation has never replaced its currency with a new currency, but if Congress authorized it, the job could be done.

For the plan to work, if the new currency (No. 2 internal dollars) got out of this country, no matter how legitimate the person or entity was who ended up with it (such as a French bank), they could not exchange these No. 2 dollars at American banks for American No. 1 external dollars or, for that matter, any other currency. No. 1 dollars (the present currency) could, of course, always be exchanged back for No. 2 dollars, or any other currency, since if they were not repatriable, no one would accept them as legal tender outside the United States. But No. 2 dollars, the new currency, would not be legal tender outside this nation's borders.*

---

*The Colombian drug lords would have little interest in defeating the problem simply by having all their profits invested in America. Since they could never come here, how would they ever enjoy their millions? (And before they could even invest their immense profits here in the States, the money would have to be laundered by their American representatives. See later discussion for ways to preclude this.) They would also be very insecure relying solely on investments over which they could exercise no hands-on control. Additionally, they would know that their investment, if determined to have been made or purchased with drug proceeds, could be seized by the government, such as the DEA seizure in 1987 of an $8,034,000 apartment complex in Plantation, Florida, and a $762,500 house in Miami Beach, both purchased by drug kingpin Pablo Escobar and transferred to a Panamanian corporation controlled by his wife and sister.

The new currency plan would neither be precluded by, nor interfere with, the way our nation transacts business (e.g., sells and pays for goods and services, etc.) with other countries, since this is not done by a physical transference of American currency anyway.

Any circumvention by the drug traffickers of the proposed monetary structure would be so inherently onerous and create such a vexatious obstacle that it is very unlikely even the attempt would be made on any significant scale. Two quixotic, purely theoretical circumventions come to mind, both of which are extremely unlikely. (1) Since No. 2 American dollars would be of no value outside the country to those who sell drugs in America, they would not sell their drugs for these dollars. So other foreign currencies which *would* be legal tender outside the United States could become the purchasing instrument for drugs here in America. Drug buyers (or the black market, which would do this work for them for a fee) could go into American banks and, posing as people who are about to travel abroad, purchase, for instance, Italian lire. The lire (or francs, marks, pesetas, as the case may be) would then be used to purchase the drugs here in this country, and the lire could be smuggled out of the country to some other country where, as opposed to our No. 2 currency, it *would* have value. (2) Drug sellers could continue to freely accept American dollars in payment for drugs. As with the drug buyers, they or their agents could pose as tourists traveling abroad, and with their American drug dollars purchase good foreign currency or American external currency at banks, and then send the foreign currency or American external dollars out of the country.

In the wholly improbable event that either of these techniques were employed, legislation could be enacted providing that American banks and foreign exchange brokers could not, at their present locations, exchange American internal currency for foreign currency. This could only take place once a traveler had bought a ticket for a foreign destination and passed through security. The U.S. government might want to operate the exchanges to prevent the mad scramble for "airport concessions" by American banks. At present, although a few American banks already operate currency-exchange units at airports, most are operated by private, foreign-exchange brokers.

Currently, American currency is being smuggled out of the country by drug traffickers in boxes and other large containers. That's the only way the process can be effective. If the traffickers had to buy foreign currency at the airport with American internal dollars, they obviously couldn't buy enough to make the operation worthwhile. And any attempt to buy quantities greater than they could comfortably put in their wallet would immediately make them suspect. We could also simply put a limit on the amount of foreign currency that could be purchased in this country, particularly by private persons.

Another solution would be to require any person or business entity who wants to purchase foreign currency with American dollars to get a permit from the government. With passport in hand, the applicant would have to satisfy the permit office that he had a legitimate reason or need for the foreign currency. Once granted the permit, the holder could take it to any bank and purchase the desired currency. This, in fact, was the precise system employed in Jamaica up to August of 1992, when Jamaica liberalized its policy toward the acquisition of foreign currency. However, under the Bank of Jamaica Act, the Jamaican Minister of Finance retains the authority to issue subsequent regulations regarding the procurement of foreign currency by Jamaican citizens. Since March 1, 1993, India has adopted an extremely restricted policy regarding the acquisition of foreign currency. Only authorized persons can purchase American dollars, for instance, and this is done at designated offices or branches of the Reserve Bank of India.

Although permit offices would have to be established, the volume of business would not be staggering, particularly since most Americans traveling abroad purchase their foreign currency once they arrive at their foreign destination. For instance, the Bank of America, California's largest bank, only averages, statewide, between 100 to 120 transactions daily selling foreign currency to Americans traveling outside the United States. In view of the enormous benefit to the nation, the requirement of a permit would indeed be a petty inconvenience for a very small number of Americans.

What about the problem of drug traffickers continuing to smuggle American currency out of the country and simply selling it at a discount to foreigners? In the first place, the discount could be expected to be substantial. Prior to 1993, all Russian rubles sold outside the U.S.S.R. were traded on the black market in foreign countries for only 10 percent of their value. But perhaps more importantly, to whom would the traffickers sell the American internal dollars? It would seem their only potential major market would be foreign tourists planning to visit the United States. But we could make it against the law to attempt to enter this country with American internal dollars. Moreover, the great bulk of foreign tourists, like American tourists, are law-abiding citizens. How many foreign tourists would be willing to purchase our internal currency knowing that they would be subject to a search by U.S. Customs as they entered our country, and if caught with the currency on them, be subject to a prison sentence in this country and blacklisted from ever entering America again?

Clearly, the mechanics and logistics of exchanging an old for a new U.S. currency would be considerable, but only in the cumulative sense, not individually. There could be a ninety-day conversion period, during which all Americans would exchange the present currency for the new. This is not unprecedented. In June, 1990, as part of the German reunification process, millions of East Germans were given three weeks to turn in all of their ostmarks by depositing them in their personal East German bank accounts. The banks had previously received $15.1 billion in new West German deutsche mark bills and coins from the West German Bundesbank (Federal Bank), and the East German banks exchanged the old ostmarks (which ceased being legal tender at midnight on June 30, 1990) for deutsche marks. Although there were long banking lines throughout East Germany, by all accounts the exchange was carried out without a hitch.

An even more recent example of currency exchange was in the Soviet Union. On January 23, 1991, President Mikhail S. Gorbachev issued a decree providing that all 50 and 100 ruble notes (the two largest denominations) were to become worthless and would have to be exchanged in three days for smaller notes, up to a maximum of 1,000 rubles. The purpose was to curb inflation and also hurt the black market, the principal currency of which was these high-ruble notes. The decree mandated that banks remain open around the clock to carry out the exchange. Because Gorbachev only gave three days for a nation of 290 million people to exchange its high-ruble currency (a few republics, such as Russia and Uzbekistan, defied Gorbachev and extended the exchange deadline to February 1), and millions of Soviet citizens lost all their savings over 1,000 rubles that consisted of 50 and 100 ruble notes, the exchange caused panic, chaos, and anger.

A currency exchange on a far greater scale than that proposed in this book is scheduled to go into effect on January 1, 1999, in Europe. The fifteen-nation European Union consisting of all the major nations of Europe, signed a treaty in Maastricht, the Netherlands, in 1992 providing that the citizens of the Union will physically exchange their currencies for a single currency, originally named the

Ecu, for European Currency Unit, but more recently named the Euro. The move for a common currency is not only seen as promoting and facilitating economic intercourse among the signatory nations, but constitutes the best insurance that Europe's major nations will never turn against each other in war. The treaty, however, is not popular among many European people. An October, 1995, poll in Germany, whose mark is the crown jewel of European monetary units, showed just over a quarter of all Germans ready to trade their marks for a common European currency.

Since most Americans actually carry little currency on their persons or in their homes, it would be a very small sacrifice—one virtually every American would be more than willing to make if it would help solve the drug crisis—for one person from every family to make just one trip to their local bank—the logical forum to make the exchange. Because the physical act of millions of Americans exchanging billions of dollars would take countless hours of bank time, the government would have to pay the banks to provide this necessary service.

There naturally would be some Americans who would be opposed to exchanging the present currency for the new; for instance, those who have large sums of cash secreted in safe-deposit boxes and would not want the IRS to know of the money's existence because it represents income for which they avoid paying taxes. The government would have to make a choice—either investigate all these people and the source of their money, or announce that no IRS monitoring will take place at the banks when the exchange is made. This type of concession would not be startling. In fact, even granting virtual amnesty has been done. From 1934 to 1951, the IRS followed a practice of not recommending prosecution in cases where taxpayers made voluntary disclosures before any investigation had begun. If the latter policy is adopted, the government would be no worse off than it was before. *Remember, either we are serious about the war on drugs, or we are not.* If we are, sacrifices and concessions are going to have to be made. Whatever they are, they don't even warrant comparison, once again, to Korea and Vietnam. The nation, particularly during Vietnam, was divided like never before or since as to the morality of our involvement. Yet in Korea and Vietnam, hundreds of thousands of young American boys were killed or maimed for life. Billions of dollars were drained from our economy. In fact, thirty-one years after the last bomb exploded in Vietnam, we are still picking up the physical and emotional debris. It is hard to imagine how the threat to this nation's security and welfare in far-away Korea and Vietnam was as great as the drug epidemic is to this nation today.

When the proposal in this book for a dual currency was first set forth in 1991, no one, other than reviewers of the book, evinced an ounce of interest in it.* But four years later, the dual-currency proposal has surfaced on a much smaller scale—not with currency, but postal money orders, which have long been a supplementary way used by drug traffickers to transfer drug money out of this country. In June of 1995, the U.S. Postal Service, believing that more than $200 million a year in drug profits are laundered through postal money orders, issued a new domestic money order that contains the words "negotiable only in the United States and possessions" in bold red letters on the front and back. Only U.S. Postal Service international money orders will be negotiable outside the United States. A Federal Register Notice went out to all American banks alerting them that money orders bearing the subject restrictive language should not be accepted if negotiated by a foreign bank and should be returned unpaid by the Postal Service. Such money orders mailed to a U.S. bank for deposit from offshore are supposed to be rejected.**

2. Interdiction of Drug-Money Wire Transfers

The remaining 50 percent of laundered money will be more difficult to cut off and, in fact, cannot be totally eliminated like the above 50 percent. However, it can be shut off to the point where it will no longer be worthwhile for drug traffickers to remain in the business, at least not in America. Before the solution is discussed, a further, more in-depth discussion of money laundering is called for.

In order for money laundering to occur, somewhere, somehow, the money has to make its way into the international banking system. Banks (including S&Ls), in this country and offshore, are the common denominator to the entire money-laundering operation.

---

*In a television debate with me on my proposal for a dual currency back in 1991, Angela "Bay" Buchanan, columnist and presidential candidate Pat Buchanan's sister, said that "Americans are comfortable" with the existing single currency, and would find the implementation of my proposal inconvenient.

**According to Al Gillum, postal inspector for the U.S. Postal Inspection Service, postal authorities are currently working on ways to alert postal clerks to drug traffickers who circumvent the new system by simply purchasing international money orders. One helpful fact is that international money orders normally represent only a very small fraction of money orders sold by the U.S. Postal Service. If these preventive measures prove unsuccessful, Gillum said his office has other options to make it difficult for traffickers to cash these money orders in foreign banks.

Although drug traffickers also sometimes use other institutions in the first step of the process (such as casinos, exchange houses, check-cashing services, and brokerage houses), eventually nearly all of even this money is introduced into the banking system.

Since money laundering is essential, it has become a cottage indus-try unto itself, and drug traffickers normally utilize professional money launderers, who usually are not themselves involved in the sale of drugs and who charge a fee for their services. Deputy Attorney General Philip Heymann says, "In the early money-laundering inves-tigations in the 1980s, the cost of money laundering to the cartels was found to be less than 1 percent of the amount laundered. The DEA estimates that the cartels now have to tolerate money-launder-ing expenses of 17 percent or more."

The amount of dirty money that the money launderers clean for the cartels is staggering. In the 1980s Beno Ghitis, a Miami laun-derer, had his office in the same building as a branch of Miami's Capital Bank, and in an eight-month period laundered $240 million, or about $1.5 million each day. The bank, which was never prose-cuted, received one-eighth of 1 percent for counting the money, and a monthly fee of $300,000.

[For years, Miami was the number-one city in the country for money laundering. One indication of this was the amount of cash surplus at Miami's Federal Reserve Bank (cash surpluses show that banks are receiving more in cash than they need for normal business; banks turn the excess cash over to the Federal Reserve System for credits on their accounts). In 1990, it was $5.396 billion, over $2 billion more than Los Angeles, which had the next largest federal reserve bank surplus in the country. However, the Los Angeles fed-eral reserve bank overtook Miami in 1992 and since then has consis-tently had the highest currency surplus among the thirty-seven federal reserve bank areas in the country. Some feel that cash sur-pluses are not always reliable indicia of money laundering; e.g., fed-eral authorities know that New York City is a major U.S. laundering center, yet the New York City federal bank frequently has a yearly deficit. Houston has also become a major money-laundering center in the last few years.]

Launderers have proven to be exceedingly creative, but by far the principal methods they have used are the following three, with varia-tions limited only by the fertility of the launderer's mind.

1. In a representative example of one method of money launder-

ing, the drug dealer here in the States will turn over to the launderer, let's say, $500,000 in cash from street sales. The launderer employs a number of "smurfs," couriers who carry the actual cash to various banks,* purchasing money orders or cashier's checks with them in amounts of $10,000 or less (more on this later)—in this case, for instance, 100 money orders at $5,000 each. The money orders are usually made payable to a front or shell corporation used by the launderer. The launderer then deposits the money orders (or, much less frequently, ships them out of the country by express mail) to one or more bank accounts of the corporation. The money is then wire-transferred by the American bank to a bank account controlled by the launderer or the cartel in Panama,** the Bahamas, Cayman Islands, etc. In a wire transfer to Panama, for instance, the American bank sends an electronic "payment order" to a correspondent bank in Panama instructing the bank to credit the Panamanian account of the sender or some other recipient.*** From this point, the money is either laundered further by way of wire transfers to other countries, or divided up—the drug lords ultimately having their money converted into pesos, kept on deposit at the bank, or transferred to secret bank accounts elsewhere, including Europe; the remainder of the funds being wire-transferred back to this country to the American trafficker.

---

* Post offices are also used by the smurfs. For instance, in Operation Clean Hands, the U.S. postal inspectors, who are relative newcomers in the government's anti-money laundering effort, broke up a ring of Colombian, Ecuadorean, and Venezuelan "smurfs" in 1991. The smurfs had purchased money orders in amounts of $1,000 or less from post offices and banks in the New York area. The total amount bought: more than $30 million.

** More cocaine drug money has been laundered through Panama in the last decade than any other nation in Latin America. Since 1979, the number of banks in Panama has grown from 9 to 10, one-third of which, the DEA estimated in 1988, were involved in money laundering. Panama became a favorite of drug traffickers not just because it is a bank and corporate secrecy haven, but because of the presence (until his removal from power in December, 1989) of Panamanian military leader Gen. Manuel Antonio Noriega, who was shoulder-deep himself in drug dealing.

*** Sometimes the wire transfer is in payment of phony invoices by fake export companies (set up by the launderer in the country to which the wire transfer is sent) for non-existent imported goods, or for goods from an actual company that are never shipped. Per Greg Passic, former chief of financial operations for the DEA and now a special agent at FinCEN (see footnote on page 189), another emerging but inherently limited way of getting drug money out of the country is for cartel intermediaries in Colombia to approach Colombian importers of American products and sell their American dollars from drug proceeds (which are still in the United States) to the importer for a discount. The transfer of money takes place in the United States between a representative of the Colombian importer and an American representative of the cartel, the latter exchanging the American drug dollars at a discount for the Colombian representative's peso, i.e., below the exchange rate. The Colombian importer's representative then smuggles the dollars out of the country or wire-

To return (called "repatriate" in drug jargon) the American trafficker's share of the proceeds, attorneys and accountants on the payroll of the American trafficker create fictitious corporate entities in,
for example, Panama, to provide false documentation that the funds
were generated through legitimate investments of the corporation.
Or, the repatriated money is disguised as a loan from a Panamanian
corporate lender, frequently a shell finance company. Since a loan is
a nontaxable event, the "borrower" has thereby avoided reportable
income to the IRS. Elevating cheek to an art form, the American
"borrower" also deducts the interest payments on his income tax
return. Through this laundering process, the now-clean funds can be
safely returned for use here in the United States, and the American
drug entrepreneur can openly enjoy his money, appearing as a credi-
ble businessman.

2. The drug money from street sales is commingled with monies
from a cash-generating business either owned or controlled by the
drug dealer or whose owner has been corrupted by the dealer for a
percentage—such as restaurants, parking lots, jewelry stores, supermarkets, or movie theaters—and the money comes to the bank disguised as legitimate earnings from the business. Once deposited, it
is subsequently moved through the same laundering process described in method 1 above.

3. A corrupted bank official facilitates for the launderer or drug
trafficker the setting up of a shell corporate account and the acceptance of money into that account. Again, once deposited, the money
is moved through the same laundering process described above. Presently, the IRS is investigating a number of banks suspected of actually having been purchased by launderers. Although buying off a
corrupt bank official, such as a branch manager, was not uncommon
in the early days of money laundering (the launderer pays the official
a percentage of the money he deposits in return for the bank's not
filing the Currency Transaction Reports, or CTRs), the consensus
today is that this type of activity, though still occurring, has decreased appreciably, and most of the billions of dollars that are being
laundered through domestic banks are done so with the unwitting
cooperation of the banks. The old days in Miami when dope dealers
carried duffel bags filled with money into the banks for deposit—no
questions asked—are long gone.

---

transfers it back to Colombia. The Colombian importer then buys his product from the
unwitting American seller with drug dollars.

Since federal authorities are well aware of the billions of dollars in drug proceeds that are annually laundered through American banks and foreign secrecy havens, what steps are they taking to prevent it? As we shall see, although the situation is improving, not nearly enough is being done.

Up until 1986, the authorities relied almost exclusively on the Bank Secrecy Act (BSA) of 1970. Congress simultaneously gave the U.S. Treasury Department a very broad statutory license to execute the BSA's provisions with implementing regulations; these regulations, set forth in the Code of Federal Regulations, have the force of law.*

Among other things, the BSA, still the centerpiece of the federal money-laundering effort (twenty-two states also have money-laundering laws), requires that specified financial institutions maintain copies of checks, drafts, money orders, and customer-identification information for five years. Most important, the Code of Federal Regulations provides (31 C.F.R. §103.22) that the financial institutions (not just banks—the main institutions the BSA is aimed at— but currency exchanges, brokerage houses, gambling casinos, telegraph companies, the U.S. Postal Service with respect to the sale of money orders, etc.) must file a CTR with the IRS for every currency transaction (deposit, withdrawal, purchase of money order with cash, etc.) "of more than $10,000." The BSA, however, gives banks the discretion to legally exempt from the reporting requirements deposits and withdrawals from businesses that traditionally generate considerable cash. When the drug traffickers control from behind the scenes one of these exempted businesses, drug money far in excess of $10,000 can be deposited without any report being completed by the bank.

The CTR (form 4789) identifies the name of the individual conducting the transaction and sets forth other identifying information. The form must be filed with the IRS within fifteen days of the transaction. A similar form (U.S. Customs form 4790) has to be filed with

---

*The problem of illicit money laundering became so complex and vast that in 1990, the Department of the Treasury established the Financial Crimes Enforcement Network (FinCEN). Centered in Arlington, Virginia, FinCEN is the Treasury Department's money-laundering control nerve center, the designated Treasury agency to establish policies and regulations to prevent and detect money laundering. FinCEN also analyzes raw money-laundering information from all sources, and their analysts provide support for more than 150 federal, state, and local law enforcement agencies as well as assisting financial-intelligence units in many foreign countries.

the U.S. Customs Service by persons taking currency or monetary instruments in excess of $10,000 into or out of this country.

IRS form 8300 has to be completed and submitted to the federal government under the BSA by persons engaged in a trade or business who receive more than $10,000 in cash or monetary instruments in one or more related transactions. The law is obviously aimed at merchants who are sought out by money launderers wishing to dispose of large sums of cash in exchange for their products (persons in a "trade or business" also include attorneys who receive their fee in cash, a common occurrence with drug defendants).

The merchants have proven to be even more venal than expected, and much more derelict and noncompliant than bankers with respect to the reporting requirement. The long-held belief that retailers were not reporting to the IRS all transactions involving more than $10,000 in cash was publicly confirmed on September 19, 1990, with the testimony of two undercover investigators for a House Ways and Means subcommittee. Posing as buyers with plenty of cash and a desire for anonymity, they found that an astounding "76 out of 79 businesses we visited nationwide expressed a willingness to accept cash in excess of $10,000 for the sale of an item and not report it to the IRS." Many sellers actually suggested ploys to circumvent the reporting requirements. The investigators bought such things as a $55,000 Persian rug, a $22,000 antique mirror, and a $73,000 Porsche. "Businesses from across our land are willing to assist others in laundering money and evading taxes for a quick buck," said Rep. J. J. Pickle (D–Tex.), chairman of the subcommittee.

Punishment for violation of BSA violations includes fines of up to $250,000 or a five-year prison term, or both.

The requirements of the BSA, when complied with, help create a "paper trail" for IRS agents seeking to learn the identity of, and build a case against, drug traffickers. But not only have a great number of banks and businesses in the past simply neglected to complete these forms through inadvertence,* the BSA requirements were easily circumvented by the smurfs purchasing money orders for $10,000 or less, thereby eliminating the reporting requirement. Smurfing,

---

* Before a packed House Banking Committee hearing room in May, 1993, representatives of two major banking groups—the American Bankers Association and the Independent Bankers Association of America—told chairman Henry Gonzalez (D–Tex.) that the reporting requirements were becoming more and more time-consuming and onerous to the banking industry, costing millions annually, and there hadn't even been "any thorough analysis of whether the law has fulfilled its intended purpose."

though still very common, has decreased somewhat since a 1986 law provided that if the smurf "structures" two or more financial transactions in one day at one or more banks (e.g., three money orders for $4,000 each, none of which by itself is reportable, though the total exceeds $10,000) for the purpose of evading the bank's reporting requirements, he is guilty of a felony. Also, if the bank has knowledge of the structuring, it is required to aggregate (add up) the separate transactions and file a CTR where the amount exceeds $10,000 in one business day.

The major defect of the Bank Secrecy Act is that it does not cover money laundering per se. If the reporting requirements are met, the fact that, for instance, the bank knew it had accepted for deposit $100,000 in cash from drug sales would not constitute a criminal violation of the Act on the bank's part. Only if the bank intentionally failed to comply with the reporting requirements would there be a criminal violation. And the maximum punishment for violating the Act was only one year prior to 1984, when it was increased to five years. Moreover, the money launderer himself, not being a "financial institution," is not covered by the Act. Further, wire transfers are not covered by the Act, since they do not involve "the physical transfer of currency," and also because the reporting requirements do not apply to interbank transfers.

Despite these gaping holes, many banks and bank officers have been successfully prosecuted under the act—e.g., First National Bank of Boston, for intentionally failing to report $1.2 billion in currency transactions.

Many of the holes in the BSA were corrected by Congress on October 27, 1986, with the passage of the Money Laundering Control Act (MLCA). The new law, under Title 18 U.S.C. §1956, provided that anyone (money launderer as well as any officer or employee of a financial institution working in collusion with him) who knows that the property involved in *any kind* of financial transaction (whether a bank is involved or not, but specifically including bank wire transfers) represents the proceeds of some form of unlawful activity, and who intends to thereby promote the carrying on of the activity, or to conceal the source of the proceeds, or to avoid the reporting requirements under the BSA, is guilty of a felony. Likewise for anyone who transports the proceeds (in the form of cash, a check, or any other kind of negotiable instrument) outside the United States with the intent to carry on said unlawful activity. The punishment is a fine of $500,000 or twice the value of the funds involved, whichever is greater; or imprisonment for up to 20 years; or both. Under Title 18 U.S.C. §1957, it is also a crime to knowingly engage in a "monetary transaction in criminally derived property that is of a value greater than $10,000 [where said property] is derived from specified unlawful activity." The unlawful activity includes not only drug offenses, but crimes ranging from espionage and bank fraud to environmental crimes and copyright violations.

Not only bank officers but the bank itself can be prosecuted criminally under the Money Laundering Control Act and/or Bank Secrecy Act. However, although banks have been prosecuted and convicted for BSA and MLCA violations (e.g., First National Bank of Boston in 1986, and the Atlantic Bank of New York in 1995 under the BSA; the Bank of Credit and Commerce International in 1991, and the Banque Leu [branch of Luxembourg bank in Sacramento, California] in 1993 under the MLCA), since in the event of a conviction the bank itself, of course, cannot be incarcerated, only fined, and since the burden of proof in a criminal trial is higher than it is in a civil trial, the U.S. Attorney far more often than not institutes civil proceedings against the bank itself, or accepts a settlement in lieu of criminal prosecution. The largest such settlement to date was for $35.2 million, paid in November of 1994 by the American Express Bank International to the federal government, resulting from five criminal money-laundering transactions for Mexican drug traffickers by two of its employees, each of whom were convicted in separate criminal proceedings and sentenced to prison. The second largest settlement by a bank in a money-laundering case was for $15.2 million, paid by the Bank of Credit and Commerce International in 1991.

Criminal, as opposed to civil proceedings, are almost always brought against the officers and employees of the bank (or casino, money exchanges, etc.). In 1993, the latest year for which statistics are available, 530 persons were prosecuted criminally (438 convictions) under the BSA for failure to file the required forms or structure currency transactions, 1,688 (only 857 convictions) under the MLCA.

On October 29, 1992, Congress further strengthened and expanded the tools to fight money laundering with the passage of the Annunzio (D–Ill.)-Wylie (R–Oh.) Anti-Money Laundering Act, amending both the BSA and the MLCA. The Act was a direct response to the worldwide banking scandal in the early 1990s involving the Bank of Credit and Commerce International (BCCI). The most notable, by far, of its new laws is the so-called death penalty for banks ("franchise shall be forfeited" is the official, euphemistic language) provision, which authorizes revocation of the charter of a financial institution convicted of money laundering. Revocation is only authorized, however, not mandatory. In deciding whether there should be revocation, federal banking regulators must take several factors into consideration, among which are these: Did the institution "fully cooperate with law enforcement authorities" in the investigation of the offense, and will the interest of the local community in the availability of "deposit and credit services" be threatened by the franchise forfeiture?

Some of the other changes: A "financial transaction" is now statutorily defined to include "the transfer of title of any real property, vehicle, vessel, or aircraft," and there is a new layer of civil penalties (up to $50,000) for financial institutions that have engaged in a "pattern of negligent activity." The Act also prohibits the firing of, or discrimination against, a "whistle blower" who reports money-laundering violations.

In 1994, Congress passed the Money Laundering Suppression Act, authored by House Banking Committee Chairman Henry B. Gonzalez (D–Tex.). The Act seeks to reduce the increasing mountain of paperwork for banks in complying with the burdensome reporting requirements of the Bank Secrecy Act. Accordingly, the 1994 act directed the Treasury Department to streamline and simplify the reporting requirements. The Act also mandated exemptions from the reporting requirements for businesses whose CTRs would have little value to law enforcement, and encouraged Treasury to enlarge the existing exemption list of other bank customers (thereby significantly reducing the CTRs filed each year), such as very large and established American corporations who the authorities are confident derive their funds from lawful activity. John Byrne, legislative counsel for the American Bankers Association, said that the Act represents "the culmination of nine years of working to establish the banking industry's credibility in proving that excessive paperwork is not the way to go."

Clearly, the most important provision of the Act was Congress focusing its statutory attention, literally for the first time in a serious way, on nonbank financial institutions (NBFIs); specifically, those that are "money transmitters"—defined by the Act as any business that provides check-cashing, currency-exchange, or money-transmitting services, and is not a "depository institution," such as a bank or savings and loan. The number of NBFIs has been estimated by the government to be as high as 200,000.* NBFIs have come under mounting scrutiny by federal authorities in recent years. Drug-money launderers have been turning to them with increasing frequency, knowing they were unregulated and finding it easier to convince them to forego filing CTRs. The biggest violators have been the *casas de cambios* (exchange houses), which have proliferated in little towns along the U.S.-Mexican border. A January, 1993, report by the Senate Permanent Subcommittee on Investigations—titled "Current Trends in Money Laundering"—estimates that there are more than 1,000 *casas de cambios* in the border states of California, Arizona, New Mexico, and Texas. Law enforcement has no handle on them (many operate out of small rooms attached to other businesses, some out of vehicles, even phone booths), not knowing how many there are, or how much drug money they launder. Although *casas de cambios* do not have the wire-transfer capacity, they of course can initiate a wire transfer through their bank.

Heretofore, NBFIs were only required to submit CTRs, an obligation they largely ignored for years. But no federal agency regulated their activities. Inexplicably, the 1994 Act still does not provide for federal regulation. Instead, it only urges states to adopt uniform laws licensing and regulating them. However, these NBFIs now do have to register with the Treasury department, submitting the names and addresses of their owners, directors, agents, the name and address of any depository institution where they have a "transaction account," etc.

With the Money Laundering Control Act, the Annunzio-Wylie Anti-Money Laundering Act, and the Money Laundering Suppression Act supplementing and closing the holes of the Banking Secrecy Act, laws are now on the books in this country to cover virtually every conceivable money-laundering act perpetrated by the drug world through financial institutions. *The problem lies not with the law but with the enforcement of it, and it is in this area that law enforcement is woefully lacking.*

In the vast apparatus of federal law enforcement involved in one way or another with the anti-drug effort (fifty federal agencies), the principal agency investigating narcotics money laundering through

---

*Western Union is the largest money-transmitting company in America. As reported in *Money Laundering Alert,* Western Union "averages 63 million transactions and 13 million payees each year. It has 19,000 agents in the U.S. and 25 countries."

financial institutions is the little-known (and little) Criminal Investigation Division (CID) of the IRS, a "pimple on the rump" of the IRS, one senior official laments. Though small, the CID has a colorful and noteworthy eighty-year history. Its successful investigations of racketeers reads like a Who's Who of the underworld: Al Capone, Frank Nitti, Dutch Shultz, Albert Anastasia, Frank Costello, and Mickey Cohen, to name a few.

Apart from managerial personnel, the CID has only 3,400 special agents in the country, and only 1,200 of them are assigned to narcotics. In terms of hours expended, only about 400 of the 1,200 worked on drug-money laundering in 1995, the remaining 800 on the frequently overlapping area of income tax evasion of drug profits. Nevertheless, the CID has more special agents working the financial intricacies of money laundering than all other federal agencies combined, and can bring more expertise to the problem than the other agencies. This is because every CID agent has to have a minimum of fifteen pure units of accounting in his background, and many are accountants and CPAs, whereas none of the other agencies have that requirement.

Although CID has proven itself through the years to be a highly professional and competent investigative agency, how can a force of 400 men and women nationwide (even in company with the support of agents from the DEA, FBI, and Customs, the latter being the second biggest federal anti-money laundering agency) even hope to make a substantial dent in the massive amount of money laundering that is going on in this country today? As hard as they are trying, they can't. Top officials at the agency concede that they are greatly understaffed, unable even to follow up on many of their tips and leads from informants. Despite these handicaps, CID does remarkably well with those narcotic cases it does pursue. In fiscal year 1994, for instance, it initiated 1,612 investigations. Of 1,265 prosecutions of these cases by the U.S. Attorney's Office, 1,110 resulted in convictions.

The current situation is not new. Harvey Eisenberg, an assistant U.S. attorney in Baltimore for the Organized Crime Drug Enforcement Task Force,* wrote Congressman Steny H. Hoyer way back on

* Established by the Reagan Administration on October 14, 1982, and in operation since 1983, the Organized Crime Drug Enforcement Task Force (OCDETF) is a federal interagency effort to investigate, arrest and prosecute large-scale drug traffickers and money launderers, as well as to seize assets and profits derived by them from their high-level criminal enterprise. OCDETF consists of thirteen regional task forces with "core" cities

July 6, 1989, pointing out that because of CID's insufficient man-power, "we have recently noted a lack of ability of CID agents to begin long-term investigations, as well as their inability to travel in pursuit of current investigations."

More and more U.S. drug officials have reached the conclusion that stopping money laundering may be the most effective way of stopping the drug cartels. Former Assistant Treasury Secretary Salvatore R. Martoche says: "From a drug enforcement point of view, there is nothing that has the potential to cripple the cartels as much as effective enforcement of the money-laundering laws. It gets us beyond the mules and even the ticket takers into the boardroom. The drug lords will put a lot of distance between themselves and their poison product, but very little distance between themselves and their money."

Since CID is the principal anti-money laundering federal agency in the drug war, how has Congress responded? By invariably treating CID like a neglected stepchild. For instance, CID's fiscal year 1995 budget for anti-drug money-laundering activities was a measley $114 million, not even the cost of one C-17 military transport plane.

In addition, although the money-laundering laws are now much more comprehensive, apart from confidential informants (CIs) and undercover operations, the basic investigative tool to combat money laundering still remains the CTR, and the form, as utilized, does not begin to serve its intended purpose well. The whole purpose of the CTR is to alert the CID to transactions that may involve the launder-ing of drug money. The form itself tells the bank that the form's purpose is to "*direct* the Federal Government's *attention* to unusual or questionable transactions." But this can't be done because CTRs are not even sent to the CID.

Walking out the door at the end of an interview with a supervising agent at CID, I asked, "Incidentally, how many CTRs come into the office here every day?" "None," he replied. "You're kidding. Why?" "They're sent by the banks to Detroit." "Detroit," I said, "what the hell is going on in Detroit?" It turns out that the banks send all

---

designated as regional headquarters—e.g., Houston is headquarters for the Gulf Coast region. Supervised by U.S. Attorneys, representatives and agents from three Cabinet-level departments (Justice, Transportation and Treasury) and eight different federal agencies (DEA, FBI, IRS, INS, Customs, Coast Guard, Bureau of Alcohol, Tobacco and Firearms, and the U.S. Marshals Service) are assigned under a control umbrella in a coordinated, long-term assault on major narcotics trafficking organizations. Because of the coordinated interagency investigations, OCDETF indictments are normally the strongest in the drug war effort.

completed CTRs to the IRS Computing Center in downtown Detroit. The Detroit center performs no examination of the forms, other than to determine if they have been filled out completely. If they have, they are put into a computer database, where, except for analysis of regional trends, etc., by the Treasury Department's FinCEN, they remain completely dormant unless a CID (or DEA, FBI, etc.) special agent accesses into the base requesting information on a particular bank or individual. When do they do that? When they are conducting an investigation of money laundering, usually based on an informant's tip. Hence, the CTR does not alert CID. CID has already been alerted by information and evidence independent of the CTR by the time the agent accesses in, and the CTRs at that point only serve to offer corroborating documentary evidence against the money-laundering bank or individual.

A 1993 General Accounting Office (GAO) review found there to be little value in the CTR filings. Testifying before the House Banking Committee in May, 1993, representatives of the congressional watchdog said that meaningful analysis of the data is difficult because millions of forms are filed (10,765,000 in 1994), access to the data is burdensome, and FinCEN had not developed any computer program to identify and segregate illicit from lawful activity. Although a follow-up GAO report in November said FinCEN had "taken steps to improve its ability to . . . identify suspected offenders," what makes this whole process even more ineffective than it inherently is, is the fact that many of the forms filed are false. For example, in July of 1991, it was discovered that the "vast majority" of forms 8300 (the forms for business transactions which, along with CTRs, are also filed with the IRS Computing Center in Detroit) submitted by a New York City jeweler indicted on laundering more than $30 million in drug money were false, the jeweler using the names of legitimate customers of his as the purchasers of his jewelry.

Despite the fact that without the ability to launder their profits, drug traffickers, everyone agrees, would be dealt a devastating, disabling blow, and the further fact that CID is the principal federal agency investigating money laundering in our nation's banks, no section in CID (or, for that matter, in Customs, DEA, or FBI), *not even one agent*, is assigned to specifically and exclusively investigate illicit *wire transfers!*

When *Drugs in America: The Case for Victory* was published in 1991, the previous paragraph was followed by these words:

And the situation only gets worse. Although there are literally hundreds of federal statutes which in one way or another deal with the drug problem, and although there are likewise hundreds of statutes regulating the banking industry, many of which are aimed at controlling the drug problem, unbelievably, *not one single federal statute regulates wire transfers!* The sole "regulation" of wire transfers is found in an obscure and never-enforced federal regulation, 31 C.F.R. §103.33. And §103.33 does not regulate or control at all. It simply provides that all financial institutions shall retain a record of any wire transfer out of the country in excess of $10,000. And there is no reporting requirement—i.e., the financial institution doesn't even have to send the record to the authorities, as they do with CTRs. With a drug problem that is ravaging our society, and with our government constantly telling us they are going "all-out" in the war against drugs,* what are the federal authorities doing about this deplorable situation! Actually, nothing at all. The main new measure contemplated is a proposed amendment to §103.33 tentatively set to go into effect in the summer of 1991 that will mandate record-keeping not just for wire transfers out of the country (as indicated, already required), but domestic wire transfers as well, and that the record contain the names of the sender and recipient of the funds, the amount and payment instructions, and the identity of the recipient's bank, *all of which would normally be on the record of a wire transfer anyway.* The Department of the Treasury still hasn't proposed that the banks be required to report the wire transfers to the authorities (*Treasury News*, page 9, October 15, 1990). However, even if the Treasury finally gets around, in a few years, to doing this, the reports will be no more useful to the authorities than CTRs presently are, and for the same reason. Under the proposed amendment to §103.33, when, if at all, will the authorities ever see the records of wire transfers kept by financial institutions? Only if they request to do so (*Treasury News*, page 37).

---

* Though 1995 polls show that Americans view crime as being the nation's number-one problem, and we know that drugs fuel crime, this nation continues to only *talk* about an "all-out war" on drugs, not actually engage in it; i.e., we refuse, as they say, to "walk the talk." Yet many in our society, even respected national figures, apparently believe the rhetoric of our leaders. For instance, in a June 20, 1995, Discovery Channel special on the nation's drug problem, host Walter Cronkite said that ten years earlier, President Reagan "had launched an all-out war on drugs, and the all-out war has continued for a decade." Can you imagine that? A distinguished former network news anchorman who has lived through many *real* wars in our nation's history unthinkingly buying into the slogan and mirage that this country's anti-drug effort is an "all-out war."

When would they do this? Obviously, as with the CTRs, only when they have already been alerted by information and evidence wholly independent of the wire-transfer record that the transfer may have been illicit.

To starkly illustrate, once again, the feeble and tortoiselike progression of this nation's anti-drug effort, an effort that occupies a low priority in the government's scheme of things, the aforementioned proposed amendment to §103.33 did not, of course, come out as it was scheduled to in the summer of 1991, nor, for that matter, in the summer of 1992. On October 29, 1992, one of the provisions of the Annunzio-Wylie Anti-Money Laundering Act specifically mandated that the Department of Treasury issue comprehensive rules regulating wire transfers by a statutory deadline of January 1, 1994. This meant that Congress was giving Treasury fourteen full *additional* months, a period of time when real wars are sometimes waged in their entirety, *to start regulating wire transfers.* But January 1, 1994, came and went, Treasury ignored the deadline, and nothing was done. Such is the sleepy attitude of a nation allegedly "at war" against the drug curse. It wasn't until January 3, 1995, over a year later, that Treasury, in collaboration with the Board of Governors of the Federal Reserve System, issued the long-awaited regulations of international and domestic wire transfers. But get this: They weren't scheduled to go into effect until January 1, 1996, a full year after they were issued, and the new compliance date has now been extended even further, to April 1, 1996. So all during the late 1980s and up to April 1, 1996, while billions upon billions of dollars of drug profits have been and are being wire-transferred out of this country—a *sine qua non* of the drug lords remaining in business—this nation, supposedly "at war" with the traffickers during the same period, has had no specific "regulation" of the wire-transfer process.*

* Remarkably, the Treasury Department, as late as October 15, 1990, did not propose that financial institutions even be required to report suspicious wire transfers. "Treasury has decided not to require reporting of suspicious funds transfers at this time" (*Treasury News*, page 15). If we are trying to win the war on drugs, how, one could reasonably ask, could this situation be possible? Under an amendment to the Bank Secrecy Act in 1992 [§5318 (g) of 31 U.S.C.], Congress provided that the Treasury Department "may" require financial institutions to report "suspicious transaction(s)." (A box for suspicious transactions in the CTR which was checked by banks was not mandatory, and has been deleted in the new CTR in effect since October 1, 1995.) Again, displaying the numbing slowness which has been the hallmark of this nation's "war" against drugs, it wasn't until July, 1995, that the Treasury announced proposed regulations that were to take effect on October 1, 1995 (later postponed to December 1, 1995), and that will now require all financial institutions to prepare a Suspicious Activity Report (SAR) for all suspicious transactions.

That would be hard enough to believe, but the new regulations, like the original §103.33, *still* won't really *regulate* wire transfers! Under §103.33, the originating bank is only required to make and retain "a record" of the wire transfer. Essentially, all that the new "regulations" require is that said record contain information such as the following: the name and address of the originator, amount of the funds transfer, date of the payment order, either the name and address of the beneficiary or that person's account number, etc. But, obviously, even without these regulations, or the original §103.33, prudent banking practice already dictates that banks keep such identifying information. What information did the Treasury think that banks normally put on their records of a wire transfer—the sender's favorite professional athletic team? It took the federal government five long years (we fought the Second World War in four) to come up with these "regulations." To convey the impression that something really new and effective has taken place, the government has added these frills to the new regulations: The threshold amount for the record-keeping requirements has been lowered from over $10,000 to $3,000, and if the sender of the wire transfer is not an "established customer" of the financial institution, the latter must verify the sender's name and address as well as secure his Social Security number before accepting the payment order.

It is important to note that the new regulations *don't even require that the financial institutions send a copy of the wire-transfer record to any agency of our government*, only that they have the records available for inspection (if requested) by law enforcement agencies for a period of five years. For the most part, we know that the government's possession of CTRs has proven to be of very marginal value. By definition, the records of wire transfers, which will not even be forwarded to the government, will naturally be of even less value.

If nothing else comes out of this book, it might serve as an impetus for the enactment of a verbal obscenity law, making it at least a misdemeanor for anyone who, with a sober countenance, asserts in a public place that this nation is fighting a "drug war."

The form will be sent to FinCEN. See also 12 C.F.R. §208.20, a general regulation in effect since 1985 requiring banks—not other financial institutions—to file a Criminal Referral Form with federal authorities for all *crimes* and *suspected crimes*. The Criminal Referral Form is to be replaced by the new SAR.

If federal agents are seeking to stop money laundering in this country when, for all intents and purposes, their investigation is still primarily based on informants and undercover operations, it is no wonder that, as dedicated and able as they may be, they are being swallowed up by the avalanche of drug money being laundered by the nation's banks.

Just a moment's reflection will reveal that the methodology employed by federal law enforcement to fight money laundering is remarkably off-base. With every major crime one can think of, be it murder, burglary, robbery, theft, arson, or what have you, law-enforcement agencies would give their arm and teeth to be present at the scene of the crime to prevent it and arrest the attempted perpetrator. They can't, because obviously they have no way of knowing when, and more important, where, the crime is going to be committed. So they have to arrive after the fact and do the best they can to investigate the crime. In those fortunate and rare situations in which they've been tipped off as to when and where the crime is to be committed, they of course are always there, waiting to apprehend the criminal. Yet with money laundering, even though law enforcement knows precisely where the crime is going to be committed—that is, the banks—instead of placing their personnel there to stop it, *they are nowhere to be found.*

RESIDENT FEDERAL AGENTS

There *is* a solution to the money-laundering problem, and it is a rather simple, quick, and relatively inexpensive one that can be accomplished in one of two ways. The first way is by placing IRS agents (or other federal agents) in residence at banks to interdict the money-laundering process (See page 215 et seq. for discussion of the number of banks and deployment of agents.) Though having an agent on duty at the banks seems like such an obvious measure to prevent money laundering, CID officials say it has never been verbally or in any other way suggested, and it appears in no internal CID document or memorandum. The wisdom of having a resident IRS agent at banks couldn't be more obvious.

1. For starters, how many smurfs (where the use of smurfs is the laundering technique employed) would be willing to go into a bank with a lot of cash if they knew that they'd be automatically referred (when attempting to purchase money orders or cashier's checks in

excess of, say, $2,000, or even less)* to an IRS agent who would question them as to the source of the money, a question the smurf could not answer without telling, in most cases, a transparent lie? Any bogus source, such as a business, could be checked out within minutes by telephone and computer, and the smurf could be placed under arrest for suspicion of violating the Money Laundering Control Act. Moreover, the money could be immediately transported to trained canines who have proven to be uncanny at sniffing traces of cocaine or other illicit drugs from bundles of currency. It is unlikely the drug people would continue to employ this technique.

The job of the resident agent would not be a difficult one. Not only would he become as adept at spotting someone who is "dirty" as INS agents, who almost routinely wave through the vast majority of cars at our nation's borders, but very few people bring in *large* amounts of cash for money orders or cashier's checks. Also, agents would work full-time at banks and would be able to recognize familiar faces who do bring in cash legitimately.

2. With respect to the more important area, wire transfers, the initial wire transfer out of this country usually goes to countries with strict bank secrecy laws, that is, countries that provide statutory confidentiality to all depositors (except by court order), and/or are lax in enforcing anti-narcotic laws, thereby ending the "paper trail" for federal agents investigating the ownership, origin, and movement of ill-gotten money. (The reason the initial wire transfer doesn't usually go to nonsecrecy haven countries, per a CID official, is that in those cases where a narcotics investigation has led to a certain person or company, federal agents can work backward by determining, through a subpoena of bank records, whether the person or company made any wire transfers, and if so, reach out to these nonsecrecy haven countries and have them identify the recipient bank account holders as well as who is associated with the account. If the latter are people federal agents know to be drug traffickers, this helps seal their case against the sender of the funds.) These bank secrecy havens for money laundering have traditionally been very small countries, prin-

---

*Already, under the Anti-Drug Abuse Act of 1988, financial institutions are prohibited from issuing or selling cashier's checks, money orders, travelers checks and bank checks (purchased with cash) in amounts of $3,000 to $10,000 inclusive (over $10,000 would require the filing of a CTR), unless the institution verifies and records the identity of the purchaser.

A 1990 Treasury regulation requiring banks to keep a chronological log of such transactions was set aside by the Treasury in October 1994 because a study showed that the information the logs contain were never used by law enforcement.

cipalities, and territories, and the list is not overly long. However, per FinCEN's Greg Passic, the cartels are getting bolder and bolder in their use of banks of the world, and the initial wire transfer oftentimes goes to countries such as Germany, England, Italy, etc. At the moment, Passic says, Colombia and Mexico, not traditional money-laundering havens, are the two main countries used by the drug cartels to launder their profits. Others, per Passic, are Panama,* Paraguay, Cayman Islands, Vanuatu, Venezuela, Ecuador, Aruba, Netherlands Antilles, Bahamas, Jamaica, the Dominican Republic, and Uruguay.**

In addition to being alerted by the wire-transferring of funds to and from countries whose secrecy laws are known to facilitate the laundering of narcotics money, there would be other telltale signs (and many less obvious ones which the agent would become adept at spotting) of illegal wire-transferring of drug money: deposits almost always being in cash, money orders, or cashier's checks, not in personal or corporate checks; large cash deposits to the account for a type of business not known to generate substantial amounts of cash, or larger deposits than would be expected of even a business that does generate significant amounts of cash; customers who use their accounts as only temporary repositories, wire-transferring the funds immediately or shortly after large cash or money-order deposits; customers who provide minimal or fictitious information, such as references, which the bank cannot verify; customers who do not request lines of credit or any of the other banking services that a legitimate customer would find valuable; and so forth.

A perfect example of how the present system is not capable of han-

---

*The 1989 invasion of Panama, and Noriega's removal from power, accomplished very little. Panama remains a laundress for the Southern Hemisphere's cocaine profits. This was so even within two years of the 1989 invasion. "Despite the removal of the Noriega regime, the money-laundering infrastructure remains largely in place" (March, 1991, U.S. Department of State International Narcotics Control Strategy Report, p. 373). In late 1994, however, Panamanian President Peres Balladares announced a new anti-money laundering policy that resembles U.S. policy. The United States has pledged training and technical assistance to help Panama attain this more aggressive plan of enforcement, and U.S. authorities are guardedly optimistic that Panama will cease to be a nation so friendly to the traffickers. Most of the money laundering today in Panama is operating out of the Colón free zone, an area near the town of Colón located about 40 miles northwest of Panama City. In the free zone, merchants can import and export without paying any custom's duties.

**Per Passic, heroin traffickers from Southeast and Southwest Asia are presently favoring Singapore, Hong Kong, and Bangkok as their chief money-laundering havens. Switzerland remains a money-laundering haven, although not to the extent it once was. The numbered account still lives, but Swiss banks now cooperate with law enforcement in the latter's investigation of money laundering, which was criminalized in Switzerland in 1990.

dling the problem is the February 22, 1989, bust of the largest money-laundering operation in U.S. history. For three and a half years, part of the money from cocaine sales in Houston and New York was shipped by armored transport cars to nine jewelry stores in Los Angeles. The firms would then deposit the money in eight Los Angeles banks as part of their legitimate jewelry store proceeds. The money was then wire-transferred to Panama or Uruguay, or to several New York banks, including Chase Manhattan and Manufacturers Hanover Trust, from which the funds were then wired to bank accounts in Panama and Uruguay. Most of the drug money ended up with Colombia's Medellin cartel, per federal authorities. Before the operation was stopped, well over $1 *billion* had been laundered. How was it stopped? One of the first tips came, as almost always, from an informant. A New York City employee of Loomis Armored Transport, hired to transport scrap gold from New York to Los Angeles, told the DEA that another employee observed a hole in one of the boxes and noticed cash, not gold, inside.

In other words, while the crime of money laundering, to the tune of *$1.2 billion,* was being committed at the Los Angeles banks, federal agents, who should have been where the crime was being committed, were everywhere but there. A New York informant had to furnish information that alerted the authorities as to what might be going on in banks in Los Angeles. Around the same time, one of the banks (officials do not suspect any of the banks of collusion), Wells Fargo Bank in Los Angeles, notified federal authorities that one of the jewelers had deposited $25 million in cash over a three-month period!

Bank employees and officials are not there to detect crime. They are there to transact business. If federal agents had been on duty at the bank, the enormous cash deposits, brought to the bank in armored trucks, and far in excess of what could reasonably be expected from the jewelry store in question, would have immediately alerted the agent. (A computerized system could be set up wherein IRS agents could be told within minutes the previous reported income of the store on its annual income tax return.) The subsequent wire transfers to Panama and Uruguay would have been an additional telltale sign.

The current, naive practice by law enforcement of viewing banks as being off-limits to them (even though they know the crime of money laundering is taking place inside the bank's doors), and of being dismissively reduced to being on the outside, trying to look in, was starkly exemplified in the 1990 case against the National Mortgage Bank of Greece. Federal agents established their money-laundering case by first, as usual, getting a tip from an informant, and then securing corroborative documentary evidence by foraging through the bank's garbage bins in alleys behind its branches in New York, Illinois, Massachusetts, and Pennsylvania.

Law enforcement's effort to fight the drug war descended to previously unimaginable depths of bizarreness with "Operation Dinero," a DEA creation in 1992 that ultimately brought in the IRS (CID) and FBI, as well as law enforcement agencies in four states and four countries. To gain a window into the money-laundering operation of the Cali cartel, the DEA actually set up their own private bank in the small Caribbean island of Anguilla, a British protectorate, and took out discreet advertisements in Colombia describing the bank as having "elite professionals" equipped to "meet your unique financial needs." The Cali cartel took the bait and for close to seven months in 1994, the DEA-operated bank actually provided the Cali cartel with a "full service bank," i.e., foreign exchange services, cashiers checks, wire transfers, U.S. correspondent accounts, etc. When Operation Dinero ended in December, 1994, the two-and-a-half-year operation had resulted in eighty-eight arrests and the seizure of nine tons of cocaine, as well as over $50 million in cash and other property. It also established a direct link between the Cali cartel and an Italian organized crime group (not the Mafia) with operations in France, Romania, Croatia, Spain, Greece, Italy, and Canada. But in the process (hold on to your seats for this one), the DEA and other U.S. federal agencies, through the Anguilla bank and related sting operations, *laundered close to $48 million in drug money for the Cali cartel*, returning the clean money back into the hands of the drug lords. And the fun and games of the drug war go on. Interminably.*

The response of the international community to global money laundering is equally unimpressive. At the December 1988 United Nations Convention Against Illicit Traffic in Narcotic Drugs and Psychotropic Substances in Vienna, Austria, sixty-seven countries, including the United States, agreed in principle to mandate interna-

---

*If Operation Dinero isn't rich enough for your taste, games played by other members of law enforcement in the drug war may be more to your liking. One example: Unbelievably, the Santa Ana, California, Police Department started manufacturing its own crack cocaine in 1994! In "reverse sting" operations, officers posed as drug dealers and arrested those who purchased the police department's own crack from them. Amidst mounting criticism, the practice was discontinued in August of 1995.

tional cooperation in the investigation of money laundering. The agreement set forth the principle that bank secrecy laws should not interfere with criminal investigations in the context of international cooperation. The signatory countries demonstrated how truly serious they were about the measures they endorsed in Vienna by the slowness with which they ratified the agreement. One full year after the convention, only four nations (China, the Bahamas, Nigeria, and Senegal) had done so. The United States didn't bother to ratify it until February 20, 1990, and it wasn't until November 1, 1990, that the agreement was ratified by the requisite twenty nations (over 100 have now ratified the agreement).

And so the significant-sounding conventions, spinning of wheels, and cosmetic war against drugs continues. It should be noted that in 1990, a Financial Action Task Force of seven major nations (U.S., Japan, Germany, France, United Kingdom, Italy, and Canada) made forty recommendations to implement the aforementioned U.N. agreement. The problem is that virtually all of the recommendations (e.g., criminalizing drug-money laundering; reporting and record-keeping requirements like those set forth in our Bank Secrecy Act and federal regulations thereunder; encouraging financial institutions to develop anti-money-laundering training programs, etc.) are already in place in the United States, and with the exception of highly publicized successes here and there in the anti-money-laundering fight, money laundering of drug profits continues through the financial institutions of America.

Since money laundering has become a global enterprise, many of the industrialized nations of the world now have anti-money-laundering laws of varying degrees of virility, and seventeen (mostly European) have financial intelligence agencies to track the flow of illicit money. But little headway has been made to thwart the ever more sophisticated techniques of the launderers. The U.S. State Department 1995 International Narcotic Control Strategy Report, though noting some accomplishments, gives mostly negative or mixed grades to the nations of the world in their anti-money-laundering effort. The report said that "far too many [nations] have still not adopted needed legislation . . . and overall, there is concern about the pace of implementation of existing laws and their inconsistent enforcement." The report noted that "too many governments still refuse to share information about financial transactions with other goverments to facilitate multinational money-laundering investigations."

With respect to the legality of having IRS agents in residence at banks and interdicting wire transfers of drug money, a whole host of legal issues present themselves, each of which can be negotiated successfully.

First, it can be assumed that every major bank in America would be more than willing to do its part in helping to solve the drug crisis and would therefore cooperate fully in providing space, among other things, for the resident agent. In the absence of industrywide cooperation, since the U.S. Supreme Court has affirmed that banks are instrumentalities of the federal government, created for a public purpose, and as such necessarily subject to the paramount authority of the United States, Congress could pass a simple amendment to the Bank Secrecy Act of 1970 (or one of the other acts, such as the Money Laundering Control Act of 1986) mandating the aforementioned cooperation.

In the principal area of IRS involvement at the bank, the wire transfer, would the bank legally be able to furnish information to the agent that, for instance, a $5 million wire transfer had been ordered by a depositor and is about to be sent to Panama? Yes. Although the depositor's legal counsel would undoubtedly challenge this, arguing that this notification is tantamount to furnishing the government with the "records" of his client—and hence be in violation of the 1978 Right to Financial Privacy Act—under §3403(c) of the Privacy Act itself (Title 12 U.S.C.), a bank may *notify* the government of information they have that "may" be relevant to a "possible" violation of any criminal statute. This allows the bank to relate the nature of suspected illegal activity and the name of the individual involved. (Moreover, the Annunzio-Wylie Anti-Money Laundering Act of 1992 contains the following provision, which gives the bank legal immunity for any disclosure: Any financial institution that makes a disclosure "of any possible violation of law or regulation . . . pursuant to this [law] or any other authority . . . shall not be liable to any person . . . for such disclosure"). With the agent and personnel from the wire-transfer section of the bank working together on a day-to-day basis, utilizing and expanding on the telltale signs referred to earlier, the already broad language of §3403(c) would be easy to comply with.

Normally, under the Privacy Act, the government would procure bank customer records by serving a subpoena or search warrant on the bank. In such a case the government would be investigating what they believe to be a crime or possible commission of a crime; i.e., the crime, if any, has *already* been committed. Here, the act of a wire transfer of drug profits is a crime that is *about* to take place. Under such circumstances, it is almost inconceivable that any court would hold that a subpoena or search warrant was required, when to do so would, in effect, permit the crime to be committed, since by the time the subpoena or warrant was secured and served on the bank, the illegal wire transfer (and hence, crime) would already have taken place. By analogy, cases are legion for the proposition that in an "emergency" or "exigent circumstances," the normal rules of search and seizure don't apply; e.g., searches and seizures without warrants are justified when there is reason to believe that a suspect is about to destroy evidence.

Even in the very unlikely event that this were not deemed to be an emergency situation, legislation could be enacted to eliminate the need for a subpoena or warrant under the narrow circumstance of a possible or suspected wire transfer of drug money. For instance, §3414 of Title 12 U.S.C. already dispenses with the need for a subpoena or warrant in cases involving the Secret Service or foreign-intelligence activities.

In light of the immense societal interest involved, it is highly probable that courts would hold such legislation to be constitutional, particularly since the entire range of rights under the Right to Financial Privacy Act was granted *by* Congress, not compelled by constitutional imperative. Being granted *by* Congress, Congress can take it away or apply exceptions to it. One example is 12 U.S.C. §3413 (L), which provides that the Right to Financial Privacy Act shall not apply when any financial institution provides "any financial record of any officer, director, employee, or controlling shareholder . . . of such institution, or of any major borrower from such institution . . . if there is reason to believe that such record is relevant to a possible violation by such person of: (2) any provision of subchapter II of chapter 53 of Title 31" (Bank Secrecy Act of 1970). Under §104 of the Crime Control Act of 1990, the above exception was expanded to include possible violations of §§1956 and 1957 of 18 U.S.C. (the Money Laundering Control Act of 1986).

In fact, the U.S. Supreme Court has already ruled (*United States v. Miller*, 425 U.S. 435 [1975]) that a bank depositor has no "legitimate expectation of privacy" that his records won't be turned over to the government in the course of an investigation, and hence, the supplying of these records to the government does not violate his rights under the Fourth Amendment to the U.S. Constitution.

If a bank were to notify the resident agent, then, that a $5 million wire transfer to Panama was about to take place, what, if anything, could the agent legally do to stop the transfer if he suspected the possible transmission of narcotics money? When I asked high-level money-laundering specialists at the CID, DEA, Customs, and the FBI this hypothetical question, they all responded, without exception, that other than asking the bank not to send the wire transfer and hoping the bank will go along with the request, there is nothing they could legally do to stop the transfer. To stop the transfer, they say, the agent would have to have *probable cause* to believe that the money was drug money (here, he would only have a suspicion); second, even if he did have probable cause (in fact, they add, even if he had *no doubt* that the wire transfer was going to be transmitting drug money), to interdict the wire transfer would require the taking of formal steps that would not be completed until long after the wire transfer had taken place. In other words, even if they *knew* the crime (here, a felony under §1956 of 18 U.S.C.) was about to be committed, the agents feel they would be powerless to do anything about it! I can think of no other crime on the books that enjoys such a charmed and privileged status.

The incongruity of the "drug war" is that our drug opposition is bound by no laws or ethical standards, and has the morals of an alley cat. Whatever works, they do. We, on the other hand, not only have to combat the formidable opposition but also overcome *our own* highly restrictive cornucopia of laws and almost elegant ethical standards. In the process, we are oftentimes severely handcuffed. At once, that which makes our nation great and honorable also makes it vulnerable.

Fortunately, the federal officials, I believe, are wrong, and I believe they are wrong because they have never verbally ordered the interdiction of a wire transfer out of this country, nor, to my knowledge, have they ever considered the possibility of doing so, and therefore this is a virgin area for them.

By normal extension from existing law, it would clearly appear that neither probable (reasonable) cause, nor even reasonable suspicion, would have to be present, nor would any formal, procedural steps have to be taken by the resident agent to interdict the wire transfer. In fact, it would even appear that the whole issue involving the Right to Financial Privacy Act discussed earlier would be moot and purely academic. Under the Fourth Amendment, which prohibits "unreasonable searches and seizures," either a search warrant or probable cause is required to conduct a search. However, courts have consistently applied a "border-search" exception to this commandment, holding that the government's sovereign authority to protect itself at its international borders justifies searches where there is neither probable cause nor a warrant. In fact, since this nation's first Congress in 1789, when the first border search statute was enacted (Act of July 31, 1789, chapter 5, 1 Stat. 29, 43), Customs officials have been authorized to stop and examine incoming persons or baggage without probable cause or a warrant to determine if something is concealed which is subject to duty or cannot be legally imported into the United States. (See also 19 U.S.C. §1581[a].)

In *United States v. Montoya De Hernandez*, 473 U.S. 531, 538 (1984), the U.S. Supreme Court held that routine searches of persons (and their effects) entering the nation's borders are not even subject to the lesser requirement of reasonable suspicion. According to Bill Odencrantz, regional counsel for the Western Region of the Immigration and Naturalization Service, "We don't need probable cause, a warrant *or any suspicion at all* to stop and search any person or vehicle crossing the border."*

The border-search exception has traditionally been applied only to persons and property *entering* the country, and by definition, the search takes place literally "at the border." In view of the fact that wire transfers deal with property leaving, not entering, the country, and that banks are invariably some distance (frequently thousands of miles) from the border, would they nonetheless fall under the border-search exception to the Fourth Amendment? Federal cases have confirmed the application of the exception to *exit* searches (see *United States v. Hernandez-Salazar*, 813 F.2d 1126, 1137 [1987]; see also dictum in *California Bankers Association v. Schultz*, 416 U.S. 21, 63 [1974], "entering and leaving"). In addition, because of the nature of international travel and the transportation of goods, courts have held that border searches may be conducted at places considered the "functional equivalent" of a border. Thus, a search by Customs agents at Los Angeles International Airport of someone en route to

---

*In the area of transporting a monetary instrument in excess of $10,000 across the border without filing the required report of such act, there is even a specific statute that dispenses with the need for probable cause before a search can be made. In 1986, §5317 of 31 U.S.C. was amended, deleting the requirement and language "reasonable cause to believe." However, under §1357(c) of 8 U.S.C., for the INS to *exclude* a *person* from the U.S., it must have "reasonable cause to suspect" that grounds exist for the exclusion.

Bogota, Colombia, was deemed to be a "border" search, and neither probable cause *nor any suspicion at all* was held to be necessary; similarly, with a search at the Minneapolis-St. Paul airport of someone en route to Calabar, Nigeria (see *United States v. Duncan,* 693 F.2d 971 [1982]; also, *United States v. Udofot,* 711 F.2d 831 [1983].* Likewise, a DEA agent's opening of a Federal Express package (containing fifteen cashier's checks sent by a drug dealer to Colombia) in Bell, California, was deemed to be a "border" search (see *United States v. Cardona,* 769 F.2d 625 [1985]).

If the border-search exception applies to the search of someone boarding a plane some distance from the border, and to the search (again, some distance from the border) of an express package—both on the rationale that the person and package will soon be crossing the border and that this would be the last chance to conduct the search—it is hard to see how wire transfers, which immediately transfer funds across the border by electronic impulse, would not likewise fall within the exception. The different method of movement across the border clearly is a distinction without legal substance. As the U.S. Supreme Court held in *United States v. Ramsey,* 431 U.S. 606, 621 (1976): "The historically recognized scope of the border search doctrine suggests no distinction in constitutional doctrine stemming from the mode of transportation across the borders."

The extension of the border-search exception to wire transfers is particularly likely in view of the consistent holding by courts interpreting the Fourth Amendment that the permissibility of a particular law enforcement practice is judged by balancing its intrusion on the individual's Fourth Amendment interests against its promotion of legitimate governmental interests. Under this balancing process, with the drug curse being the most serious internal crisis this nation has faced since the Civil War (the U.S. Supreme Court in the *Montoya De Hernandez* case has already referred to the drug problem as "a veritable national crisis"), it is difficult to imagine how appellate courts would rule in favor of the drug traffickers on the proposed IRS practice set forth in this chapter.

What the IRS agent would do at the bank when he suspected a possible wire transfer of drug money is simply instruct the bank not

---

*The well-publicized U.S. Supreme Court case of *United States v. Sokolow,* 109 S.Ct. 1581 (1989), requiring "reasonable suspicion" of drug activity to even stop and interrogate a passenger who had deplaned, does not apply. The suspect in that case had flown from Miami to Honolulu, i.e., *within* the United States, and hence no border search was involved.

to wire-transfer the funds, and then question the sender as to the *source* of the money and the purpose of the transfer. (Since we have seen that under the border-search exception, not even reasonable suspicion is needed to conduct a search, stopping the transmission of the money and questioning the sender would certainly be legally permissible, being a lesser invasion of one's person and privacy than a physical search. Furthermore, in the wire-transfer situation, though not necessary, reasonable suspicion *will* frequently be present.) If, in fact, the sender is a drug-money launderer, this fact, and probable cause to believe that he is about to make an illegal wire transfer of funds, will most likely be established during this interrogation of the sender and other preliminary investigation, such as determining if the sender has any record of narcotics or other unlawful activity. Since at this point the authorities could lawfully prevent the bank depositor from wire-transferring his funds, they could likewise prevent the depositor's agent (the bank) from doing so.

The next step for the IRS agent would be to seize the funds. This can be achieved in several ways. In a situation analogous to the "securing of the premises pending issuance of a search warrant" cases (e.g., *Segura v. United States*, 468 U.S. 796 [1984]), the agent's order to the bank not to wire transfer the funds would remain in place pending the arrival of a seizure warrant, which can normally be obtained within hours. Under Rule 41(c) of the Federal Rules of Criminal Procedure and 18 U.S.C. §981 (b) (2), the agent would prepare an affidavit setting forth his probable cause for the issuance of the warrant, and after clearing it with a local assistant U.S. attorney, present it to a federal magistrate. If the magistrate finds probable cause, he would sign a seizure warrant ordering the bank to issue a cashier's check in the amount of the money to be seized payable to the Department of the Treasury, and to deliver the check to the federal agent that serves the warrant.

Though the foregoing is the traditional way of seizing funds at a bank, it would clearly appear that 18 U.S.C. §981 (b) (1) would allow an agent to make the above order to the bank *without* a seizure warrant if the "seizure is pursuant to a lawful . . . search," as would be the case here. Warrantless searches have to fall within one of the recognized exceptions to the Fourth Amendment's requirement of a search warrant. Here, it would be the "exigent circumstances" exception. In *United States v. Dascarett*, 6 F.3d 37, 49 (2nd Cir 1993), the court noted that "electronic funds transfers [wire transfers] can be completed in a matter of minutes . . . because the property . . . is capable of rapid motion due to modern technology," and hence, these transfers "present greater exigencies than the seizure of a conveyance . . . or any other kind of property" (see also 21 U.S.C. §881 [b] [4] for similar authority).

The Electronic Communications Privacy Act (ECPA) of 1986, 18 U.S.C. §2510-20, which prohibits the interception of "electronic communications," would also not be violated here. Admittedly, although the ECPA is primarily directed at regulating surveillance activities (i.e., wire-tapping), the legislative history of the Act indicates that Congress intended to also protect "funds transfers among financial institutions" (see S. Rep. No. 99-541, 99th Cong. 2d Sess. 0 [1986], reprinted in 1986 U.S.C.C.A.N. 3555, 3562). However, we're not dealing here with one financial institution transferring funds to another financial institution, a common occurrence. We're dealing with a financial institution being the agent of a private person or entity sending funds to another private person or entity. Moreover, in addition to the fact that arguably there would not even be any "interception" of the wire transfer here, the ECPA defines "intercept" as the "aural or other acquisition of the contents of any wire, electronic, or oral communication through the use of any electronic, mechanical, or other *device*." And no "device" is being used in the conduct of the IRS agent proposed herein.

Continuing the scenario, the seized funds would then be placed in the "Asset Forfeiture Suspense Account," a trust fund of the Treasury Department (the U.S. Marshall's office is used as the trustee if the seizing agency is the DEA or FBI) pending the outcome of forfeiture proceedings. If the government prevails at the proceedings, the funds would be forfeited to the Department of the Treasury and transferred into its asset forfeiture account. If the government loses, the funds, of course, would be returned to their original source.

Under the proposed practice, once the funds are seized, existing law is heavily weighted against the drug trafficker. This is so because although *criminal* forfeitures of drug money and assets, which are still being done, can only be made if the owner of the property is *convicted* of the drug-related crime, most U.S. attorneys proceed by way of *civil* forfeiture, which can be utilized even where there is *no* arrest or criminal conviction. The reason is that the proceedings are *in rem*—that is, against a thing (here, the money, but in many instances, a car, boat, or even home or office building), not a person. In fact, asset forfeiture in drug cases has become an important weapon in the fight against narcotics trafficking. Concomitantly, it is also a major source of revenue for many local, state, and federal law enforcement agencies (the federal forfeiture take for fiscal year 1994 was $730 million), who use the funds to increase their capabilities by, for instance, purchasing new and better equipment to use against drug traffickers.*

Moreover, with a civil as opposed to a criminal forfeiture, the government does not have to prove, *beyond a reasonable doubt*, that the money is drug-related. In U.S. District Court proceedings, it only has the burden of showing *probable cause to believe* that the money is "substantially connected to narcotic activity" (and evidence gathered by law enforcement *after* the seizing of the funds right up to the time of the forfeiture proceeding is admissible to show probable cause). The burden of proof then shifts to the party whose funds were seized to prove, by a preponderance of the evidence, that the money is not drug money (or that the property seized was not used in, or purchased with proceeds from, illicit drug activity). If the money truly is drug money, as is nearly always the case, the party rarely even contests the forfeiture proceedings, and the government wins by default, enabling it to keep the funds.

But the principal benefit of the interdiction of the wire transfer would not be the forfeiture of the money. The overriding purpose for the interdiction would be its chilling and deterrent effect on the money launderer. By and large, the money launderer is not involved in drug trafficking, and far more often than not is ostensibly a respected member of the community, such as a CPA, lawyer, or businessman.

"The drug people and the money people run in different circles," says Mike Orndorff, former chief of the DEA's Financial Intelligence Unit and presently assistant director for the office of liaison support

---

*But abuses have not been infrequent. A private commercial pilot flew a man he had never previously met from Arkansas to California. Unbeknownst to him, the man was a drug trafficker carrying $2.8 million in cash. Although the pilot wasn't convicted of any crime, and the authorities found no evidence that he was involved in drug trafficking, his Learjet was seized. More common is seizing the home of absentee landlords who have no knowledge that their tenants are selling narcotics out of their homes. This, despite the fact that the civil forfeiture statute, 21 U.S.C. §881 (a) (6) specifically protects owners of property who have no knowledge of the criminal use to which their property is being put. Finally, in the U.S. Supreme Court case of *United States v. 92 Buena Vista Avenue*, 113 S. Ct. 1126 (1993), the Court held that the property of one who satisfied the "innocent owner" defense was not subject to civil forfeiture. Also, to prevent abuse, in April of 1993 the U.S. Department of Justice issued an ethics code to all federal agents titled "Code of Professional Responsibility for Asset Forfeiture." The guiding principle of the code is that "law enforcement is the principal objective of forfeiture," not "potential revenue."

at FinCEN. Orndorff adds that 80–85 percent of the launderers have no previous drug record. For instance, in December, 1994, a $70-million-drug-money laundering operation was dismantled by the DEA, FBI, and New York City Police Department. The launderers included two lawyers, a stockbroker, three bank officials, a New York City police officer, a New York City fire fighter, two rabbis, a hospital administrator, and the Honorary Consul General for the Republic of Bulgaria. Just the mere knowledge that there is a high probability his wire transfer is going to be investigated by the Criminal Investigation Division (CID) of the IRS will almost assuredly have a deterrent effect on such a launderer, discouraging him from even making the attempt.

If, for instance, you're a businessman with no criminal record (in fact, if you have a record, even more so), and you'd like to wire-transfer $5 million to an account in Panama, and you know there's a strong likelihood that a CID agent is going to call you on the phone and ask you the dreaded question, "Where did this money come from?" (along with a hundred other questions you can't answer), are you going to jeopardize your life and career by ordering the wire transfer? Under these circumstances, one would almost have to be consciously self-destructive to attempt an illicit wire transfer, which carries a penalty of up to twenty years in prison.

And without the money launderer, virtually all federal drug officials believe that cocaine drug trafficking in America would be dealt an incapacitating blow.

Would agents have to be in residence at every bank and savings and loan in America? There are 58,106 national- and state-chartered banks, including branches, as well as 12,318 savings and loans, including branches, in the United States, for a total of 70,424. CID and DEA officials estimate that less than 1 percent are involved in money laundering; in other words, far less than 1,000 financial institutions—and those mostly in Miami, New York City, Houston, and Los Angeles. Money laundering in cities like Topeka, Duluth, or Boise is out of the ordinary. Obviously, resident agents would not be necessary, for instance, at the First Sierra National Bank in Truth or Consequences, New Mexico, or even Banker's Trust in Des Moines, Iowa. In fact, since 1977, a total of only 82 U.S. financial institutions, nearly all of which were banks, not S&Ls, have been prosecuted through CID investigations of Bank Secrecy Act and Money Laundering Control Act narcotics violations. In April, 1990, as a result of Operation Polar Cap (developed jointly by IRS, Customs, FBI, and DEA), the largest drug money-laundering investigation ever conducted by U.S. law enforcement agencies, the Department of Justice obtained federal court orders requiring 173 banks in 23 states to turn over bank records on specific accounts believed to have been utilized to launder drug-money profits. Most of these banks, none of which was suspected of knowing the true source of the deposits, were in just two cities—Miami, 81, and New York City, 50. The entire state of California was a distant third, with 8. Although there are undoubedly more banks in the United States being used to launder drug profits than those specific ones suspected by the federal authorities, this relatively small number (173) gives some sense of the feasibility of the proposal herein set forth.

Unless an expansion proved necessary, agents would initially have to be assigned only to the major banks (some of which would require more than one agent) in the major money-laundering cities. Not every major bank would even have to be staffed, for the simple reason that word of the IRS practice would travel like greased lightning among drug-money launderers, and the launderer could never be sure that the bank he was using did not have an agent. The absence of one yesterday would be no assurance that one wasn't there today. And the mere *possibility* of an agent being there, intercepting the wire transfer, then calling and asking about the source of the money, would have a chilling effect.

Are we confronted here with the same maddening phenomenon that makes interdiction of drugs and eradication of coca crops and cocaine laboratories impossible—to wit, if you eliminate one area, the problem simply surfaces somewhere else? No, because, as opposed to infinite smuggler routes, coca cultivation, and cocaine laboratories, the number of banks *is* finite. Moreover, the money launderers, choked off in the nation's major cities, simply aren't going to move their bases of operation to places like Omaha, Nebraska, or Portland, Maine. But theoretically, if they did, the federal government has the capacity to employ, train, and place an agent in every bank and savings and loan in America.

Would the cost of all this be prohibitive? If this proposal for solving the drug problem were adopted as a substitute for much of what we're doing now, to the contrary, it would result in the saving of literally billions of dollars. But even if all the current expenditures (for law enforcement, interdiction, eradication, etc.) remained in place, and this was in addition, the cost would not be prohibitive at all.

Let's take the worst-case scenario, one that is even silly to contemplate. An agent is required at each of the nation's 70,424 banks and savings and loans. The government would either have to hire thousands of extra IRS agents or establish a new investigative agency, the members of which would be trained in the exclusive and very limited area of wire transfers. Assuming a starting salary of $25,000 per year, 70,424 resident agents would cost close to $2 billion ($1,760,600,000) a year. This sounds like a large sum, but the importance of comparison is that it reduces things to their true dimensions. Spending close to $2 billion to substantially solve the drug curse is not much when the $12 billion $14 billion we've been spending annually has achieved precious little. Spending close to $2 billion to substantially solve the drug problem is not much when just one B-2 Stealth bomber costs approximately $2.2 billion.

The foregoing discussion, of course, is irrelevant, since it is difficult to imagine any scenario that would require more than 1,000 resident agents deployed in banks throughout the nation. This is so because the vast majority of bank branches in America do not even have the wire-transfer capacity. And even those that do, have it only to a limited extent. A representative example is Wells Fargo Bank in California, which has 634 branches. Before 1993, a customer could make a wire-transfer request at any of the subject branches of the bank in the state, but the branch had to pass the request on to the "central wire room" in Southern California (El Monte) for ultimate transmission. Since 1993, wire transfers can now be "electronically originated" at most of the branches, but the transaction information (i.e., sender of the wire and his debit account number, amount of the wire transfer, beneficiary bank, beneficiary's name and account number, any special instructions, etc.) is still electronically forwarded to the bank's central processing site in El Monte, where the transaction is subject to controls that could stop it from leaving the bank—e.g., various databases look at the available debit balance or any other special flags that may have been put on the debit account. Once it is cleared in El Monte, the wire-transfer transaction is transmitted to one of the banking clearinghouses. Rather than establish individual and thereby different communication links with innumerable foreign banks to send and receive wire transfers of funds and debit and credit their respective accounts, banks utilize "clearinghouses" (which have uniform arrangements with banks throughout the world) to transmit payment orders and instructions for them. Well over 90 percent of all out-of-country wire transfers go through these banking clearinghouses, such as S.W.I.F.T. (Society for World-Wide Inter-Bank Financial Telecommunications) and "Chips" (Clearing House Integrated Payment System). "Fedwire" (Federal Reserve System) is another major clearinghouse, but it is primarily used for domestic wire transfers. So the presence of a federal agent, in this very representative example, would only have to be at El Monte, not at each of the 634 branches of the bank.

But to be conservative—and even excluding reassignment from the present workforce—even an additional 5,000 employees at $25,000 each would constitute an added expenditure of just $125 million for an entire year. With the necessary concomitant cost of approximately $140 million to print up a new currency (see page 180) and the estimated $50 million or so that the government would have to pay the banks to exchange the old for the new currency, we are talking about approximately only $315 million to dramatically reduce the nation's drug problem. This sum is a lot of money. But again, by comparison, on the national economic stage it is a rather small sum. The young boy next door may seem like a giant at 6 feet 6 inches tall, but on an NBA team, unless he can jump like a hunted kangaroo, he'd be too short to play two of the three positions. Three hundred and fifteen million dollars to substantially solve the nation's drug problem isn't much when, as indicated, just *one* of the highly controversial B-2 Stealth bombers costs $2.2 billion (twenty B-2 Stealth bombers are presently being built at a cost of $44.4 billion, $24 billion of which was spent on research and development). *Meaning: The cost of just one B-2 Stealth bomber is about seven times as much as the cost of the entire new currency and IRS agent in residence at bank proposals set forth herein to end the nation's drug crisis;* $315 million isn't too much when just six Peacekeeper LGM (formerly called MX) missiles cost $420 million; when just two (there will be forty) C-17 transport planes cost $350 million; when just one (there are fifteen) Trident submarine costs $1.462 billion; when just one (there will be eight) Arleigh Burke DDG-51 destroyer costs $906 million. Three hundred fifteen million isn't too much when this is almost $200 million less than the $500 million this nation is paying the tiny island of Palau (800 miles southwest from Guam) for the right to use it as a military base over the next fifteen years. "We have no military presence on the island, nor are there any plans for one," says Phil Savitz of the U.S. State Department's Office of Pacific Island Affairs.

Consider as well the cost of farm subsidies, historically intended to "preserve the family farm." Today most of the subsidies (grants that do not have to be repaid by the farmers) go to large farms and farm corporations—in effect they are welfare payments to people who don't satisfy the normal criteria for welfare. Three hundred fifteen million dollars to substantially solve the nation's drug problem isn't much when in 1994 alone, farmers in Iowa—just one state—received $732,567,001, over two times the proposed cost of substantially eliminating the drug problem in America. Illinois farmers received $303,158,452. The total U.S. farm subsidies in 1994 were $7,865,090,160. Three hundred fifteen million dollars to force the drug lords out of the drug business isn't much when in 1986, $709 million worth of contracts were approved for the cleaning, painting, and repairing of federal buildings.

On March 9, 1989, a brief article on a back page of the *Wall Street Journal* announced that GTE Corporation had received a $945.8 million contract for supplying "eight army divisions and certain signal battalions" (actually, per a GTE spokesperson, eight signal battalions, and one signal and seven maneuver brigades) with new communications gear similar to cellular phones in automobiles, designed to allow soldiers to better communicate with each other while moving quickly through a battlefield. This scandalous sum of $945.8 million for cellular phones for only eight battalions and eight brigades just happens to be virtually identical to the sum ($962.2 million) spent in 1989 by the federal government in the *entire drug interdiction* effort. To repeat: The entire amount this country spent in 1989 to keep drugs from entering our nation's borders was no more than the GTE defense contract for chic cellular phones for a handful of battalions and brigades! Unbelievable, but unfortunately true.

Put another way: Eliminating money laundering of drug profits through our nation's banks would go a very long way toward eliminating this country's drug crisis. Yet the GTE phone contract was more than eight times larger than the entire amount of money ($114 million, which is 28 percent of the CID's total 1995 budget of $409 million) presently allocated to the principal federal agency engaged in stopping money laundering in America.

Many of our nation's leaders have compared the drug war with the declared military wars this nation has fought. For example, President Bush said that we have to "mobilize all our resources and wage this war on all fronts. We have to go all out." That is the symbolic rhetoric. This is the reality: At the very moment former President Bush made that remark in 1990, the defense budget, during *peacetime*, was approximately $300 billion, over thirty times larger than the fed-

220

VINCENT T. BUGLIOSI

eral drug budget that year (1990) of approximately $9.5 billion. The 1995 defense budget (again, during *peacetime*) was $241.55 billion, as opposed to a 1995 drug budget of $13,264 billion. (The recently approved 1996 defense budget is $265.3 billion; the requested drug budget, $14.5 billion.) And we're supposed to be engaged in a current "war" on drugs.

COMPUTERIZED CENTRAL COMMAND POST

The second alternative way to interdict drug money wire transfers (and the one which ultimately should be aspired to) would be to eventually have a completely computerized central command post staffed by federal agents that employs the latest automatic data processing system for every region of the country. The resident IRS agent proposal could be employed while the new computerized command post was being developed.

The "Outgoing Wire Transfer Request" by the sender of funds is made in various ways, such as by phone, by making a request in person at the bank or, increasingly, by the sender instructing his personal computer to tell his bank computer to make a wire transfer. In this latter method, there is "no human intervention" at the bank to edit or monitor the request and funds transfer. The resident IRS agent solution, by definition, contemplates such human intervention. But human intervention could be deferred to a later point in the wire-transfer process by the command post concept.

An emerging form of advanced technology being used today by the military and big business is the "SMART" systems, or as they are sometimes known, "Artificial Intelligence," and they could be employed to interdict the wire transfer of drug profits. By relying on programmed historical data (i.e., any past information available on the person or entity initiating the wire transfer, the beneficiary, etc.), and an authentication system to determine that the parties to the transaction are who they purport to be, this computer-based technology could be utilized to watch for warning signs that would identify potential money-laundering activity. This could be done by including combinations of control points in the "SMART" system such as the following: names of money-laundering haven countries;* names of

---

* Since most *initial* wire transfers of drug money out of the United States go to these countries, and since, as the head of the wire-transfer section of a major national bank told me, "wire transfers to these countries are a very small percentage of all transfers," being alerted to these relatively few transfers, which would be easy, could alone have a possibly

businesses and individuals already targeted by the DEA, CID, Customs, etc.; knowing whether this is the first wire transfer initiated by the sender; whether this is the first wire transfer initiated for the beneficiary; whether previous wire transfers from the sender are for the same amount; whether the sender is a company transmitting to an individual beneficiary as opposed, typically, to another company; whether the wire amount is above a certain threshhold; whether the wire amount is out of pattern with normal activity for the type of business engaged in; whether the sender has an account at the bank.

The list can go on and on. For example, as mentioned earlier, if the sender has an account at the bank, are his deposits almost always in cash, money orders, or cashier's checks?; have there been large cash deposits to the account for a type of business not known to generate such amounts of cash?; does the sender use his account as a temporary repository of his funds, wire-transferring them shortly after large cash deposits?; does the sender request or require the broad spectrum of banking services? And so forth.

If any number or combination of programmed control points were present, the wire-transfer transaction would immediately be taken out of the normal stream and put into a special category meriting additional review and attention by the monitoring federal authorities at the command post. In other words, the computer system would sound an alarm for the wire-transfer monitors at the command post, and set forth the reason it believes the wire-transfer request is suspicious.

Because of the border-search exception to the Fourth Amendment alluded to earlier, even though probable cause to stop the wire-transfer for questioning of the sender would not be required, surely, once

---

significant impact on the wire-transferring of drug proceeds.

For example, what in the world would the ABC parking lot on Flagler Street in Miami be doing wiring $100,000 to a Cayman Islands corporate account? Five hundred and twenty-five international banks and trust companies have branches in the Cayman Islands (three islands in the West Indies), which have a population of only 26,000, nearly 10,000 of whom are non-Caymanians. The Cayman Islands have no income tax, corporation tax, capital gains tax, withholding tax, or estate tax. They have a strict bank secrecy law that makes it a serious criminal offense to disclose financial information.

In a related vein, it should be added that the Department of Treasury's Office of Foreign Assets Control (OFAC) is required under 31 C.F.R. 500 et. seq. to prohibit American companies and persons from doing business with specified countries because of trade and economic sanctions against these countries by the American government. American banks, for instance, are presently prohibited from wire transferring to these countries. OFAC's current list of embargoed countries are: Iraq, Cuba, Libya, North Korea, Iran, Federal Republic of Yugoslavia (specifically, Serbia and Montenegro), and, for arms and oil only, Angola.

the "SMART" system produced a finding that the incipient wire-transfer was suspect, the federal agents at the command post would have probable cause or, at minimum, a "reasonable suspicion" to provisionally halt the wire-transfer subject to further investigation.

One is reticent about relying on cliches, but sometimes they make immense sense. "If we can put a man on the moon," surely we can come up with sufficiently sophisticated computer technology to alert federal authorities to most illicit wire-transfers. This isn't something that is unrealistic and completely theoretical. In fact, WJM Technologies of Petaluma, California, a company that develops software for the financial services industry, already has a "SMART" software system of theirs in many of the largest banks and S&Ls in the country called "Early Warning." The system alerts these financial institutions to customers and account holders whom the bank might not want to deal with. On July 25, 1995, I asked Wayne Johnson, president of WJM Technologies, if his company would have the technical capacity to develop a "SMART" system to detect illegal wire transfers of drug money. "Yes, it would not be difficult at all," he replied without hesitation. He went on to say that he had no doubt that the system his company could develop would be able to detect "most" of such transfers and would have a "substantial impact" on drug-money laundering. He said his company could develop such a system for as low as a half-million dollars. He would contemplate charging banks an annual license fee of around $50,000 to use the system.

Even if the contemplated WJM system or other like systems missed 75 percent of all drug-money wire transfers, how many launderers here in America, as indicated earlier, would be willing to send drug money out of this country when they knew that each time they did so there was even a 25 percent chance that they would be caught and have to face twenty years in prison? I can't imagine many. To all the federal officials who tell us that drugs are destroying millions of American lives, and love to mouth the words "drug war" to whoever will listen, maybe one of them, just one, will deign to read what has just been written, and further, bother to pick up the phone and call Wayne Johnson. I will even provide his phone number. It's (707) 769-2699. He's waiting for your call.

Because banks are wary of any program that will increase their operating costs and in any way impede the flow of dollars through the banking system—the Federal Reserve estimates that 1 trillion U.S. dollars in international wire transfers occurs each business day—unless the foregoing proposal were mandated by law, it could not be expected to be consistently implemented throughout the banking industry. We, of course, should automatically do this, but again, *we will only do so if we are serious about solving this nation's drug crisis.*

Parenthetically, other preclusive measures should be taken in company with the command post system. One example among many could be an amendment to the 1986 Money Laundering Control Act requiring that the "Outgoing Wire Transfer Request" to the bank by the sender (by whatever method employed, such as telephone or personal computer) include a statement, under penalty of perjury, as to the *ultimate* destination of the funds. By agreement with nonsecrecy haven countries, if, for instance, the ultimate destination of a $1 million wire transfer was listed as Italy, but the Italian bank to which the initial wire transfer was sent notified the American correspondent bank that the funds were subsequently wire-transferred to Colombia, the sender would immediately be subject to investigation for perjury. And, of course, the perjury would give rise to an investigation of money laundering.

For those who would say that the new currency proposal and resident IRS agent at the bank (or computer command post) proposals would, in some instances, necessarily infringe on the personal liberties of even law-abiding citizens, such minor infringements would be more than justified due to the severity of the problem, and because this nation, through its presidents, has declared a "war" on drugs. Indeed, the "war on drugs" language has been uttered by virtually every police chief, sheriff, and governor in America. And as former Customs Chief William von Raab said in his May 26, 1988, letter to then–Attorney General Edwin Meese, "in time of war, the entire nation focuses its energy on the war effort. The national drug war should be no different—*we must put our nation on a war footing.*

Unless the "war on drugs" language is just vacuous political rhetoric to allay the national angst over the crisis, certain consequences flow therefrom; namely, that war is a notorious interferer with liberty, and that during war, extreme measures are lawful and authorized—even those, the courts have held, that violate cherished constitutional rights and protections. This is so because the Constitution authorizes *war* (Congress's power to declare war) and protects *freedom* (the Bill of Rights). When these two constitutional provisions collide, the balancing of interests almost invariably favors the war power, not the whole panoply of constitutional rights and protections.

Even if the Constitution did not authorize war, personal rights would have to take a back seat. As President Lincoln aptly and rhetorically asked, "Is it possible to lose the nation and yet preserve the Constitution?" Everyone would agree, says noted constitutional scholar Edward Samuel Corwin, that sometimes it is necessary to "suspend the Constitution." For instance, as sacred as freedom of the press is, no one would challenge the government's right to forbid publication of statements that would convey valuable information to the enemy. Thus, censorship of news having military importance becomes inevitable in wartime, while it would not be tolerated in time of peace.

The history of infringements of constitutional rights during wartime, including civil war, are replete with examples—e.g., the Civil War Confiscation Acts of 1861–1862; Lincoln's suspension of the habeas corpus privilege in 1862; government operation of all transportation systems in World War I; rationing of food and gas, and relocation and internment of 120,000 Americans of Japanese ancestry during World War II.

If there truly is a war on drugs in America, as we are told ad nauseam, then wartime measures, with corresponding inconveniences and sacrifices, are called for.

And infringements on personal liberties are not limited to wartime. The *banking crisis* during the Depression, when thousands of banks throughout the country failed, caused the rapid passage through Congress on February 25, 1933, of the Couzens resolution, by which there were limitations on depositor withdrawals—the percentage of the bank's assets that were liquid determined the percentage of the depositor's money he was allowed to withdraw. On March 5, President Roosevelt went a step further and actually closed all of the nation's banks for four days. He then extended the closure for an additional five days, thereby stemming the rush by Americans to withdraw deposits. Penalties were also fixed for hoarding gold or gold certificates.

Of more recent vintage, at the height of the *energy crisis* and gas shortage, brought about primarily because of an embargo by the Arab oil-producing nations, on January 2, 1974, President Nixon signed into law the Emergency Highway Energy Conservation Act, which lowered the speed limit on the nation's highways to 55 miles per hour. This, of course, was a significant inconvenience for millions of

Americans who found it difficult to drive their cars on
ways at the reduced speed.

Whether it is the banking crisis, the energy crisis, or
sacrifices have to be made by the American people. B
nation's citizens know drugs to be such an enormous
Americans would most likely be more than willing to make these
sacrifices. A September, 1989, *Washington Post*–ABC News poll
found that to help solve the drug problem, 62 percent of Americans
were even willing to give up "a few of the freedoms we have in this
country", for example, 52 percent said they'd even be willing to have
their homes searched without a warrant or probable cause; 67 percent said this about their vehicles. And a December, 1995, Gallup
poll showed 54 percent favoring mandatory drug testing of high
school students and 71 percent favoring mandatory drug testing at
work.

In the case of the IRS agent at the bank (who would rarely have any
need to question a law-abiding citizen), the infringement of rights
(in this case invasion of privacy,) is infinitely more benign than the
emerging practice at insurance companies, factories, and so on
throughout the land of employing private undercover agents to pose
as employees and gain the confidence of fellow employees to learn
who is and who is not using drugs. And, of course, there is random
drug testing of employees by many American corporations and, since
Presidential Executive Order 12564 in 1986, of many categories of
federal government employees. Also, as of January 1, 1995, there can
be random drug testing of truck drivers, railroad workers, pilots, and
other safety-sensitive transportation workers, which affects 7.4 million workers. And on June 26, 1995, the U.S. Supreme Court ruled,
in an Oregon case, that high school athletes may be subjected to
routine, random urine tests to determine if they are using illegal
drugs. All of this is a far, far greater invasion of one's privacy than
would be involved in the proposals set forth in this book.

Actually, when viewed in the context of a genuine, as opposed to a
half-hearted, war on drugs, the sacrifices and infringements of rights
implicit in the new currency and resident IRS agent at bank proposals
are very, very mild indeed—just one trip to the bank to exchange
currency, and questioning by an IRS agent if one buys a money order
or cashier's check with over, let's say, $2,000 in cash—something
very few Americans ever do anyway; and, if you happen to be an
innocent person sending a $1 million wire transfer to the Cayman
Islands, answering some questions by the IRS agent. These intru-

sions can hardly be too much to ask of our nation's citizens if they would help solve this monstrous social condition that has caused immeasurable grief and misery and shows few signs of abating.

Moreover, no relaxation of the Fourth Amendment protection against unreasonable searches and seizures with respect to a person's body, home, or vehicle would even be involved, a discernible trend presently taking place that is highly alarming to most civil libertarians.

Former President Bush, in his 1989 inaugural address, said, "Take my word for it. This [drug] scourge will stop." Of course, the scourge will not go away by itself. It has already proven itself to be by far the most durable, serious problem of any kind this nation has ever faced, and it is here to stay unless revolutionary steps are taken. Subsequently, the president said he was determined "to do *everything* in the federal government's power to eliminate this scourge." Like the words of lovers, these words should have been written on the wind.

There is much, of course, that our government has the power to do that it is not doing. The proposals recommended herein (or any others that may be advanced of similar potency and potential efficacy) will only be pursued by this nation's leaders if we are really and truly serious about finally solving this country's catastrophic drug problem. If we are not, we should at least have the decency to stop the posturing.

PART THREE

FINAL THOUGHTS

Legalization

Although it has been categorized as such by many, legalization is *not*, as opposed to the two previous proposals, a solution to the drug crisis. This is so because with legalization, the likelihood is that drug use will either remain the same or, more probably, increase, at least temporarily. Since the use of drugs, *all by itself*, is so harmful to the user and ultimately society, legalization can hardly be said to be a "solution" to the drug problem.

However—don't be judgmental at this point—the countervailing benefits legalization may bring about in the enormously important area of drug-related problems may very well justify a modest increase in drug use, particularly if temporary in nature.

Legalization (or decriminalization, which involves civil penalties, such as a fine, but no arrest or incarceration) is the principal solution or approach to the drug problem that has been advanced by the social engineers and political pundits. Articles urging this approach appear on a rather regular basis in the editorial sections of major metropolitan dailies. *Time* magazine's cover story for May 30, 1988, was titled "Thinking the Unthinkable"—to wit, making drugs legal.

The reason, I submit, that such an approach is perceived to be "unthinkable" is a misconception that most people have about the use of drugs, which is fostered by a lack of knowledge and thinking on their part. The misconception is that using drugs is a *true* crime and hence, *morally* wrong. In fact, even many of my legal brethren

229

have not only forgotten their first-year criminal law class, but have apparently done no thinking on the matter. A noted law professor, no less, urging legalization, recently wrote, "It is not sound policy to criminalize all *immoral* behavior."

Some basic criminal law is in order. Essentially, there are two types of crime, *malum in se* and *malum prohibitum*. *Malum in se* (wrong in themselves) crimes are the only true crimes, such as robbery, rape, murder, and arson. Without exception, they all involve morally reprehensible conduct. As the U.S. Supreme Court said in *Morissett v. United States*, 342 U.S. 246 (1952), the criminal act by the perpetrator is always accompanied by an "evil state of mind," an "evil purpose." You don't need a statute or a law to tell you it is wrong to do these things. They have been wrong since the beginning of recorded time and will never cease being so.

Malum prohibitum (wrong because they are prohibited) crimes—more properly called "public welfare offenses," "civil offenses," "quasi crimes," or "regulatory offenses"—on the other hand, are not true crimes and do not involve morally reprehensible conduct with an "evil mind." They are "wrong" only because they are prohibited by statute, and for no other reason; i.e., you *do* need a law to tell you they are wrong. Louis XIV of France was once asked by a puzzled member of his court why a particular act was against the law, and he replied, "It's against the law because I want it to be against the law."

Unlike true crimes, *malum prohibitum* offenses, then, are not intrinsically wrong. For example, if sexual intercourse between consenting adults is not considered wrong—and is lawful—only a perversion of logic can make it wrong and unlawful for one of the consenting adults to pay the other for the act. *Malum prohibitum* offenses include conduct (it is thought that the prohibition of such conduct promotes the public welfare in an ordered society) such as selling liquor after a specified time of day, hunting during the off-season, prostitution, gambling, and yes, unequivocally yes, the use of drugs. The latter is unquestionably a *malum prohibitum* crime because if there were no statutes forbidding it, no rational person would condemn, as an evil and morally reprehensible person, someone who, for instance, is snorting cocaine or injecting himself with heroin. Under certain circumstances, one might feel sorry for such a person, feel him to be unwise, or sick, or hedonistic, or what have you, but unless you would likewise consider immoral or evil someone who is hurting himself by smoking a pack of cigarettes, drinking himself blind-drunk, or hitting his head against a wall, you would have no reason to consider the drug user or his act evil.*

If the use of drugs were a true crime, it would always and universally be against the law and frowned upon in all civilized societies, as is the case with true crimes such as rape and robbery. Yet at the turn of the century, the sale and possession of cocaine and opiates in nearly all states was not unlawful, and, as was discussed earlier in this book, they were sold openly in pharmacies and even grocery stores throughout the country. By the end of the first decade of the twentieth century, however, 38 states had made the *sale* of these drugs ("excepting upon the written order or prescription of a physician, dentist, or veterinary surgeon,") a crime, usually only a misdemeanor. But as of 1911, only four states had made *possession* of cocaine and opiates a crime: Michigan, California, South Carolina, and Wyoming (Michigan was the first state, in 1909; however, Ohio, in 1880, enacted a law against smoking, not merely possessing, opium). In fact, as late as 1931, there were still twelve states that did not do so. On the federal level, it wasn't until the Comprehensive Drug Abuse Prevention and Control Act of 1970 that straight possession of cocaine, as well as heroin and other narcotic drugs, became a criminal offense. Prior to 1970, under statutes like the federal Boggs Act of 1951, it was only a crime to "import any narcotic drug into the U.S. contrary to law . . . or receive, conceal, buy, or sell" an imported drug "knowing the same to have been imported contrary to law."

It's not as if the use of cocaine was so minimal during the early years that no one even cared. In fact, at the federal level, the Harrison Narcotic Act of 1914 specifically dealt with the regulation of the sale of cocaine by pharmacists, and the prescription of the drug by physicians. And in those situations where Prohibition of alcohol was effective, as the *New York Times* reported on January 11, 1923, "cocaine in particular is greatly in demand." The drug was popular enough in the 1930s to be mentioned in the lyrics of Cole Porter's great standard "I Get a Kick Out of You."

> I get no kick from cocaine. [later changed to "champagne"]
> I'm sure that if
> I took even one sniff, [later changed to "sip"]
> It would bore me terrifically, too.
> But I get a kick out of you.

---

*Like all propositions, the notion that it is not a morally reprehensible act to use drugs has exceptions; for instance, a pregnant mother who is not an addict, and who with full knowledge of the dangers of cocaine to her unborn child, nonetheless takes the drug.

Likewise with marijuana. First brought to this country in 1910 when Mexican farmers began smuggling it across the border into Texas, and used, though not extensively, in American cities throughout the 1920s and 1930s, there was no *federal* legislation even dealing with marijuana until the Marijuana Tax Act of 1937,* which required anyone selling marijuana to register and pay an occupational tax as well as a tax on each sale.

Robbery, rape, burglary, and other *malum in se* crimes were never, at any place or at any time, lawful in this country, nor could they ever be. The use of drugs became "wrong" only when laws were eventually passed that made their use a crime.

And just as a law can create a *malum prohibitum* crime, a law can just as easily be passed making the heretofore illegal conduct legal, which could never be the case with a true crime. In other words, true crimes can never be legalized in a civilized society, but *malum prohibitum* crimes can and are. For example, between 1975 and 1990, it was lawful in Alaska (yes, Alaska *is* a part of the United States) to grow and possess up to four ounces of marijuana for one's personal use at home. Before 1975 it was a crime, as it is once again today. Until recently, lotteries were against the law in every state. Today, they have been legalized in thirty-four states. And if selling or imbibing alcohol were a true crime, how is it that it was only against the law during the Prohibition era (1920–1933), and suddenly became lawful with the repeal of Prohibition?** Could murder, robbery, or rape ever become lawful?

How is it possible for prostitution to be against the law nearly everywhere in this country, but not in some counties in Nevada? Why is carrying a concealed weapon strictly against the law in twenty-two states (as of December, 1995, fourteen of the twenty-two states have legislation pending to permit the carrying of a concealed weapon), yet twenty-eight have a liberal permit policy? Likewise, if gambling is generally unlawful throughout the nation, how is it law-

---

*The first prohibition of the possession of marijuana was an amendment to the New York City Sanitary Laws of 1914. The first states prohibiting possession of marijuana were New York and Utah in 1927. Michigan and California followed in 1929. As of 1931, the majority of states (twenty-six) still did not prohibit possession of marijuana.

**The Eighteenth Amendment to the U.S. Constitution, prohibiting "the manufacture, sale, or transportation of intoxicating liquors," was ratified in 1919 and went into effect in 1920. The Volstead Act, an act of Congress to implement the Eighteenth Amendment, was passed in 1919, and it extended Prohibition by making it unlawful to "possess or use" any intoxicating liquor, defined as being any beverage containing one-half of one percent or more of alcohol. The Twenty-first Amendment in 1933 repealed the Eighteenth Amendment.

ful in places like Nevada and Atlantic City, New Jersey? And even in those states where gambling is unlawful, how is it that in some of these states racetrack betting is lawful? Or that in Oregon, citizens can lawfully bet on professional football and basketball games, with the state serving as the official bookmaker? Could rape, robbery, or murder ever be lawful, anywhere?

No state would likely be inclined to substantially reduce, if reduce at all, the punishment for a true crime such as robbery, rape, or murder; in fact, the trend is to stiffen the punishment. Yet eleven states have already decriminalized the use of marijuana. For instance, at one time in California, possession of marijuana in any amount was a felony, punishable by imprisonment for one to ten years. Today, possession of not more than 28.5 grams (slightly more than 1 ounce) is a simple misdemeanor that carries a maximum penalty of a mere $100 fine.

On September 14, 1988, ABC's Ted Koppel hosted a several-hour panel discussion on the wisdom and efficacy, or lack thereof, of drug legalization. There could never be a panel discussion on whether to legalize any true crime. On a 1988 Barbara Walters special of past interviews, Bing Crosby is shown taking the extremely conservative position that if he knew any of his children had had sexual relations before marriage, he'd disown them and never speak to them again, and is next heard to say we should legalize marijuana. On the same special, Richard Pryor told Walters he "enjoys" snorting cocaine with friends. Many other celebrities have casually admitted their drug use on television. Would television, movie, and sports stars ever appear on television and say, "I've been raping women, and stealing other people's property"? If so, would we interview them (as we do those who freely admit to drug use) as if they were perfectly decent human beings?

Not just liberal thinkers, but some deep-dyed conservatives like columnist William Buckley, the patron saint of modern-day conservatism ("Prohibition works no better on drugs than on liquor," he says); Raymond Kendall, secretary general of the International Criminal Police Organization, better known as Interpol; free-market economic guru Milton Friedman; and The Economist, the London-based, right-of-center international weekly, have come out in favor of legalization. As stated, no one has or ever will come out in favor of legalizing rape, arson, and burglary.

If drug users are true criminals, were the great numbers of young American men in Vietnam who smoked marijuana, and who fought and died for this country, true criminals? In the last half of the 1960s, over 50 percent of our nation's children on many college campuses experimented with marijuana. Were they true criminals? Are the millions of Americans who presently use drugs in America, including doctors, lawyers, politicians, judges, and athletes, true criminals with all that that term connotes?

The reason for spending so much time discussing these seemingly obvious matters is that so often in life, things are only obvious once they are stated. If the "obvious" matters discussed above were in fact obvious, would *Time* magazine, because of its awareness of the mind-set in our society, have felt compelled to title their article "Thinking the *Unthinkable*"? Would an intelligent law professor who favors legalization feel the need to concede that drug use was "immoral"? Would Congress, in the Anti-Drug Abuse Act of 1988, deem it necessary to say that legalization would be an *"unconscionable* surrender in a war [where] there can be no substitute for total victory"? Would, in fact, all polls show that the decided majority of Americans are unalterably opposed to the legalization of drugs?

If those who advocate the legalization of drugs hope to make any yardage in their endeavor, it is unlikely to come about unless they start adding to their arsenal, almost off the top, the argument that there is nothing inherently immoral or criminal about the use of drugs. The acceptance of this reality by the American public is the *sine qua non* to any legislature legalizing the use of drugs. Before the American public understands the essence, if not the legalese, of *malum prohibitum*, all the other arguments of the abolitionists (those who want to repeal laws prohibiting drug use) will fall upon deaf ears. And it's the American people who have to be convinced, not the legislators. Though many responsible Americans have publicly urged the legalization of drugs, you'll find more $100 bills on the floor of a poorhouse than you'll find governors, U.S. representatives, or senators doing so. Legislators (for the most part politicians, after all, not statesmen) can't be expected to recommend legalization when their continued political existence depends on the will of their constituents, the vast majority of whom are opposed to legalization.*

Why are they opposed? Apart from their belief that legalization would be dangerous, the general public simply doesn't understand the true nature of the "crime" of drug use. Without having ever bothered to analyze the thought in their minds, their reflexive, instinctive reasoning is that drug use *must* be "wrong" and "immoral" because it's

---

*A 1995 Gallup poll showed 85% of Americans opposed to legalization.

a crime. And obviously, it would be wrong to legalize a crime. (It may be difficult for many to accept the notion that just because a law is on the books prohibiting certain conduct does not, perforce, make the law right or rational or worthy of enforcement. Though extreme examples, it might be helpful for those with such congealed states of mind to know, for instance, that it is against the law to wear suspenders in Nogales, Arizona; to shave in the daytime in Poplar Bluff, Missouri; or to own both a cat and a bird in Reed City, Michigan.) Thus, in this line of reasoning, since all crime is bad to the average, law-abiding citizen, tolerating or condoning drug use is leftist, radical, and un American. When presidential candidates George Bush, Bill Clinton, and Ross Perot couldn't get the words out of their mouths fast enough in their October, 1992, debate that they were *very much* opposed to legalizing drugs (as if there wasn't even another side to the issue), they were either mindless (hardly), hadn't given any *serious* thought to the matter (possibly), or simply realized that it would have been political self-immolation to recommend legalization.*

Now that the true nature of the act of drug use is hopefully understood, we can proceed (where those who have heretofore recommended legalization have started) to discuss the issue of drug legalization, not turning on the question of its morality vis-à-vis its immorality—which, as we have seen, is an invalid debate—but on the ultimate question that has to be answered in all *malum prohibitum* crimes: Is the prohibition of the conduct (in this case, drug use) of more benefit to society than the absence of said prohibition?

---

* There is one immutable principle of politics that towers over all others—the old Turkish proverb that whoever tells the truth is chased out of nine villages. For this reason, one can't be too critical of the great run of politicians being as known for their courage as nuns are for their promiscuity. Speaking to a group of alumni of the Stanford Business School in Palo Alto, California, on October 7, 1989, former Secretary of State George P. Shultz, noted for his sober and cautious intellect, stunned his audience of buttoned-up conservative businessmen when he said: "Now that I am out of government, I can say this. We need at least to consider and examine forms of controlled legalization of drugs." Shultz went on to say: "No politician wants to say what I just said, not for a minute."

There is a definite trend among the nations of the world to either legalize the use of drugs or to decriminalize them. On May 5, 1994, the Colombian Supreme Court, in a five-four ruling, legalized the use of small amounts of drugs, e.g., up to 20 grams of marijuana and 1 gram of cocaine. Colombia's then–Prosecutor General Gustavo de Greif, who led the hunt for Pablo Escobar, had publicly urged the ruling. "As long as the drug trade is illicit, the narco-trafficantes will continue to receive immense profits that will allow them to corrupt everyone," he said. On April 28, 1994, Germany decriminalized the possession of small amounts of marijuana. The country's most populous state, North Rhine-Westphalia, has extended the tolerance to all other drugs. On April 18, 1993, the Italian people, by referendum, voted to decriminalize the use of small amounts of all drugs.

Invariably, a balancing process ensues, and this, it appears, is what it comes down to on the legalization issue.

Since the current policy of illegality has been monumentally ineffectual in preventing the widespread use of drugs, other alternatives must be considered; thus *Time*'s "Thinking the Unthinkable." Many who consider the alternative of legalization are as strongly opposed to drug use as the prohibitionists are. It's just that they are earnestly seeking an answer to a national dilemma, whereas their adversarial counterparts seem content with hand-wringing and righteous indignation. Or, to be more charitable to the latter, if a conservative is one who is enamored of existing evils, as distinguished from a liberal, who wishes to replace them with others, whose position is the lesser of two evils—the prohibitionist position of the conservative, or the liberal's abolitionist one?

The prefatory observation should be made that the *only* rationale for making the use of drugs illegal is that we want to protect people from themselves.* There is no other *defensible* justification.

The corollary argument that by protecting people from themselves, we are also protecting those around them, such as their families and society as a whole, necessarily falls of its own weight, since this argument could equally be applied to the lawful drug of alcohol, which has not only destroyed an incalculable number of families but is also responsible for a carnage on the nation's highways (approximately 25,000 deaths per year) that drugs such as marijuana and cocaine has never even approached.** Likewise, the argument that drug users are immoral because by their use of drugs they support the drug industry with all its horrible consequences, is a hollow one, unless we are willing to say that all cigarette smokers are also immoral because they keep the tobacco industry going, an industry that produces a product responsible, according to the national Centers for Disease Control, for hundreds of thousands of deaths from cancer per year.

Protecting people from themselves creates a serious problem. In a

---

*By making the use of drugs a crime, the anomaly is created of the perpetrator and victim of the crime being one and the same person.

**A favorite argument of the prohibitionists for treating alcohol differently than drugs like marijuana or cocaine is that alcohol has a long tradition of being the main drug of choice in America, and it would literally be antithetical to our culture to prohibit its consumption. But this notion seems intrinsically un-American and in contravention of the equal protection clause of the Fourteenth Amendment to the U.S. Constitution in that it discriminates against Americans whose "drug of choice" is not as common as alcohol. In other words, if your drug of choice is not the same as that of the majority of Americans, you should be treated as a criminal.

nation whose core value is individual liberty, does not each American citizen have an inalienable right to engage in conduct that others may consider harmful, foolhardy, or even perilous to himself (examples of the latter are activities such as hang-gliding, skydiving, and race-car and speedboat racing)? Stated another way, in a free society, does the government have the right to prohibit conduct that is only dangerous to the party engaging in it? In the same vein, but narrowing the scope of the inquiry to drugs, if protecting people from themselves is the justification for drug prohibition, how can we then not be consistent and outlaw tobacco (a drug we know causes cancer, arteriosclerosis, and emphysema, along with a host of other ailments) as well as alcohol (which causes, among other ailments, cirrhosis of the liver, congestive heart failure, hepatitis, brain damage, and dementia)? In fact, it is estimated that approximately 400,000 Americans die every year from the use of tobacco, and close to 100,000 die from alcohol-related illnesses.* Deaths attributable to marijuana, in contrast, are virtually nonexistent. Harvard Professor Lester Grinspoon, coauthor of the 1993 book *Marijuana: The Forbidden Medicine,* says that "if you scour the medical literature, you cannot find a death due to cannabis."

Harvard Law School Professor Alan Dershowitz argues, "We've already decriminalized two drugs, alcohol and tobacco." Now it's time, he says, to decriminalize the other drugs. "We adults," says former Omaha Chief of Police Robert Wadman, "are staggering around with a vodka in one hand and a cigarette in the other, telling our kids they shouldn't use mind-altering substances that are bad for their health. Now, what's the lesson you would draw from that?"

Even if we can negotiate the substantial hurdle of intrinsic rights in a free society, and a glaring lack of consistency, we still must address ourselves to the deterrent effect of current laws banning the use of drugs. After all, behind these laws is the assumption that in the absence of them, far more Americans would use drugs than do today. This argument incontestably is valid with respect to true crimes. If people could rob, rape, or kill with total impunity, everyone agrees our society would have a much higher incidence of such conduct. With laws on the books prohibiting such conduct, only a small part of 1 percent of Americans are robbers, rapists, or murderers.

---

*See J. Michael McGinnis and William Foege, "Actual Causes of Death in the United States," *Journal of the American Medical Association* 270 (18) 1993, pp. 2207–2212. The authors put drug-related deaths at 20,000 per year. The National Drug Abuse Warning Network puts the number of deaths from drug overdoses, mostly from heroin and cocaine, between 7,000 and 8,000 per year.

But when it comes to drugs, the deterrence argument would appear to be a *non sequitur*.* We have empirical evidence that for all intents and purposes, drug legislation has virtually no deterrent effect. Our experience with marijuana is instructive. The 1994 National Household Survey on Drug Abuse (NHSDA) showed that 17.8 million Americans used marijuana in 1994, and an incredible 65.2 million Americans have at one time experimented with the drug. The U.S. Census Bureau estimated the 1994 U.S. population to be 260,341,000. Excluding children up through the age of eleven, a group (with an estimated population of 46.7 million) not likely to have many users of the drug, this means that 30 percent of all Americans, an astonishingly high percentage, has tried marijuana. During the counterculture movement of the 1960s, surveys showed that on some college campuses, as many as 90 percent of the students had tried marijuana. The NHSDA further estimated that as of 1994, 71.9 million people in America age twelve or older—almost one out of every three Americans (32.1 percent)—have used an illegal drug of some kind, not just marijuana, at least once in their lifetime.

These startling and alarming figures are very persuasive evidence for the proposition that drug laws do not have much of a deterrent effect, if any at all. The argument that if we legalize drugs we'd have a crazed nation of hopped-up drug users is a rather weak one, because it necessarily is anchored on the unproved premise that there are great numbers of people in America who would very much like to use drugs but aren't doing so because of their illegality. In light of the incredibly large number of Americans who were not deterred at all by existing drug laws, one should not be too confident about that hypothesis.

Available statistics speak loudly that, by and large, whoever wants to use drugs has in fact done so.** Coupled with the fact that drugs are readily available for the asking, in a sense, *de facto* legalization has already taken place. There's also the known phenomenon that when something is forbidden, its allure is increased. As conservative

---

*The *Economist* argues that illegality is not needed to dissuade people from harming themselves, noting that for alcohol and tobacco, "the idea of dissuasion without criminal sanctions is broadly accepted."

**The virtual impossibility of keeping drugs away from those who want them is exemplified by the fact that even behind bars, a completely restricted environment, drug use is very prevalent. For example, urinalysis revealed that in 1992, 35 percent of the inmates at the Joseph Harp Correctional Center in Lexington, Oklahoma, had used illegal drugs. It should be realized that much or most of the remaining 65 percent may simply not have wanted to use any available drugs, not being drug users.

French intellectual Guy Sorman, a proponent of legalization in his country, says: "By wiping out the prohibition, you make the drug banal." The thrill of breaking the law and getting away with it is a very real one, particularly for young people.*

Even given the aforementioned realities, no argument for the legalization of drugs can fail to concede that, at least initially, the abolition of drug-prohibition laws may very well generate an increase in the use of drugs, a very unfavorable condition. And for the purposes of this book, the working assumption will be made that drug use can be expected to increase from drug legalization.**

How much? No one, of course, knows, but it's reasonable to believe that most Americans will not use drugs whether or not they are legal because they know how harmful drugs are and don't want to have anything to do with them. Those who don't care—those who feel that the pleasure or high from drug use is worth the risk of harm—are most likely already using drugs, or at least have tried drugs once or twice and have no further interest. That 32.1 percent figure tends to prove this. So realistically, it would seem that drug use will probably increase very little, if at all, with legalization. There's just been too much education in this country in schools and through the media of the dangers and perils of drug use for it to go up dramatically with legalization.

This ultimate question has to be asked: Notwithstanding increased drug use, are there countervailing benefits that would accrue from legalization that would *more than compensate* for the increased use? This is the type of question and balancing process that we as a nation have to ask ourselves on virtually every issue, whether it's to raise taxes, limit the term of elected officials, or commence a foreign war. Are there more benefits than liabilities?

Even the fiercest opponents of drug legalization usually acknowledge that certain benefits would most likely result from legalization.

---

*Comparative figures are available for 1993 between the use of marijuana in the United States, where it is illegal, and Holland, where it is also illegal, but where the law applicable thereto (one month in jail) is not enforced. Per the Dutch Ministry of Welfare, Health, and Cultural Affairs, a national sample in 1993 of school children between the ages twelve and eighteen showed 6.5 percent using marijuana. A University of Michigan national survey of marijuana use in the United States in 1993 showed 5 percent of eighth graders using marijuana (up to 7.8 percent in 1994); 10.2 percent of tenth graders (up to 14 percent in 1994); and 15 percent of twelfth graders (up to 19 percent in 1994).

**Dr. Lee Brown, the nation's former drug czar, didn't restrict himself to assumptions. In a May 21, 1994, speech on drugs and crime at Harvard Law School, he said: "Legalization is a formula for self-destruction, and this administration is unequivocally opposed to any 'reform' that is *certain* to increase drug use."

It is simply their contention that these benefits do *not* outweigh the danger of drug legalization, which, they say, is increased drug use.*

What are some of the benefits that can reasonably be expected to be derived from legalization?

1. Prohibition creates a black market, increasing the cost of drugs far beyond their natural price. "Cocaine is expensive not because it is scarce like caviar, or difficult to produce like plutonium, or nonreproducible like a Van Gogh painting," writes Antonio Caballero in the Colombian weekly *Semana*. "Despite the fact that it's as easy and cheap to produce as sugar, it's expensive because it's illegal." It is estimated (e.g., 1989 National Drug Control Strategy report, page 6) that if cocaine were legalized and sold by the government or by competing private companies, the cost of cocaine powder would drop to $3 or $4 per gram, *twenty to twenty-five times less than the current U.S. street cost!* In fact, today on the streets of Colombia, a gram of pure cocaine goes for just under $4.

With the greatly increased cost brought about by prohibition, two inevitable consequences result. First, just as Prohibition gave rise to bootlegging and organized crime (which in turn led to a succession of gang wars and murders)** in the 1920s, when profits from the illegal sale of alcohol were so high, the prohibition of drugs has not only given rise to the international drug cartels but has also spawned a dramatic increase and proliferation of violent gangs like the Bloods, Crips, and Jamaican posses warring over drug turf and terrorizing urban areas. With the legalization of drugs, street pushers, gangs, and the international drug cartels would most probably be put out of business overnight, since it is highly unlikely that they would try to stay in business by selling on the black market below the legalized price. Again, our experience with alcohol prohibition is instructive. With the repeal of the Eighteenth Amendment in 1933, speakeasies closed overnight and organized crime got out of trafficking in alcohol. In fact, since 1933 right up to the present time, illegal trafficking in

*If Holland is any example, these fears are not warranted. By electing not to enforce drug laws against users, Holland has, in effect, legalized drugs. Yet the use of marijuana has actually gone down, and the use of cocaine has increased only marginally, as opposed to dramatic increases in the United States in the past decade. Moreover, Holland has the lowest percentage (of total population) of hard drug addicts in all of Western Europe.

**According to a May, 1989, Cato Institute Policy analysis by attorney James Ostrowski, "there can be little doubt that most, if not all, drug-related murders are the result of drug prohibition. The same type of violence came with the Eighteenth Amendment's ban of alcohol in 1920. The murder rate rose with the start of Prohibition, remained high during Prohibition, and then declined for eleven consecutive years when Prohibition ended. . . . The murder rate during Prohibition reached levels not surpassed until 1973."

alcohol in America is virtually nonexistent. Is there any reason to believe that drugs would be substantially different? To illustrate, if you've been selling cocaine for $80 a gram, and suddenly, to beat the government price of $3 or $4 a gram, you have to drop your price from $80 all the way down to $2 or $3 per gram, are you going to stay in the drug business? The very low profit margin would provide no incentive whatsoever for you to do this. Drug dealers would no longer enter school grounds to sell drugs to our children (conduct that would remain a serious crime) for the same reason that no one now enters school grounds to sell alcohol to them—the profit to be realized from doing so would be so small it wouldn't be worth the risk of punishment if caught. Even as uncompromising an opponent of legalization as former drug czar William Bennett concedes this. Page 7 of his 1989 National Drug Control Strategy report reads: ". . . to destroy the cocaine black market *entirely*, we would probably have to make the drug legally available at not much more than ten dollars a gram." As we've seen, with legalization, this would be very easy. So legalization would end all the drug-related violence committed by gangs, drug pushers, etc., committed against each other.

Second, and most importantly, with the elevated cost of drugs caused by prohibition, the addict feels compelled to commit other far more serious crimes (e.g., theft, burglary, robbery) against innocent third parties to support his habit. So we're talking about hundreds of thousands of felonies, each of which has an innocent victim, committed every year in this nation to finance the drug habit. These crimes include the ultimate crime, murder, in many cases committed to get just a few dollars for a quick fix. There can be little question that drug prohibition has given rise to an epidemic of crime and violence in America.

Would the far lower price of drugs during legalization merely result in increased purchases on the part of addicts, so that they would still have to rob and steal just as much as before? Number one, the majority of the cocaine-using population are not addicts. Moreover, even with addicts, the consensus is that today, without legalization, they are *already* using as much or nearly as much as they desire. Since the cost of cocaine during legalization would be approximately twenty to twenty-five times cheaper than it is today, they would have to desire twenty to twenty-five times as much cocaine as they are presently using (and therefore, commit twenty to twenty-five times as many robberies, burglaries, etc.) for this theory, it would seem, to be viable.

Inasmuch as the cost of drugs would significantly plummet with legalization, there would most probably be a concomitant substantial reduction (not elimination, however, since drugs would still cost *something*) in the commission of crimes like burglary, robbery, and murder by the addict.* Given this high probability, shouldn't this question be asked: By insisting on continuing to treat drugs as illegal, are we not completely, almost blithely, ignoring the hundreds of thousands of American citizens who we know are going to be robbed, burglarized, and, yes, murdered every year by addicts needing money to support their habit? *And do we have a right to do this?* Is the argument that we have to protect people from themselves strong enough to ignore these other prospective victims of the drug addict? And which number is even higher—the additional number of people who we *assume* will use drugs with legalization, or the people we *know* are going to be victimized in the absence of legalization? Moreover, between the two victims, whom should society want to protect the most—the user, who, after all, exercised his free will in starting to use drugs, and hence, voluntarily did the harm to himself, or the victim of the robbery or murder, who had no culpability whatsoever in contributing to the awful harm that befell him?

Although they may not actually state this, those opposing legalization in the drug debate are almost necessarily arguing elliptically: "Legalization may reduce crime, but more people in this country would use drugs, and this is an unacceptable price to pay."** In fact, to listen to the strident rhetoric of some of the prohibitionists, one would believe that legalization would precipitate this nation's inevitable and *irreversible* descent into disaster and ruin—the ending of the Republic as we know it. Are they being sophistic when they speak such prattle? Or is it possible that the obvious is not obvious to them; namely, that legalization does not have to be permanent, that it can end as quickly as it began. James Wilson, professor of public policy at UCLA, argues that "if cocaine is legalized and if the rate of its

*The prohibitionists correctly point out, however, that although those addicted to regular cocaine commit nonthreatening crimes such as embezzlement and forgery to support their habit, most burglaries, robberies, and murders to support cocaine addiction are committed by those addicted to crack. And they do this, the prohibitionists note, even with vials of rock cocaine selling for as low as $10 or even $5. In other words, even $5 is more money than the crack addicts have. What the prohibitionists fail to consider is that a $5 vial of crack cocaine contains approximately one-twentieth of a gram of pure cocaine. With legalized cocaine selling for $3 to $4 a gram, a vial would sell for around 20 cents.

**The prohibitionists, *above all,* hate the big drug dealers and drug lords, yet they unwittingly pursue policies that can only serve to perpetuate these very people. In fact, were one to ask members of Colombian cartels who their very favorite people were next to their families, it would have to be those who fight so tenaciously to keep drugs illegal.

abusive use increases *dramatically*, there is no way to put the genie back in the bottle"—i.e., what do you do with the addicts who become addicts *because of* legalization? However, for the experiment of legalization to be costly to our society, one has to presuppose that the rise in the abusive use of cocaine would be *dramatic*. And this, it would seem, is highly problematic. Moreover, as Wilson himself quotes the abolitionists, "the costs of having more addicts around would be largely if not entirely offset by having more money available with which to treat and care for them." But much more important, when a nation is plagued by a crisis or disaster causing untold tragedies and adversities, to demand a complete nirvana as a guarantee before agreeing to alter its approach to dealing with the crisis is senseless. In other words, "We've got twenty problems now, but if your different approach can't assure us of no problems at all, we want to keep our twenty problems."

What the prohibitionists are also not verbalizing, but nonetheless saying, is that they would rather have a greater number of thefts, burglaries, robberies, and murders than see more people use drugs—in effect they are saying that a new drug user is committing a more serious crime and causing more harm to society than one who commits, say, armed robberies to support his habit.

If we know, as we do, that addicts finance their habit by street crime, and if an addict needs, say, $80 rather than $3 or $4 (for the same amount of drugs) to satisfy his habit, doesn't he have to commit twenty to twenty-five times as many burglaries, thefts, and robberies? And if legalization gives the theoretical promise of reducing crime in America dramatically, as columnist Joseph Sobran says, "It's hard to imagine any consideration on the other side to contravene it."

To summarize, if we look upon drug use as the problem, and treat laws prohibiting drug use as the cure, do we not have a classic example of the cure being worse than the problem? In other words, as bad as the use of drugs is, aren't the property and violent crimes committed to sustain it far worse? Particularly when the victims, as opposed to drug users, are completely innocent?

2. Enforcement of drug prohibition laws by local, state, and federal law enforcement agencies, our courts and prisons, etc., costs the nation an estimated $30 billion a year, a significant drain on this nation's economy. Legalization would eliminate that drain, and hence be economically beneficial.

3. Some of the billions now spent on enforcing drug laws could be

utilized for expanded and improved drug education among the nation's youth, and for treatment of all indigent addicts who request it. Public rehabilitation centers around the nation are not only few, but bursting at their seams. Addicts who desperately want treatment to end their addiction can't get in because of horrendous waiting lists. A typical waiting period in most major cities is between four and six months, and private rehabilitation centers are beyond the reach of most addicts, charging $6,000–$15,000 for one month's in-residence treatment. Though drug treatment on demand will be costly, the amount spent to treat an addict is dwarfed by the cost to society of his continued addiction: loss of economic productivity; the commission of crimes to support his habit; the costs of arrest, prosecution, and incarceration; the social cost for additional drug-damaged babies for years to come; etc. The latter cost includes the more obvious expenditures not only in the treatment of the child's physical ailments and abnormalities, but in the need for special education services when he or she reaches school. For instance, the Los Angeles Unified School District spends $15,000 per year per child on teachers, speech therapists, aides, and social workers for such children, compared to $4,000 annually to educate the average child. As indicated earlier in this book, a 1994 State of California study concluded that treatment of drug addiction is very cost effective, paying for itself over time by saving $7 in education, criminal justice, health care, and welfare costs for every dollar invested.

Perhaps the best place for treatment is behind bars, where so many addicts are. But *New York Times* reporter Joseph Treaster, writing in the July 3, 1995, edition of the paper, found that "only a fraction of inmates—about 2 percent—undergo the kind of serious rehabilitation [normally in prison "therapeutic communities," where the addict inmates are segregated and receive concentrated drug treatment] that can change destructive behaviors which have been congealed for a lifetime." And he cites the lack of available funds as one of the principal reasons.

Through legalization, then, enormous resources would be released to fight drug use by other means. One area, among many, that cries out for funds is biomedical research to develop an addiction-reversing chemical agent that will relieve addicts of their compulsive need for a fix.

4. Even a small tax on legalized drugs would bring in much-needed revenue to state and federal coffers.

5. Law enforcement and our courts, set free of the obligation to

enforce drug laws, could devote all of the millions of man hours now tied up in the drug war to apprehending and prosecuting rapists, arsonists, and murderers. Former San Jose Police Chief Joseph McNamara, for instance, estimates that his department spent 80 percent of its time trying to enforce drug laws and combating drug-related crimes. "The fight against drugs for the past seventy years has been one glorious failure," he says. "The courts are overflowing, there is violence on the streets, and the problem seems to be getting worse."

A 1988 American Bar Association report concluded, after a two-year study by an ABA committee, what exists to this very day: "Police, prosecutors, and judges told the committee that they have been unsuccessful in making a significant impact on the importation, sale, and use of illegal drugs, despite devoting much of their resources to the arrest, prosecution, and trial of drug offenders. These extraordinary efforts have instead distorted and overwhelmed the criminal justice system, crowding dockets and jails, *and diluting law enforcement and judicial efforts to deal with other major criminal cases.*

In major cities throughout the land, drug cases have gridlocked the courts, with trial and appellate courts unable to handle the soaring load. And because criminal defendants have a constitutional right under the Sixth Amendment "to a speedy trial," drug cases take priority over civil cases, threatening access to the courts for civil litigants. One example among many: In 1990, all civil trials in San Diego had to be suspended for three entire weeks because the judges assigned to these cases were needed to handle criminal cases, over 50 percent of which were drug cases. "We're becoming drug courts," says Philadelphia Federal Appeals Judge Edward R. Becker, noting that because of the enormous volume of narcotics cases, "it's making it very difficult in many jurisdictions to hear civil cases." New York's federal courts are so overloaded with drug cases that in 1995 many civil litigants reported they had literally been waiting for years (one as long as eleven) for judges to find time to reach a decision in their nonjury trials. Again, overnight, legalization would automatically clear up our terribly congested courts. They would instantly be able to more effectively handle the wide diversity of legal matters and disputes that come before them.

6. Deaths from sometimes impure, toxic drugs sold on the street would be eliminated if the production of drugs were federally regulated. Moreover, the criminal element that otherwise law-abiding citizens frequently have to deal with to secure their drugs on the street

(to which exposure can beget other, more serious antisocial behavior) would be eliminated.

7. Legalization would permit the compassionate prescription, for example, of heroin to relieve the needless agony and suffering of thousands of Americans dying from cancer. Heroin, unlike cocaine and morphine, has not been authorized for use in medical treatment under the Controlled Substances Act of 1970.

The reality of our loved ones dying of cancer and crying out in agony over the unbearable pain, being denied heroin (an analgesic three to four times more powerful than morphine), which would permit them to live the last days of their lives with their family relatively free of pain, would seem to be inexcusable. The irony, of course, is that in hospitals, where heroin is sorely needed to lessen suffering for dying patients, it is not available, while on the streets just outside the hospital, where heroin can only cause harm, it is easily obtained.

The United Kingdom (England, Scotland, Wales, and Northern Ireland) already permits the medical use of heroin as a painkiller. Likewise, marijuana has been found to have a therapeutic effect on epilepsy, glaucoma, asthma, and hypertension, and the movement for the medicinal use of marijuana has been gaining support and momentum in several states.* Hemp, or *Cannabis sativa*, of which marijuana is a byproduct, can also be used to make fiber, paper, paints, varnishes, plastics, and even fuel. In 1916, the Department of Agriculture released a study on hemp paper (Bulletin #404), reporting that one acre of hemp produces as much paper as four acres of trees. To help the war effort in 1943, a U.S. government film, *Hemp for Victory*, encouraged farmers to grow it. On November 10, 1995, Representative Barney Frank (D–Mass.) introduced legislation (House of Representatives Bill 2618) which would permit doctors to lawfully prescribe marijuana for treatment of certain medical conditions.

8. Though in the minority percentage-wise, numerically the drug laws are widely ignored by great numbers of American citizens in every socioeconomic segment of our society. This widespread disap-

*Curiously, there is one legal marijuana farm in the United States, and the little-known "plantation" is run by the federal government on the periphery of the University of Mississippi in Oxford, Mississippi. At an annual cost of $250,000, the federal government provides about 300 marijuana cigarettes monthly to eight Americans, including a stockbroker and former torch singer. These eight were grandfathered from a now discontinued (1992) federal program to provide marijuana, free of charge, to those who could prove it alleviated the effects of their medical problem. The original member of the group won an acquittal on marijuana possession charges in the District of Colombia in 1976 when he provided persuasive medical evidence that he needed the drug to treat his glaucoma.

proval and violation of the nation's drug laws can only breed cynicism and disrespect for the rule of law *in general,* a negative consequence. Many people view the use of drugs, like the use of alcohol and tobacco, as something that should be left up to each individual's personal discretion. As Stephen J. Morse, a professor of law at the University of Pennsylvania Law School put it, in fighting the drug war, "we are fighting an enemy that large numbers of Americans do not consider their foe."

9. Legalization would spare millions of Americans the anxiety, grief, and public embarrassment and shame of being branded criminals. Many believe that drug abuse should be treated as a public health problem, not a criminal justice problem; that those who are hooked on drugs need help from our society, not law enforcement adding immeasurably to their problems by arresting them, forcing them to go through the judicial process, and punishing them by fines or incarceration.

The very term *enlightenment* connotes a certain tolerance, or relaxation, if you will, of heretofore narrow and restrictive views of minority conduct not harmful to others. Both as a nation and as a people we take pride in being enlightened—it is almost a predicate to a civilized society. But in the area of drugs, it could be said we've retrogressed. Witness the Tennessee Narcotic Act of 1913, which provided for the registration of addicts to enable them to have their narcotic needs satisfied on a state-regulated basis by prescription from a pharmacist "to minimize suffering among this unfortunate class" and to keep "the traffic in the drug from getting into underground channels."

10. Legalization would give more protection to the most basic and cherished right in a free society: the right of privacy. Invasion of privacy by way of random drug testing (justified, for example, in areas like national security and transportation employment) and police searches, oftentimes without probable cause, would be eliminated in the area of drug use. "The government seems to be doing a better job winning the war against the Fourth Amendment than winning the war against drugs," says University of Michigan law professor Yale Kamisar.

11. Although not extensive in this country, the prohibition of drug use has nevertheless created significant corruption among the very elements in our society charged with enforcing the laws. Though not of Miami Police Department nor New York City Police Department dimensions (instances of which are too numerous to mention), nor

even numerically prevalent, virtually every major police department in the nation has been infected with drug corruption. For instance, the Los Angeles County Sheriff's office, along with the Los Angeles Police Department one of the finest and least corrupt law enforcement agencies in the nation, has been tarnished. In 1989 and 1990, thirty-two veteran Los Angeles County deputy sheriffs from four elite anti-narcotics squads were indicted for allegedly skimming hundreds of thousands of dollars of drug money from raids. Twenty-eight were subsequently convicted, one was acquitted, and three cases are still pending. In 1994 and 1995, fifty-six drug convictions were set aside in Philadelphia because of corruption on the cases (stealing drug money, planting drugs, tampering with evidence, falsifying records, etc.) by six Philadelphia officers who pleaded guilty.

Rural America has also been corrupted by the drug cancer. Per a September 6, 1992, article in the *Atlanta Journal—Constitution*, since 1981, thirteen Georgia sheriffs in several counties have been convicted of drug-related crimes. Georgia sheriffs are not atypical. As of 1995, seven sitting and two former sheriffs in eastern Tennessee have been convicted of accepting bribes from drug traffickers.

And the DEA, the vigorous lead federal agency in the nation's war against drugs, hasn't been spared. Two Los Angeles DEA agents pled guilty in 1991 to drug-trafficking charges and a third was convicted. And on August 14, 1989, a decorated supervising agent at DEA headquarters in Arlington, Virginia, was arrested at Boston's Logan International Airport with $560,000 worth of cocaine in his suitcase. The agent pled guilty and was sentenced to six years in prison. In 1993, the Miami DEA supervisory agent who handcuffed and escorted to jail Panamanian dictator Manuel Noriega in 1989 pled guilty to attempting to launder $700,000 in drug money. The eleven-year DEA veteran, whose wife was also a DEA agent (since resigned), was considered to be an outstanding agent, per the Miami DEA special agent in charge. When one takes into consideration the number of DEA agents, their shamefully low pay, and the enormous temptation for very easy money they are exposed to almost every day, the DEA has remained remarkably clean.

Not even our military has been exempt. A 1991 Department of Justice probe revealed that in 1990 about half of the fourteen Coast Guardsmen stationed at Islamorada base, a key South Florida outpost, were peddling drugs and aiding traffickers (by selling codes, disabling patrol boats, and so on) while on anti-drug duty in the Florida Keys. Even prison officials have proven to be corrupt. For instance, since 1992, more than two dozen corrections officers and other staff officers at the District of Colombia prison in Lorton, Virginia, have been convicted of smuggling drugs into the prison. And on October 27, 1995, four prison guards at the federal prison in Atlanta were indicted for smuggling drugs to inmates.

Currently, a federal grand jury in San Diego is taking testimony on allegations that eight present and former U.S. Customs service employees, including two criminal investigators, have been assisting Mexican drug traffickers in shipping tons of cocaine into the United States. Even the bench has been sullied. In 1993, a U.S. District Court judge in New Orleans was convicted of taking a $100,000 bribe from a drug smuggler seeking leniency.

The headline stories of corruption in the past several years go on and on: "Texas Sheriff Convicted of Taking $150,000 in Bribes from Drug Dealers"; "Two District of Columbia Police Officers Arrested in Crack Sales"; "Winston-Salem Police Officers Convicted on Cocaine Charges"; "Florida Circuit Court Judge Arrested for Taking Bribes in Drug Cases"; "Florida Sheriff (Hendry County) Pleads Guilty to Cocaine Trafficking"; "Three U.S. Customs and an FBI Agent Charged in Florida with Stealing Cocaine and Laundering Drug Money. Hidden Cameras Recorded Theft of Cocaine, Cash"; "Three U.S. Border Patrol Agents Convicted of Conspiracy with Drug Traffickers"; "Dallas Police Officers Convicted of Extorting $50,000 from Drug Dealers"; "INS Inspector Convicted of Taking Bribes from Drug Traffickers"; "Maryland Police Officer Convicted of Selling Crack"; "Nine New Orleans Officers Arrested in Drug Sting Operation"; "West Texas Sheriff Convicted of Importing $48 Million Worth of Cocaine"; "Two Inspectors [one INS, the other U.S. Customs] Indicted on Charges of Conspiring with Traffickers to Smuggle Drugs through Calexico Port of Entry."

The above are just a small sampling of the corruption in law enforcement engendered by the illicit drug trade. The motivation behind all of it, of course, is money, which for all intents and purposes would be lacking if there were legalization. *

---

* The Brockton, Massachusetts, police department had a different problem. Its chief was addicted to cocaine, and because of it, in June, 1990, the Plymouth County district attorney had to dismiss 380 drug cases due to lack of evidence. The chief had stolen the evidence (cocaine) from the police department's evidence room to support his habit. He said he used cocaine every day for five years after trying some of the samples he took to anti-drug lectures. Cocaine "possessed me like a demon," he said.

At least on paper, and most probably in reality, the *many* arguments for legalization are compelling when arrayed against the lone, sole argument against legalization—the need to protect people from themselves. The multiple benefits seem to simply outweigh the liabilities.

However, since we know that not infrequently large chasms exist between theory and reality, if we go in the direction of legalization, there is a first, more cautious step we should take, and that is to keep all the drug laws intact on the books but simply not enforce them for a given, limited period of time. This is not as conceptually farfetched as it may sound at first blush. Contrary to popular belief, Holland has not legalized drugs. Its conservative government simply does not enforce many existing drug laws, taking a very pragmatic, and ultimately benevolent, view of drug use. In Amsterdam, for instance, marijuana and hashish are generally sold right next to the drinks and snacks in the city's extensive network of coffee shops and "cannabis cafes" (the police, however, strictly enforce laws against the sale and possession of even small amounts of hard drugs like cocaine and heroin, and the sale of all kinds of drugs to minors). As the Dutch minister of justice said at the United Nations Conference on Drug Abuse and Illicit Trafficking in 1987: "We always bear in mind that the drug abuse problem is basically and principally a matter of health and social well-being. It is not, in our view, primarily a problem of police and criminal justice." In 1988, Dr. Frits Ruter of the University of Amsterdam explained on Capitol Hill: "These users and addicts are part of our Dutch family." Dutch policy drug adviser Mario Zap says: "We try not to make our people criminals. What will it take to convince other countries, especially America, about the high cost of repression?"

In fact, right here in America, we don't always choose to enforce existing laws, primarily in the area of sexual activity, where at least two acts between consenting adults, heterosexual as well as homosexual, are against the law in most states but rarely, if ever, enforced—even where, as with homosexuals, the acts take place at public bathhouses with the full knowledge of the police. Adultery is a crime in twenty-seven states, yet prosecutions for it are almost unheard of. With the crime of prostitution, although the customer is also committing a crime, only rarely do the police elect to arrest him. It's the prostitute they go after.

Another example is gambling. Again, the person placing the wager with the bookie, according to law, is also committing a crime. Yet police arrest only the bookie, rarely the bettor. As Steve, a football bookie, said before Super Bowl XXIII, "Everyone has something on the game, the butcher, the baker, the candlestick maker. There's a certain hypocrisy about betting. On the one hand, what I do is illegal, and yet nearly every newspaper publishes the betting line, the football sportscasters talk about the line on national television, and people aren't ashamed to boast that they won their bets." An even more common example is gambling among private citizens. Though private, it is still a crime, yet virtually never prosecuted. It is estimated that 20 percent of the adult population wagered on the last Super Bowl, much of it right out in the open in office pools, including those at police stations—yet another example of unlawful conduct that we overlook without repealing the law. Another example is the sale of cigarettes to minors. Although it's illegal in forty-four states, the laws are widely unenforced. And the list goes on.

If, during this trial period, it appears from all the available evidence that more harm than good is resulting, then enforcement can commence once again without missing a beat. No laws would have had to be changed.

If, on the other hand, the opposite is true, then new legislation repealing existing drug prohibition laws could be enacted. It must be added by way of important footnote that during legalization, it would still be against the law for any unauthorized person to sell drugs. And when the sale is to a minor, the punishment should be increased over what it is today. It would also be against the law, of course, to operate any conveyance (car, plane, etc.) under the influence of a drug.

One of the leading prohibitionists is Rep. Charles B. Rangel (D–N.Y.), who chaired the House Select Committee on Narcotics Abuse and Control before it was disbanded in March of 1993. Rangel makes the argument that "legalization would only send a message to our young people that we encourage drug abuse." But surely our legalizing alcohol and tobacco is not a statement by our nation that we encourage people to drink and smoke. And young people could hardly form this opinion when they not only would be informed time and time again by expanded educational programs about the dangers of drug use, but would know that any adult selling drugs to them would be committing a serious crime.

Mathea Falco, president of Drug Strategies, a nonprofit group that studies the nation's drug problems, eloquently argues in her recent book, *The Making of a Drug-Free America,* that the drug laws "play a critically important role . . . by conveying social values and defining

the limits of permissible behavior. Legalization would signal a fundamental change in American attitudes, implying tolerance rather than
disapproval of drug use." Her observation has undoubted merit, although it doesn't necessarily follow, as she suggests, that legalization
would cause many more Americans to use drugs than currently do.
The fact that a staggering 32 percent of the American people have
used illicit drugs indicates that prohibition (i.e., Ms. Falco's "disapproval of drug use") hasn't served as a deterrent to those who for
whatever reason seek out the drug experience.

However, if Congressman Rangel's and Falco's assumption that
legalization will greatly increase drug use is correct, it alone would be
sufficient justification for not legalizing drugs. Even the mere possibility of their being correct is all the more reason that before making
the decision on legalization, we should experiment with it by first
taking the cautious step of not enforcing existing drug laws for a brief
and specified period of time.

A discretionary adjunct to legalization would be the registration of
addicts with local health authorities. Under a doctor's supervision in
a government facility, the addict (as in Britain, where the addict reg-
isters with the Home Office, the British equivalent of our Department of Justice)* would be given a "maintenance" amount of the
drug during efforts to wean him or her from its use. *Since an addict
is going to continue his or her use of drugs anyway,* having the addict
receive a maintenance amount of the drug free (or at a greatly reduced
price) under medical supervision, during which time consultation
and other forms of treatment would be given, would seem to be pref-
erable to committing crimes to enable him or her to buy the drugs
on the street.

---

*One often hears, in arguments against legalization, that the "British experiment" did
not work. But Britain has never legalized drugs. What they did do between 1959 and 1968
was permit any British doctor to prescribe heroin to *addicts* as part of their treatment.
Michael Snell, second secretary at the British Embassy in Washington, D.C., says, "We
quickly learned what we should have guessed—that our doctors are pretty much a reflection of the general population. There are many good, but also many bad people out there."
In the mid-1960s, too many doctors started prescribing heroin to nonaddicts, as well as
prescribing excessive amounts to addicts and not reporting, as required (to prevent addicts
from going from one doctor to another), what addicts they were treating. The result was
that heroin addiction more than doubled. The right of *any* doctor to prescribe drugs such
as heroin was discontinued in 1968, and only doctors licensed by the Home Office and
working in special government treatment centers are now authorized to prescribe these
drugs to addicts, who must be registered with the Home Office. Presently, less than 400
heroin addicts are being prescribed heroin under the program. Approximately 17,000 heroin addicts in Britain, however, are being maintained on methadone, a common situation
in the United States also.

If there were legalization, presumably drugs would be sold by licensed dealers and regulated by local, state, and federal authorities, including the Food and Drug Administration, the way alcohol and tobacco presently are. Admittedly, the mechanics of legalization are fuzzy, but there is every reason to believe that good minds would be able to devise workable methods to ensure the sensible and controlled production, sale, and regulation of drugs. Conceivably, private enterprise might end up producing and selling drugs. This may sound bizarre, but how bizarre is it really? Isn't this the precise situation we have right now with two other drugs—alcohol and tobacco? But it doesn't follow that the marketing would have to be the same. Part of the regulatory measures could be that commercial advertising of drugs (radio, TV, print, billboard) would be prohibited. If we can presently prohibit the use of drugs like cocaine and heroin, we certainly can prohibit something far less—the advertising and promotion of these drugs.

Or, the federal government itself could purchase the drugs themselves from foreign governments and the drugs could be sold generically at government-operated stores or, as would most likely be the case if they were produced by private enterprise, in pharmacies. As we have seen, there is a precedent in this country for the unrestricted sale of narcotics in pharmacies. Some pharmacies in the late nineteenth century and early twentieth century sold *only* narcotics. On a very limited and different scale, our government is already involved with foreign governments in the marketing of the drug opium. Because the cultivation of opium is unlawful in the United States, three American pharmaceutical firms (Johnson & Johnson International, Penick Corp., and Mallinckrodt Inc.) are licensed to purchase opium on the world market for processing into the painkiller morphine, an opium derivative. The U.S. government has guaranteed India and Turkey that 80 percent of American opium purchases will be from these two countries. By a DEA regulation, the remaining 20 percent can be purchased from five other opium-producing countries—Australia, France, Hungary, the former Yugoslavia, and Poland.

On the evening of December 18, 1990, two Detroit drug dealers stormed into the home of five-year-old Katherine Staples in Highland Park, a Detroit suburb, and shot the child repeatedly in the chest. Police said her murder was revenge against another youth in the home who stole some of the dealers' cocaine. Katherine (her nickname was "Pinky" because her favorite color for the dresses on her dolls was pink) was a cheerful, particularly pretty little girl with large, expressive brown eyes who was eagerly waiting to see what toys Santa Claus would bring down the chimney for her in a matter of days. As tragic as her murder was, it was not unusual, and is mentioned here in lieu of others only because it is representative of the type of brutal, senseless, and seemingly endless murders that take place every day in our nation's cities. Not just five-year-olds, but toddlers, even unborn babies in their mother's supposedly protective wombs, have had their precious lives snuffed out as a direct result of drug prohibition.

No one is spared. Members of law enforcement year in and year out have valiantly given their lives in the futile war against drugs. This book is dedicated to them. And innocent civilians who try to help the law enforcement effort are ruthlessly cut down too by the drug traffickers' bullets. One example among a great many: On March 4, 1993, in South-Central Los Angeles, a drug addict's bullet-ridden body was found in an alley, the victim of an argument over the sale of crack. Gloria Lyons, age thirty-one, and Georgia Denise Jones, age thirty-three, witnessed the killing. LAPD homicide detectives persuaded them to testify in court against the alleged killer, a cocaine dealer named Charles Lafayette, even though this made them vulnerable to being silenced or killed in retribution. Both were murdered. Jones had accepted witness relocation assistance from the district attorney's office, while Lyons declined, moving in with relatives instead. As reported in the *Los Angeles Times*, "It didn't matter. On April 3, 1994, Lyons was shot in the head" a few blocks from where she had witnessed the murder. She had yet to testify. "Two months later, Jones, who had testified days earlier at Lafayette's trial, was shot repeatedly in the head and upper body."

It is an accepted reality that thousands of murders every year are drug-related. That means that every day of the year, human lives are brutally extinguished, and grieving parents, sisters, brothers, and other loved ones are left behind, oftentimes to have nightmares for the rest of their lives over what happened to those who had been dear to them. And the victims aren't only children like Katherine Staples or young adults like Gloria Lyons and Georgia Jones. They include elderly men and women found shot or bludgeoned to death out on the street for the few dollars in their purse or wallet that can buy the killer a fix. Do we really care? Oh, we say we do. We look at the pictures in the newspapers of someone like bright-eyed Katherine Staples and say things like, "How terrible," "How sad," "What a tragedy," and then we turn to the next page, never giving it another thought.

"There should no longer be any question as to how much of a catalyst for crime the lust for illegal drugs has become in America. Drug users will beat, rob, and kill anyone for drugs," says former Attorney General Richard Thornburgh. If we know this to be true, and if we also know that with drug legalization, the strong likelihood, almost the certainty, is that these drug-related violent crimes would be substantially diminished, don't we owe it to the future Katherine Utaplcoco, Gloria Lyonvov, and Georgia Joneses of our country to give serious thought to legalization?

As previously indicated, this writer is not categorically recommending immediate legalization. Such a position without further study and serious consideration would be irresponsible. The problem is that no such study or even fleeting consideration by our government is going on in America today. Legalization has been rejected categorically, and our legislators, many of whom are thought to be privately in favor of it, are afraid to take a position publicly.

Like affirmative action to overcome centuries of discrimination and prejudice against black Americans, the arguments for legalization in this section of the book are perhaps overstated to help surmount the Procrustean inflexibility and attitude ("don't confuse me with the facts—I've already made up my mind") that this nation has adopted with respect to the legalization issue.

One step in the right direction toward a more open and intelligent dialogue on the legalization question would be the presidential appointment of a panel of distinguished Americans from outside of government (where politics and political survival will not be factors)—representing every major field and discipline and from every point of the political spectrum—to study the feasibility of legalization, or at least, as recommended herein, the experimentation with it by way of nonenforcement of drug laws for a period of time. Someone of the unimpeachable stature and credibility of an Elliot Richardson or (if it hadn't been for the position he's already publicly taken) a George Shultz should chair the panel. Augmented by a staff of experts in the field of narcotics, the panel's findings and conclusions, including the bases for them, should be presented in depth by the president to the American people in a nationwide television address, not just in a ten-second soundbite on the evening news and one buried article in the daily newspaper. If the panel's recommendation is legalization, then even if the president does not accept the conclusion of his appointees, the vast audience and the imprimatur of a presidential address would probably stimulate, like never before, a serious and long overdue debate and dialogue on the issue of legalization not just by political and social pundits, who have been debating the issue for years, but, for the first time, by public officials.

At a minimum, instead of thoughtlessly continuing prohibition for the same reason that hens continue to lay eggs—that's what they do and have always done—we owe this to the memory of little Katherine Staples, and those many innocent victims like her who pay the ultimate price for this nation's effort to protect people from themselves.

Conclusion

I f either one of the two relatively simple, inexpensive, and direct proposals (military search-and-find mission; new currency and interdiction of wire transfers) recommended in this book were implemented, the probability is that the supply of cocaine in the United States would be minimal. If both were implemented, the high probability is that the supply of cocaine in this country would dry up like water on a hot skillet.

The response I have received to my proposals is far too prevalent to ignore in this book. Thus, with minor variations, the following is a conversation I have had with many people.

"But if we succeed in keeping cocaine out of this country, people will simply turn to some other drug," I keep being told.

Apart from the fact that the proposals set forth herein can be applied to drugs other than cocaine—even, with proposal number two, those drugs grown or synthetically manufactured in this country—and apart from the fact that cocaine is the source of crack, responsible for much of the drug-related violence in this country, I have answered, "If what you say is true, then I take it you recommend that this nation dismantle all of its present multi-billion-dollar effort to keep cocaine from entering the country. I'm referring to our efforts in the area of interdiction as well as our efforts to prevent the growth of the coca crop in the Andean nations. In other words, we should immediately discontinue our war against cocaine."

257

"Why do you think I would be willing to recommend something as drastic as that?" they respond.

"Well, would you agree that however ineffective the effort has been, our nation is trying to keep cocaine from getting into this country?"

"Of course."

"I understood you to say that if we in fact succeeded, people will simply turn to some other drug. If that's so, there's nothing to be achieved by winning the war on cocaine. Therefore, why make any effort to win it in the first place? Doesn't this logically follow from what you've said?"

"Well, I don't know. I guess so."

On the opening page of this book I mentioned the phenomenon that when it comes to the drug problem, for some unfathomable reason this nation refuses to change its policies, despite the fact they have proven to be a failure. In the war on drugs, the mind-set seems to be: I came, I saw, I concurred. An effort is called for to at least speculate on the dynamics behind the intellectual inertia (and hernia) that has caused our government to continue to employ an ineffective battle plan, and that will most likely cause it to refuse to employ the revolutionary changes recommended in this book.

For one thing, the proposals contained in this book are such a totally different way of attacking the problem that even if the federal government were finally amenable to change, it would most likely be uncomfortable with these specific proposals because they are just too stark, too much of a departure from established policies. Though there are few tyrants like blind custom, we all feel comfortable with old habits and ways, even if they aren't always fruitful, because at least the future failure does not shock us. The fear of the unknown which change represents so inhabits mankind that it is believed, of course, to have given birth to the world's great religions.

But there are perhaps a host of other, less extenuating reasons why it is most improbable that any revolutionary measures, such as those contained in this book, are apt to be carried out, one or more of which are probably exerting their influence on a subconscious level.

One reason is that our nation's leadership (the executive and legislative branches), the very people who have the authority to implement these measures, are not personally threatened by the drug crisis, and likely never will be. The most powerful motivating influence to human behavior, we all know, is that of self-preservation, and though the drug crisis could hardly be a more serious one, to those in power it is no problem at all. The drug problem is so much a part of this nation's existence that it was not even mentioned in President Clinton's 1995 State of the Union address, nor is it mentioned in the Republicans' Contract with America.

Since the drug crisis is perceived to be incapable of solution and a virtual accepted staple of our existence, no one has lost his job because of it. Try to think of one president, or even one governor or mayor in America, who was thrown out of office by the electorate because he wasn't doing a good job fighting the drug problem.* Clearly, political pressure, the principal force that motivates politicians, as opposed to statesmen, is virtually nonexistent. Furthermore, the drug curse has not changed our leaders' comparatively affluent, privileged lifestyle one particle, and never will. True, now and then the errant child of one of our leaders will succumb to the drug craze, but that is the closest it will ever come, and when it does, the finest rehabilitation centers in the country, like the Hazelden Foundation in Center City, Minnesota, can be counted on to minister to the needs of the leader's son or daughter.

This is not to suggest that unless personally threatened our leaders don't routinely take steps which, in their minds, will promote the country's welfare. This, in fact, is what they are presently, but blindly, doing in the nation's war against drugs. But to get them to take revolutionary and drastic measures, it may be that the threat has to at least have the potential of touching their own lives, which the drug curse does not have.

In April of 1989, the *Wall Street Journal* reported on a typical day in our nation's capital. In the Rayburn House Office Building "a harpist is playing Schumann's 'Traumerei,' the bartenders are tipping the top brands of Scotch, and two huge salmon sit on mirrored platters." The scene was a reception on Capitol Hill thrown by lobbyists for the wood-preservation industry. But there was, and is, another reality just a number of city blocks away from the sparkling-clean grand edifices of our nation's capital. On the mean, squalid streets of Washington, D.C.'s inner city, just blocks from the Capitol, shots ring out, sirens shriek, and blood flows daily in that city's violent and convulsive drug scene.

---

*Washington, D.C., Mayor Marion Barry lost his grip on City Hall a few years ago not because he wasn't doing a good job combating the city's drug problem, but because of his being videotaped by the FBI smoking crack cocaine in a downtown Washington, D.C., hotel room and his subsequent conviction for drug possession.

Unlike the Russian regiments on the outskirts of Berlin closing in on Hitler's bunker in another April, fifty years ago, those few city blocks of Washington, D.C., real estate are never going to shrink, and the Scotch and the blood will never interfere with each other. But let a ragtag group of leftist guerrillas take over the government of Grenada, a tiny, remote island in the West Indies thousands of miles from Capitol Hill that most Americans had never even heard of, and within days, 6,000 American troops supported by planes, tanks, and heavy artillery invade the island. Why? Because pre-Gorbachev, although the leftist regime in Grenada posed as much threat to this nation's security as Dolly Parton does to Mike Tyson, the potential was there, however extremely remote, that in confluence with other leftist winds it could someday, even years later, personally affect the lives of our leaders. *Self-preservation.* Communism could change the expensive Scotch to cheap beer, the salmon to bologna sandwiches. Communism could take away the limousines, the second homes on Martha's Vineyard, the pricey country club memberships. The drug crisis has never posed such a threat, it doesn't now, and it never will.*

The heart of capitalism is our nation's banks. In recent years, American banks have loaned *billions* of dollars to Third World countries ($97.7 billion) to shore up sagging economies, thereby hopefully enabling them to resist Communist aggression. A substantial percentage of the money loaned frequently is merely a euphemism for a gift, since considerable portions of the loans are eventually written off or forgiven. *Self-preservation.* How many billions of dollars do you think our nation's banks would contribute toward paying for and improving the effectiveness of this nation's war on drugs? How many millions? Even, how many thousands?

At a level just beneath that of our nation's leaders (a level that has no power to determine our anti-drug policy, only the responsibility

---

* Or perhaps the reason for our failure to deal with the drug cancer resonates beyond the nation's corridors of power to the country as a whole: that the economic fat this nation has enjoyed and luxuriated in for so many years has finally invaded the marrow of its core, inducing almost a constitutional indifference to problems (e.g., the staggering yearly deficits and trillion-dollar national debt; massive foreign takeovers of our corporations; by far the highest crime rate of any modern industrialized nation; the shameful, lowering quality of our children's education, etc.), no matter how severe, as long as they haven't yet interfered with a continuation of its high standard of living; and that if we ever become a second-rate actor on the global stage, it will not be due to any enemy from without, but from a weakening palsy within.

to carry it out) is another facet of the self-preservation condition. Relatively speaking, the recommended solutions to the drug crisis contained in this book require very little manpower or money. What this means is that if they are successfully carried out, many bureaucracies and federal agencies won't be needed anymore, at least not anywhere near their present strength. And human nature and the instinct for self-preservation being what they are, this cannot fail to cause ambivalent emotions among many, particularly the leadership of these drug-fighting fiefdoms.

In fact, a common but unfortunate consequence of vested interests is the interagency competition and infighting for federal drug funds and jurisdiction, which, some say, hinder the drug fight. "I think the competition in law enforcement is extremely distasteful," opines DEA head Thomas A. Constantine. Already, some of the rivalries have produced budgetary and turf battles that are the stuff of legends. A few examples should suffice. Max Mermelstein, the government's key witness against the Medellin cartel, testified before the Senate Judiciary Committee on August 17, 1989, that "the FBI won't tell the DEA [information they have], the DEA won't tell the FBI, and nobody wants to talk to Customs. Everyone has his own budget priorities." When, in August, 1993, Vice President Gore recommended merging the DEA into the FBI as part of the Clinton Administration's effort to streamline government and cut federal expenditures, the DEA predictably mounted a very strong offensive in Washington to prevent this, and on October 21, 1993, Attorney General Janet Reno rejected the proposal. She added, however, that she was concerned about turf disputes between the two agencies that hampered the anti-drug effort. Reprising Mermelstein's charges, she said there was evidence the FBI and DEA were failing to share all intelligence information in the counter-narcotic effort. When CID proposed in 1992 (the proposal was adopted) placing a small number of its agents in U.S. embassies in several countries, U.S. Customs opposed the plan, arguing that foreign money laundering was its domain, and CID should content itself with domestic money laundering. *Money Laundering Alert* quoted an "informed source" as saying Customs viewed CID's modest entry into foreign operations like a camel with his nose in the tent. "Nothing is as certain in law enforcement," *Money Laundering Alert* said, "as the maxim that agencies protect their turf as fervently as they seek its expansion."

This is not to suggest that these are bad people. They are anything but. But one has to realize that there are a number of people in this country who, although they genuinely abhor the drug scourge and have admirably dedicated themselves to being as effective as possible in fighting it, nonetheless are personally leading very satisfying lives because of it. It may not be realistic to expect people who have years of seniority, a sometimes glamorous, even potentially heroic job, to desire the adoption of a plan that will, in effect, either terminate their employment or substantially eviscerate their sphere of influence.*

An analogy could be drawn to the end of the Cold War. At its zenith, many scientists, engineers, etc., in the defense and aerospace industries diligently sought to invent ever more powerful weapons to destroy the "evil empire." But there was an unconscious and inherently contradictory elliptical clause to this desire: "as long as they (the enemy) are still there," i.e., "I want to destroy you, as long as you are still there for me to continue to try to destroy you." Though these people are good, decent human beings who are just as patriotic as you or I, how many of them do you believe were truly happy about the end of the Cold War, when that ending forced them out of their jobs and caused so many of them to lose their homes because they could no longer make their monthly payments? A significant number of them, unable to find comparable employment elsewhere or, at their age, any kind of well-paying job, have felt fortunate to land work as a waiter or driving a taxi. Several in-depth newspaper articles have examined and chronicled this phenomenon. "We did too good a job [winning the Cold War]," a depressed, laid-off aerospace worker told a reporter for the *Los Angeles Times* in March, 1992. "It's phenomenally depressing," another unemployed worker said. In other words, very few humans have the ability to rise above their own self-interest. This observation is not meant to be critical, for this is a malady that afflicts most of mankind. It is only to state a reality.

For the recommendations contained in this book to be adopted by the federal government, it would be most helpful, perhaps critical, to have the support of those people in our country who are presently entrusted with conducting the drug war. But to expect the support of some of them to be anything more than tepid might be pipe-

---

* Moreover, there is the phenomenon of enjoying and deriving satisfaction out of continuing to fight something or someone you detest. Tell me that Gen. George S. Patton, Jr., did not like the Nazis, but don't tell me that he didn't enjoy the war against them. As Patton wrote in a letter to his hero, Gen. John J. (Black Jack) Pershing, at the time of the First World War: "War is the only place where a man really lives." Again, though it may be indelicate to say it, don't tell me that Generals MacArthur and Montgomery did not like war.

dreaming. As far back as 1973, the Shafer Commission, which President Nixon empaneled to study the burgeoning drug problem in America (and which unsuccessfully recommended the decriminalization of marijuana), had this to say about the drug fight: The result of the drug war "has been the creation of ever-larger bureaucracies, ever-increasing expenditures of monies and an outpouring of publicity so that the public will know that 'something' is being done. Perhaps the major consequence of this . . . *has been the creation of a vested interest in the perpetuation of the problem among those dispensing and receiving funds* In the course of well-meaning efforts to do something about drug use, this society may have inadvertently institutionalized it as a never-ending project."

In examining the reasons for our nation's failure to effectively combat drugs, there is another factor that has to be considered in the equation. With any presidential administration confronting the endemic crime and violence in America, drugs provide an ideal patsy. Though drugs unquestionably are the principal *immediate* cause of most property crime and much violent crime in America, just as unquestionably, the *proximate* cause of a goodly percentage of it, particularly in the nation's ghettos, is poverty. The inexcusable condition of poverty in a nation as rich as ours* can be conveniently tabled without political injury as long as drugs dominate the front pages and the nation's consciousness.

For whichever of the above reasons, this nation is likely to continue fighting the drug cancer with the same prescriptions it has always used, only in heavier dosages. But to those who advocate the continued and uncompromising utilization of currently accepted techniques, is it not proper to say: "You've had your chance. In fact, you've had it for a great number of years, and your policies have met with monumental failure. Don't you think that it's high time, after decades of failure, that we try something new?"

I've previously characterized as draconian the measures this nation has to adopt if it ever hopes to be triumphant in its prolonged struggle with the drug plague. Actually, proposals 1 and 2 in this book are draconian only because they are such a dramatic departure from this nation's modus operandi of fighting drugs for over half a century.

---

*The federal census bureau reports that in 1994, 38,059,000 Americans (14.5 percent of the population) were living below the official poverty level of $11,821 for a family of three; $15,141 for a family of four.

Comparatively speaking, they are the most modest of measures. To illustrate, if either had been the method of combating drugs these past many years, the present system of fighting the drug war—billions of dollars being spent annually; a principal job of law enforcement throughout the nation being to ferret out and arrest the user and pusher; our crammed courts struggling to handle not only untold numbers of drug cases but also hundreds of thousands of robbery, burglary, theft, and murder cases that are drug-related; our stuffed jails and prisons trying to shoehorn additional inmates in; together with a litany of other execrable conditions—would be viewed as draconian, an utterly mad and unhinged strategy to defeat the drug epidemic. When viewed from this comparative perspective, proposals 1 and 2, particulary proposal 1, can immediately be seen for what they are: simple, logical, and highly *conservative* measures to fight the drug war.

Winston Churchill once said that the solution to every problem, no matter how complex, is common sense. Contrary to forecasts of doom and futility, I do not believe the war on drugs cannot be won. To believe this is to believe that the most powerful nation on Earth, inexorably being eroded and deformed by a small band of thugs, *does not have the physical means to do anything about it.* This, on its face, is absolutely preposterous. Of course we have the physical means. The challenge to this nation at this fateful hour in its young history is not a physical one. It's whether we have the common sense, the will, and most important, the spine to do what has to be done.

As with any war (the Second World War, today's alleged drug war, etc.), in addition to the unspeakable carnage and tragedy, there is the inherent glamour in the fight and the inevitable heroes. The Hollywood war pictures of John Wayne, as with today's Hollywood staple, the formula cop drug dramas like *Tequila Sunrise*, attempt to capture and markedly glorify the patina of excitement, danger, and romance that is an integral part of the good and true fight. Witness just a few illustrative quotes from the men on the front line of America's drug war: "Lots of crime, lots of drugs—this job's got everything"; "They [smuggler pilots] get a lot of money for what they do. But I also feel some do it for the excitement. Just like us"; "I don't see it as a frustrating job. I think it's a lot of fun"; "It was like a John Wayne movie. We got one"; "I've always said that the flying we do, chasing the dopers, I call 'em bad guys, is the best flying in the world outside of combat flying"; "It's a cat and mouse game. We try to figure out each other's next move"; "I think it's a thrill. It's the only satisfaction I get."

But sooner or later, there's got to be a Hiroshima (actually, nothing remotely close is even required) to put an end to the misery, and yes, the war games with their heroes. Sooner or later, there has to be a Truman who says, "That's enough of that." And if this nation's president or Congress finally takes that attitude, one that's quite a few *Tequila Sunrises* overdue, we'll be startled to find that the drug monster is not only slayable, but will be slain.

Index